What Parents Are Saying About Carol's Child Whisperer and Energy Profiling Techniques

"In just one short week of learning and applying Carol's parenting techniques, I have learned more about how to parent my children in ways that really work than I have learned in 28 years of life. I have also had amazing 'light bulb' moments, not only about my children, but also about my childhood, my parents, and my siblings. I can already tell that Carol's formula really is THE better way to parent. I can hardly wait to learn more!"

—Suzette Pace

"Your system has probably been the biggest influence on my parenting than any other book, website, system, etc. I have a PhD in clinical psychology with a specialty in family and couples' therapy. You can imagine that I have extensive training in that area, but your system is the one I refer to on a daily basis. It completely changed how I relate to my own children and often how I relate to their father. It also helps me relate to clients professionally and help them in the changes they are trying to make in their lives and relationships."

—Elizabeth Bonet

"I am always saddened by how conditioned parents are to be more concerned about what other people think (strangers, even) than what is best for their child. Thank God that is changing! We are in a whole different energy and your parenting book is 'right on!' in supporting and feeding this change. A parenting book that respects the children and heals the parents—love it!"

—Kristine Bolstridge

"Where do I begin? Carol's system has transformed my life, and my family's life. I am a better mom, wife, sister, daughter and just a better human being. If I had to narrow down how Energy Profiling has helped me as a parent to just one thing it would be how it has saved the relationship between my 10-year-old Type 4 daughter and myself (Type 2). Now that we understand each other we respect and like each other a lot more. I shudder to think of the path we would still be on if I had not been blessed with Energy Profiling."

—Tausha Hansen

"Your message of Energy Profiling is needed in the field of education at all levels. As my 10-year-old said in May as she attended our annual homeschool convention for the first time, 'Energy Profiling needs to be here, Mom. All these people need to learn about it!' That is just one of many places it is needed, and for that I have to concur with her wholeheartedly."

—Sheila Sierts

"I have a Type 4 son, and from the time he was 14 months on, I was baffled by how to raise him. I looked in the community and medical fields for answers, but they had no real suggestions; so true to my Type 4 nature, I went back to school for a masters degree. Surely academia had the answers I was searching for.

I certainly did find answers, but the most enlightening was when my friend recommended your book. It brought insight. . .and aided me in better understanding the research I was composing. Following the completion of my Master's paper and graduating, I've been able to continue to study the principles you teach, and I appreciate so much the simplicity and applicability they bring. I even cited your book in my paper—look at that, you're even in academia (although I'm sure it won't be the first or last time!). Thank you."

—Jenny Jones

The Child Whisperer

The Ultimate Handbook
for Raising Happy, Successful, Cooperative Children

CAROL TUTTLE

*Best-selling author of Remembering Wholeness
and It's Just My Nature*

LIVE
YOUR
TRUTH
PRESS

The Child Whisperer™, Dressing Your Truth®, Energy Profiling®, Energy Type™, and Type 1™, Type 2™, Type 3™, and Type 4™ are trademarks or registered trademarks of Carol Tuttle Enterprises, LLC.

ISBN: 978-0-9844021-3-7

Library of Congress Control Number: 2012916781

Printed in the United States of America

8 9 10 11 12 — 25 24 23 22 21

Cover Photo: Debra Macfarlane

debramacfarlane.com

Cover Design: Timothy Kavmark

kavmark.com

Text Design and Layout: Sea Script Company

seascriptcompany.com

Live Your Truth Press

support@liveyourtruth.com

liveyourtruth.com

LIVE
YOUR
TRUTH
PRESS

Other books from Carol Tuttle

The Path to Wholeness

Remembering Wholeness:
A Personal Handbook for Thriving in the 21st Century

It's Just My Nature:
A Guide to Knowing and Loving Your Truth Nature

Mastering Affluence:
6 Lessons to Create a Life You Love

The Modern Chakra Guide:
7 Steps to Awaken Your Energy in Today's World

Contents

Author's Note
by Carol Tuttle

As you read this book, you will notice that many sentences pair the singular word *child* with the plural pronoun *them*.

For example: *When you understand your child's nature, you can better help them develop their natural gifts and talents.*

I recognize that the singular noun and the plural pronoun do not match up, but I have chosen this usage deliberately. No singular, gender-neutral pronoun exists in English, and using *he/she* throughout would interfere with the book's conversational tone.

Most importantly, this book is meant to be a comprehensive manual for parents of all children, regardless of gender. I chose to use the word *they* to avoid any misunderstanding about which gender this information applies to. Every time you encounter the word *they* in reference to your singular child, I hope you recognize that I honor your child as a unique and singular individual.

As you read, you will also find stories of children and their parents. The stories' purpose in the text is to illustrate specific principles and provide real-life experiences you may identify with and learn from. While they are an important supportive element, this book can also be read from start to finish without them.

Acknowledgements

My deepest and most sincere gratitude goes to my editor, Kathy West. Kathy spent many hours helping me put this amazing book together. True to her Type 2 nature, she took all the content and stories that we gathered over months of research and helped me compile it to flow so beautifully. Thank you, Kathy, for living your truth and helping me write this amazing book, which we both know will help many parents.

Thank you to my husband, Jonathan, for being the great father he has always been to our five children.

Thank you to my parents who did the best they knew how with very little insight on how to raise a go-get 'em, Type 3 daughter like myself.

I appreciate the assistance of the other editors who worked on this book, Mike Fitzgerald and Beth Farrell.

Thank you to our amazing graphic artist, Timothy Kavmark, for his beautiful cover design. And to our entire team at Live Your Truth, LLC—especially my son Chris, our CEO; my son-in-law, Tanner, our President; my son Mark, our Social Media Manager; my daughter Anne, and daughters-in-law, Sarah and Jaleah, who are Experts in our programs. Thank you for your dedication to helping people worldwide live their truth and love it.

Thank you to my amazing customer support team, especially Kristine, who helped gather numerous stories.

My love and thanks to my growing nest of grandchildren who show me every day what it is to live our truth simply and clearly.

My many thanks go out to the parents who shared their stories and insights with me. You and your families are living proof that this information can transform lives and relationships. You are an inspiration to every parent who aspires to become a Child Whisperer!

The Child Whisperer

Why Every Parent and Grandparent Should Read This Book

People joke that children don't come with a handbook, but they're wrong.

Every day, children tell their parents exactly how they need to be parented. Your children are trying to tell you *who* they are so you can recognize and treat them in a way that honors them uniquely. All you have to do is learn to read the clues that they are naturally giving you.

Your children are their own handbook. This book that you are reading right now is your guide to understanding them and their true natures more clearly.

By true nature, I mean your child's innate, inner self—their natural quality of moving, thinking, feeling, and relating to the world. Your child's true inner nature expresses itself outwardly in appearance, body language, tone of voice, and choice of words. Your child's true nature is inscribed in the shape of their face, eyes, nose, and eyebrows. Every day, your children *move* in a manner true to their nature, expressing their core intrinsic movement in their play, their walk and talk, and their physical characteristics. From sun up to sun down, your children give you giant clues about who they really are and the personalized parenting they need from you.

. . . .

BROCK'S STORY
Children Tell Us Who They Are

Brock is a determined little guy. Ever since he could walk, he just went for whatever he wanted, rather than ask for it. He climbed up the furniture or went outdoors, always after a goal. His mother says, "I've never seen such a determined child."

One Sunday morning, when Brock was three years old, he heard that the family planned to go to church. But it wasn't time to leave yet. That didn't matter to Brock.

Just a little while later, his dad got a phone call from a neighbor, saying that Brock was at the church. Brock had left the house wearing only a diaper and his favorite rubber boots. He'd walked across a very busy road, and down the street to the church, where he was knocking on the door. It didn't matter that he wasn't dressed and that the family wasn't ready yet—he went anyway! Without saying a word, Brock told his parents that he has a willful, determined nature that naturally moves others into action.

Many parents might see this determination as "bad behavior" that requires discipline to change. But Brock's parents have become Child Whisperers, so they have the tools they need to direct Brock's strong will in a way that helps him develop it as a gift in his life and the lives of those around him.

. . . .

Understanding your child's true nature will help you better recognize their natural gifts and talents, more clearly see their personal challenges, and know how to guide them more easily.

You will feel empowered as a parent to raise your child with more understanding, more joy, and the confidence that you're helping them fulfill their special purpose in the world.

Why Child Whisperers Discipline Less

After applying the concepts you learn in this book, you will also need to use less discipline. Do you have a difficult kid? A rebellious teen? You won't anymore. Your children actually want to be cooperative, not defiant. When honored for who they really are, children will cooperate more easily as a by-product of parenting efforts, and you will experience increased cooperation and harmony in your parent-child relationships.

. . . .

KAELA'S STORY
More Cooperation, Fewer Fights

Kaela is a six-year-old who used to get out of control when she felt upset. She threw things. She kicked. She didn't handle frustration well. Her mom used to put her in her room and shut the door so that Kaela would learn to control herself, but it only made things worse.

Now that her mother understands Kaela's naturally methodical nature, she's become a Child Whisperer. She knows how deeply Kaela values plans—even at an age as young as six. Her mother even said, "I have realized that I inadvertently caused much of this tantrum stress by jumping quickly from one activity or requirement to another." When she communicates her plans to her daughter, those tantrums just don't happen much anymore.

Whenever Kaela starts to get out of control, her mother approaches the situation differently now. She gets down at her daughter's eye level and asks, "What is causing you so much stress?" Kaela feels immediately validated. She expresses why she feels upset or unprepared. Mother and daughter have now changed their pattern from struggle to cooperation. Kaela's mom says, "We've really cut down on the screaming and throwing fits."

· · · ·

A Note to Grandparents, Aunts, Uncles, Educators, and Friends

To grandparents: If you are a grandparent reading this book, you most likely do not have the primary responsibility to raise your grandchildren (if you do, please read this book from the perspective of a parent). As a grandparent, you play a supporting role in how your grandchildren are raised. Understanding your grandchild's true nature helps you be a support and create many endearing moments for your grandchild to bond with you. As a result, your grandchild will see you as the best grandparent ever!

To educators, friends, aunts, uncles, and anyone else who wants to become a Child Whisperer: As you read this book, consider the children you come in contact with regularly. This book will give you the insights and tools you need to support them in living true to their nature in whatever capacity or situation you interact with them.

The Ultimate Goal of This Book

As I mentioned earlier, we have bought into the cliché that children don't come with a handbook. Well, it's high time that changed. It's high time we start understanding what our children are trying to tell us every day.

The goal of this book is to help you become a Child Whisperer—someone who recognizes the messages children send every minute, even when they don't know how to say their needs out loud. When you become a Child Whisperer, you will understand what your children's tantrums, rebellions, friendships, and joys are telling you about their true self.

As a result, you will develop a unique parenting approach that honors and supports your child, eliminating a high percentage of conflict and discipline. You will recognize your own child's unique priorities and point of view. This book will also show you the specific desires your child *needs* you to fulfill in order to feel truly loved and honored. When you fulfill those needs, you will fill up your family life with joy and understanding you may never have experienced. . .until now.

How Our Parenting Can Change Humanity

A change in our parenting approach doesn't stop at our own families.

What you will learn in this book has the potential to dramatically change the way we raise children and how we understand others and ourselves. Parent by parent, child by child, we will change humanity.

Many of today's parenting models provide parents with if/then scenarios: "When a child does A, then you do B." "If a child acts out this way, then you discipline this way." This sort of advice is reactionary and conditional. And it just plain doesn't work. It focuses on reacting to behaviors rather than understanding and honoring the root of those behaviors.

Many of us were raised under a hierarchical pattern of parenting. In other words, "Do what I say because I am the parent!" As children, we were led to believe that our parents knew best for us, simply because they were older than we were. This model no longer works (and, quite frankly, it never worked).

It allowed parents to get away with a lot of bad parenting and less effort to instruct their children or to truly know who their children were.

Children are not responding to this threat anymore. They are not bowing down and submitting themselves to a parent's sense of false authority backed with little understanding. Children are coming to this world more fully expressive and committed to living true to their natures. This is GREAT, as these children are less willing to be repressed and wounded by parents, grandparents, and other adults in their lives.

The challenge, then? If you don't understand and honor your child's true nature in your parenting approach, you will most likely experience unpleasant, frustrating, or even painful interactions with them.

You don't have to stay locked in frustration or struggle forever. You don't need to wonder when your child will stop going through this "phase." As a parent or grandparent, you can unlock the secrets of your child's true nature, discover their specific motivations, and let them show you exactly what they need. You can raise a child who feels capable, confident, and valuable in the world. You can start today.

Just imagine. . .

. . .a world in which the "Terrible Twos" do not exist.

. . .a world where teenagers don't rebel.

. . .a world where families support and honor each other and peace prevails effortlessly.

This kind of world is possible. It starts with understanding and honoring your child's true nature. It starts with becoming a Child Whisperer. And when you become a Child Whisperer, you don't just become a better parent. . .you create a better world.

Could You Be Wounding Your Child And Not Even Know It?

Some approaches to parenting are "wounding parenting styles," meaning they inadvertently wound children. They are not intentionally hurtful—in fact, any given parenting style may work for certain children. But standard parenting practices just don't take into account your child's true nature. The easiest way to wound a child is to ignore, judge, or squash that nature!

Just like children express a unique nature, so do their parents. Most parents are naturally drawn to parenting approaches that honor their *own* true nature, rather than their child's, just because that approach feels more natural to them.

· · · ·

SYDNEY'S STORY
Slow It Down

Sydney's mother has told her many times in her life to hurry up. She wanted Sydney to move quickly and finish things a little faster. Ever since discovering Sydney's true nature, she's stopped asking that.

Sydney's mother has learned that she herself naturally expresses a more swift, dynamic energy. And Sydney's own natural movement is more gentle and flowing. The two of them have come to understand that they express different natural energy and movement—and both are okay.

Sydney's mother says this about those former power struggles: "I could see the goal, be it cleaning her room or finishing her homework. I couldn't understand why she couldn't just do what needed to be done (and quickly). I could have avoided many conflicts and tears had I just realized that she could take her time and still complete what was important. My greatest joy in raising this child is seeing her sweet, honest concern for others blossom into a mature appreciation of the gifts everyone brings to the table."

Now that mother and daughter understand each other's own unique energies, they can honor each other as Sydney becomes an adult and they move into a new phase in their mother-daughter relationship.

. . . .

Why the Self-Help Industry Exists

In the current billion-dollar self-help industry, millions of adults spend loads of time and money trying to find themselves, looking for healing and self-understanding. For most, this healing involves recovering from the wounds and traumas of their childhood.

Why do we have so many wounded, insecure adults running around? Yes, there are those who experienced traumatic and abusive childhoods. (Not to be dramatic here, but I throw myself into that group! I have personally spent a few decades and many thousands of dollars in pursuit of finding and living the true Carol!) But others who experienced relatively good childhoods still feel like something's missing, like they are not free to be their best selves.

In the more than twenty years I have worked in the field of self-help and personal development, I have assisted hundreds of thousands of adults in re-discovering their true natures. I have found that it does not take trauma or abuse to wound a child! All it takes is not seeing them for who they really are and parenting them in a manner that goes against their true nature. Over time, this pattern of parenting finally convinces a child that they are inherently flawed.

That is why adults all over the world mistrust their true natures. Because their true natures were never validated and honored, they did not allow themselves to develop a personality congruent with who they really were. These adults have trained themselves to "be" someone they are not! Somewhere deep inside, they believe they are not really good enough. How painful and limiting! This is no fault of our parents. They were raised by people who didn't ultimately understand their true natures either!

What All the Frustration Really Means

I have helped parents worldwide discover that most of the conflict between them and their children is just the result of lack of understanding. They can resolve that conflict easily by understanding who their children really are.

Parents all over the world encounter situations that stump them, and many of their dilemmas boil down to one frustrating pattern. Children resist parenting styles that run contrary to their true nature. Parents feel frustrated and confused because their approach *should* work because it "feels right" to them, or because it worked for their parents. The parent then tries to get a child to comply through discipline. This may achieve the short-term result the parent wants, but it does not support a child in creating inner confidence and self-love.

Here's Your Parenting Pop Quiz

Answer these questions honestly to discover whether you are inadvertently wounding your child by not knowing how to parent them true to their nature:

- Have you ever wished your child would just stop doing something they always do?
- Does your child ever withdraw from you, either physically or emotionally?
- Do you ever feel drained and frustrated as a parent at the end of the day because of a way your child behaves?
- Do you ever look at other people's kids and wonder what's wrong with yours?
- Do you wonder how to get your children to stop fighting?
- Have you ever said, "I just don't understand this kid"?
- Do you want your child to respect you and listen to you?
- Are you experiencing a child that is rebellious?
- Does your child seem distant from you?
- Are you experiencing your child throwing tantrums on a regular basis?
- Do you ever say to yourself, "I just don't know what to do with this child!"?
- Do you ever perceive your child as a "problem child"?
- Do you talk to others on a regular basis about how hard your child is to deal with and that you just don't understand why?

- Do you get angry and yell at your child more than you would like?
- Do you feel you have to threaten your child a lot to get them to respond and behave?
- Do you feel you have to constantly stay on top of your child to get things done?

If you answered *yes* to one or more of the questions above, don't worry or feel bad. Just recognize that it's time—time to stop accidentally wounding your child and time to start raising them in a way that honors and supports you both.

You may not see how your answers to those questions may wound your child. Or maybe you do. Either way, you will know what to do about them by the end of this book. You will see that parenting doesn't have to be a frustrating experience. You will learn how to encourage and support the very best in your child easily and joyfully—and true to their nature. You will be a Child Whisperer and your children will be grateful that you are.

What is a Child Whisperer?

The term *whisperer* became popular when the 1998 movie *The Horse Whisperer* depicted a philosophy of working with horses based on an understanding of how horses think and communicate. This philosophy trained both horse and human to accept one another and work responsively together. One of the goals of a horse whisperer is to make the animal feel secure around humans so that horse and rider can achieve union and increased cooperation.

After the horse whisperer's popularity waned, we were introduced to Cesar Milan. He became famous for his work in rehabilitating problem dogs on his popular television show, *The Dog Whisperer*. The same philosophy applied to working with dogs—that if the owner could intuitively read their animal's needs and respond correctly, the animals would cooperate.

Your Children Are Not Animals or Pets

There's a big difference between horse whispering and child whispering: Your child is not an animal or a pet. Your child is a person and I do not see you as "owning" them.

However, this same principle applies in all instances: When

you know how to read the messages you are being given and you respond to them in kindness and with inspiration, you will experience more cooperation and mutual respect. I have witnessed amazing changes when parents apply the same Child Whispering techniques I will teach you in this book. Try them and your children will be happier, more successful, and cooperative.

How Child Whispering Works and What it Does

"Child Whispering" is my philosophy of working with children based on the model of Energy Profiling. Energy Profiling is an assessment tool that considers body language, communication, learning processes, personality, physical characteristics, and numerous other qualities. This model provides parents with an intuitive understanding of how their children see the world and innately express themselves.

As a result of identifying your child's true nature—or Type—based on my Energy Profiling system, you will become your own "Child Whisperer." You will more clearly understand the pattern of your child's thoughts, feelings, social interactions, motivations, and priorities. You will learn what they are naturally designed to express and experience, as well as what honors and supports them. As a result, you will be able to parent in a way that creates a greater degree of mutual cooperation and deep bonding with your child that significantly decreases the need for discipline.

Most parents have been trained and convinced that disciplining children is the way to get a child to cooperate. But let's look at the definition of the word discipline:

> *"The practice of training people to obey rules or a code of behavior, using punishment to correct disobedience."*
> —*Webster's Dictionary*

Consider how backward this approach is! Yes, children need to understand appropriate behavior, but do we really believe that they could not learn through any other means but punishment? Do we really need to teach them by coercion? No. In fact, children learn more positive lessons through other means. For example, a two-year-old who imitates her mother isn't trying to help because she was punished. She just chooses to help because she wants to.

Instead of trying to discipline and train children into a certain way of being, parents will be more effective when they recognize their children's natural way of being and parent them according to their individual needs. Every child is innately different. I often hear parents say how different their children are, even though those children grow up in the same house!

· · · ·

MARK AND MARIO'S STORY
Each Child is Different

My two sons, Mark and Mario, are perfect examples of how two children can be complete opposites of each other. If I hadn't understood their true natures through the model of Energy Profiling, I could have easily judged certain tendencies and behavior traits they each expressed naturally as flaws.

Mario, our fun-loving son, has a natural gift for spontaneity, bright ideas, friendliness, and an upbeat, hopeful attitude. His nature expresses itself as randomness that can be judged as irresponsible. Mark, our more serious son, has a natural gift for structure and focus. He prioritizes being his own authority, which can bring out others' judgment that he's a know-it-all. The same parenting approach DID NOT work for these two sons.

Once I discovered how to parent each of them true to their natures, I was able to honor both boys in the way they needed. Becoming a Child Whisperer gave me the insights I needed in the exact moments that made a difference.

I worked with these two very different children based on an understanding of their true natures and primary needs. Their unique natures showed up in their thoughts, feelings, communication, learning style, and even body language and facial features. Believe me, they were motivated by very different needs, and they each perceived my love through different eyes! As a result of child-whisperer parenting, both my sons felt safe, secure, honored, and understood—a gift I felt grateful to give. This experience has increased cooperation and harmony in our relationships to this day. That's what Child Whispering is all about.

. . . .

Why Anyone Can Become a Child Whisperer

My friend has a young son who gets very excited to talk to me when he knows I am coming over. I have had four-year-olds ask me for my autograph. Recently an 11-year-old girl told me she had prayed to be able to meet me. Parents frequently tell me their children want to meet me and they really love and appreciate me. I find this to be one of the greatest honors of my career. To have children so endeared to me is incredibly humbling.

These experiences do not happen because I am special. They can happen to you, too—and I want them to! On a deep, unspoken level, children naturally respond to adults who know who they are and respect and love them for their true selves. How could they not want to be around someone who helps them feel understood and at ease? How could they not want to connect with a Child Whisperer?

To many children, I am a Child Whisperer, with a natural ability to see and relate to their innate nature. But this is not a special gift unique to me. In fact, it's not even a special gift. Anyone can become a Child Whisperer with the information in this book. In fact everyone *should*. As I said, children are telling us all day long how to be Child Whisperers.

I wrote this book with the intent to help you become a "Child Whisperer" with your children, grandchildren, and any other children in your life. I want to help you understand this approach so clearly that you trust yourself and open up to receive inspiration on behalf of the children in your life. Ready to be a Child Whisperer? It's time to get started.

What Is Your Goal as a Parent?

Your journey into the Child Whisperer parenting style starts with your own answer to this vital question:

"What is my ultimate goal as a parent?"

The answer to this question matters very much. And if you and I are not on the same page about the purpose of parenting, you will not use the information in this book very effectively.

I believe that *the purpose of parenting is to raise children true to their natures so they can grow up feeling honored, confident, and free to be themselves.*

That's a big goal. How could any parent know if they've succeeded? What standard of measurement should we use? I would like to offer three vital questions that will help you evaluate your success as a parent. Come back to these indicators as you practice and hone your Child Whisperer skills to see how you're doing.

Three Questions to Measure Success as a Child Whisperer

1. *Do my children know who they are and accept themselves?*
   It doesn't matter who understands and accepts your child

if your child doesn't understand and accept him or herself. Your children cannot maximize their potential gifts and future happiness if they do not feel that their inner natures are worthwhile and valuable.

This does not mean that you should praise your children for every single thing they do from the second they wake up to the second they go to bed. This just means that you can consciously point out their natural tendencies and express appreciation and love. Believe that those tendencies can develop into your child's greatest strengths, rather than judging them as frustrations that get in your way.

The most powerful gift you can give your child is the permission to be their best self.

2. *Do my children use their natural gifts and trust them?*
As your children grow up, they will face challenges and take on responsibilities. The best way to prepare them is to help them develop and optimize their natural gifts to best serve them in the future.

Use your family experience to create those opportunities. You ask your children to carry out tasks all the time. Make them count! Ask yourself, "Am I aligning what I ask my children to do with activities and experiences that will help them develop their natural gifts and talents?"

3. *Are the things I think are important really important?*
This is the big one that gets a lot of us stuck. As parents, we obviously love our children and we want them to succeed. But focusing on success (however you define it) before you focus on the true root of success will automatically undermine all your efforts.

Here's the real trouble: Some of our highest expectations for our kids are more self-focused than we like to believe. Even if you define success as your child's happiness, who's to say that you've measured their happiness in the way that best honors them? You might find certain actions important that are actually hurtful to your child!

Let me give you an example. I spoke with the mother of a four-year-old boy who would not look at strangers when they talked to him. She worried that he was being rude and needed to practice social skills for later in life. She wanted to know how to encourage him to engage with people. Social interaction is obviously a good skill to learn, but consider one other part of the story with me.

This young boy's true nature is naturally more serious and quiet in new social settings or around unfamiliar people. Because of his naturally still energy, he needs time to observe before participating in a new environment. He prefers to engage in life in his own way and his own time.

At four years old, this boy could not yet have an agenda to be rude. He was merely living true to his innately serious and reflective nature. These are some of the messages he might take from the demand to engage socially before he's ready: "I need to please others to be loved. I need to change my nature to accommodate others. I need to do what others want me to do so they can be comfortable, even if it makes me uncomfortable."

Teaching this boy that he needed to live contrary to his true nature was hurtful to him—even though the skill being taught was supposed to contribute to his later success. Here's the trick: Teaching him this skill would probably create the opposite effect by causing him to withdraw even more! In fact, the adults I've worked with who still can't look people in the eye are most often those who were shamed about who they were as children.

By allowing her son to just be in a new space in his own way, this mother will communicate that he is more important to her than the potential reactions of other people. She will actually help him develop more self-confidence to interact by expressing her own trust in him that he can make the choice when he feels ready.

Do not misunderstand this example. I am not saying that we should allow children to do whatever they want, whenever they feel like it. I am not saying that we shouldn't bother teaching our children social skills or appropriate boundaries. As parents, we have an extraordinary responsibility to guide and to teach.

What I *am* saying is that we need to reevaluate the expectations behind our guidance and our teaching. Why do we *really* place certain expectations on our children, especially in social situations? How much do our expectations serve our parental egos, and how much do they honor our children's specific needs? Do we want to *look* like good parents—or do we want to actually *be* good parents?

Children who experience genuine support as they grow up naturally express themselves in pursuits congruent with their true expression. The natural byproduct of parenting this way is a child's future happiness and personal success.

Tiger Moms and True Success

At the time of this writing, the recent book *Battle Hymn of the Tiger Mom*, by Amy Chua, has received a lot of attention. It's one of those books you either love or hate. I do appreciate that it has brought a lot of attention to the question of what makes a good parent. It has opened up the conversation about parents who raise children to be high-performing, high-achieving adults. I personally think that such an approach is one of the primary reasons for widespread childhood depression.

Consider how many high-performing, depressed adults we already have in this world. They know how to do, do, do—but do they know how to just *be*?

Where did we go so wrong to accept the belief that our *doings* give us value? The truth is, we are enough just as we are. And so are our children. They were born with infinite value inherent in their being. We send our children one of the biggest false messages we ever could by teaching them to base their self-worth and value on performance.

The pursuit to do enough may look different, depending on your family culture (how high are your grades, how clean is your room, how long did you practice, how many friends do you have?), but the resulting exhaustion and discouragement for both parent and child is the same. And it creates a void in a child's life that no amount of doing will ever fill.

. . . .

KAYLEE'S STORY
Do, Do, Do

Kaylee was overdoing it! As an adult, she felt pushed to do, do, do and go, go, go, even when she didn't want to. And when she sat down to get to the root of the problem, she discovered a pattern that went back to her childhood.

As a child, she had always tried to tone down her big, vibrant energy so she wouldn't overshadow her sisters. She didn't feel she had permission to just be who she was, and so her repressed energy came out in frenzied efforts to prove herself in other ways. As an adult, she overworked herself, feeling like she had to make up for lost time.

She needed to reframe her experience to let those childhood hang-ups go (which she did!) and tell herself, "I am now being my amazing self. My energy is purposeful. I am here to make a difference, just by being me."

. . . .

Where Our Value Really Comes From

When we believe that high performance is the standard of success—both for our children and for our parenting—we encourage our children to grow into over-achieving adults, conditioned to believe that their achievements create their value. Then, sometime in their adult lives, they have to face and undo that lie in order to find that their true worth is a unique and constant part of their being, and that they are lovable and valuable, just because they exist.

I am not against supporting a child in becoming a high achiever. I value success and achievement. In fact, my own children achieve great success and I cheer them on and support them in their many endeavors.

Here's the key: Outward successes are not measurements of my children's inner worth or my worth as a parent. What matters most when we parent is the way we help our children develop their abilities true to their unique nature. When we have this focus, success and high achievement just become natural by-products in your children's lives. Our children don't have to struggle, stress and overwhelm themselves to feel valuable. Their accomplishments just become a natural, outward manifestation of how inwardly confident these children feel about themselves and their own abilities.

Whose Success Do You Actually Have In Mind?

Consider for a moment:

- Which standards have you set for your children that actually satisfy your *own* needs?
- Do you need your child to be or look or act a certain way in order for you to feel like a good parent?
- What motivates you to want your child to be a certain way or accomplish certain things?
- Do you need your child to look good so you feel good?
- Or do you really believe that what you are doing has value to your child's development and personal happiness?

This is a big one: If you have ever worried about your children missing certain opportunities, take a look at yourself. Are you trying to avoid dealing with failures or regrets in your own life? Your child is not responsible to protect you from uncomfortable emotions.

The best time (and the trickiest time) to ask yourself all these questions is when your buttons get pushed, when you feel your child is really stirring things up.

Whenever you experience parent-child conflict, or your child does not want to cooperate or comply with something you've requested, STOP and ask yourself:

Is this about me or is this really about my child?

Just put yourself in that frame of mind as you read the rest of this book and right away, you'll find shortcuts to some healthy responses. My goal for you is to help you create a genuinely happy family—one that operates through joy and understanding and love. The key is choosing a perception that honors your child's true nature.

. . . .

ADRIA'S STORY
You Can Create a Happy Family

Adria is a three year-old with a LOT of energy. Her naturally bright, bubbly nature is very animated and random, so much so it sometimes exhausts her mother. Adria often climbs on people and jumps and shouts. When she feels upset, she can get loud and stubborn! Her tantrums were a real challenge for her parents, but something's changed.

Her mother has identified Adria's dominant Type through Energy Profiling and has embraced and honored it. She's given her daughter the kind of attention that Adria needs and they naturally experience fewer tantrums in their home.

*For example, Adria came home from nursery school one day with a picture she was excited to show off. She immediately interrupted something important her mother was doing and wanted her mom to celebrate her picture with her. Another time, her mother might have acted irritated or frustrated, but she decided to honor Adria's energetic delight. She didn't just give Adria attention— she gave Adria **the right kind** of attention, specific to her Type. As soon as that happened, Adria calmed down and snuggled up to her mom. They spent the next few minutes together, basking in the joyful moment.*

Adria's mother said, "I imagine that if I hadn't acknowledged her in this moment and continued to do what I wanted, I might have destroyed her confidence in doing what she enjoys and made her feel less important. I love her!"

. . . .

How to Increase Your Gross Family Happiness

Have you ever heard of the country of Bhutan? A few decades back, they started talking about *Gross National Happiness*—the idea that *being* is more important than *doing* (more important than "success"). Why don't we take on that standard and parent according to our child's level of happiness? What is your *Gross Family Happiness*?

The first step to creating happiness in your home and becoming a better parent can be summed up in two simple statements that I encourage you to tell your child today. No matter how young or old your child is, no matter how many struggles you've had or misunderstandings you've experienced, say these two statements to your child:

"I want to help you be happy being YOU."
"I love you, just the way you are."

If you mean them when you say them, you're already on the right path to becoming a Child Whisperer.

How to Become a Child Whisperer

Your children entered this life equipped with their own deeply rooted, innate gifts and talents. And so did you. I call this energetic configuration that every person is born with an Energy Profile.

What does Energy Profiling have to do with becoming a Child Whisperer?

Everything.

Becoming a Child Whisperer involves identifying your child's Energy Profile, understanding what their Energy Profile tells you, and applying what you've learned in order to make everyday interactions with your child effortless and enjoyable for you both.

What is an Energy Profile?

Every person alive has their own unique Energy Profile—a natural movement that expresses itself in body language and earliest sounds from the day a child is born. In fact, it even starts earlier than that. Have you ever heard a mother say that her pregnancies each felt different? That's because she was carrying children with different energetic movements.

Most parents default to the assumption that their children's personalities are the factor that makes them different. I suggest to you that personality is actually just a by-product of something much deeper, much more innate in a child's expression. I suggest that a child comes to this life with a natural expression of movement that profoundly influences personality. If this natural expression is ignored or stifled, children's personalities can develop in contradiction and conflict with their true nature. The goal of every parent should be to help a child develop a personality consistent with their true nature and natural movement, rather than one that contradicts it.

In other words, your goal as a parent is to become a Child Whisperer.

When you are a Child Whisperer, you don't have to wait for the tantrum, the rebellion, or the crisis to happen. You already know your child's deepest motivations and you know how to honor and support them so the crises just don't exist. You have all the tools you need to intuit your child's needs, rather than react to them. Not only that, you know how to create a home environment that honors each Type in your family so that everyone feels happier and more fulfilled.

. . . .

COLE'S STORY
Their True Nature is Already There

When ten-year-old Cole started to play basketball, his coach told him that the more he practiced, the better he would be. He took that advice to heart. And true to his deeply committed nature, he did something about it.

When Cole went home later that day, he told his parents he planned to shoot 100 baskets a day. They reminded him that they didn't have a basketball hoop. He said that was fine. He had already gone across the street and arranged with the neighbor to use their basketball hoop daily. He had taken initiative and already committed to his plan. His parents didn't need to force or even encourage him— they just needed to support him in being the committed, authoritative person he already was!

. . . .

An Energy Profile is an Inner Blueprint

I recently heard a parent say she needed to "instill" into her children the right values so they would grow to be good people. But to instill suggests that we have to "put into" children something that is not already there. I believe children come with a blueprint, an inner design of who they really are.

You may choose to teach your children your particular belief system or cultural norms, but there is nothing you need to instill to make your child good—just a true nature to bring out! Your children already came to your family with natural gifts and talents of intuition, compassion, and love.

Your natural movement may look different from your child's, but *you also* possess unique gifts to aid you in the incredible journey of parenting your children true to their natures. Open yourself up to your own intuitive gifts and abilities.

With that in mind, it's time to talk about the Energy Profiling model so you can revolutionize your parenting and support your children in feeling more loved and confident than ever.

Introduction to Energy Profiling

Energy Profiling is an intuitive model to describe the configuration of movement and energy your child was born with. Your child is a unique and wonderful person, and Energy Profiling is a supportive tool to help you understand the truth of who your child is—inside and out.

As you determine your child's Energy Profile, it will be worthwhile for you to remember that Energy Profiling is *not* a personality test. Personality is only one of several factors used to identify someone's Energy Profile. Some of those other factors are actually more reliable because they cannot be altered or faked.

Children will adapt their personalities to the expectations put on them. They often receive messages or are parented in a way that encourage them to develop a personality at odds with their nature and natural movement. It's one of the biggest reasons we have such a huge self-help industry today. Think about your own childhood. There were probably rules or expectations from someone (whether parents, friends, teachers, or otherwise) that demanded that you alter your personality to fit in or survive.

. . . .

KATHY'S STORY
Rules and Expectations

Kathy was not parented true to her nature as a child. She was a bright, animated child with a naturally buoyant, random nature. At a young age, she connected with the belief that she had too much movement, too much energy, too much noise for her parents. She believed that she needed to behave, and behaving meant that she couldn't live life in the fun, unstructured, spontaneous movement that came naturally to her.

This belief brought on so much shame about her inner nature. She felt ashamed of who she truly was and is! Her body responded by playing out that belief as she grew up. She gained a huge amount of weight and apologized for it constantly. She made jokes about herself, as if she were saying, "Yes, I know I'm too much. I take up too much space. I'm ashamed that I want to live life as big as I do."

You know what? It's not okay! When children are told that they are too much or not enough, they are shamed into acting contrary to their nature. It's not okay that this brilliant, beautiful woman was shamed about who she was. I'm proud of her. She came to me after she had already lost 70 pounds. Since then, she's taken even more steps on the path to healing, happiness, and living true to her nature.

. . . .

A child's inner nature exists before personality ever develops! Your job as a parent is to honor your child's nature so their personality develops in harmony with who they really are. Identifying your child's Energy Profile is one of the most important steps you can take in understanding and honoring that true nature.

How to Identify Your Child's Energy Profile

In Energy Profiling, there are four Types of natural movement. Each Type is labeled with a number—Type 1, Type 2, Type 3, and Type 4—to avoid negative judgment associated with descriptive titles. These four Types each describe different qualities and levels of movement that children naturally express.

As you read through each of the Types' descriptions, observe your child's natural gifts and talents, personality traits, thought and feeling processes, communication, behavioral tendencies, learning tendencies, physical development, body language, and physical characteristics. Use all these factors to determine which of the four Types best describes your child. There is no test to take—this system is designed to be intuitive, personal, and empowering.

As you read the next four sections (one for each of the Types in my Energy Profiling system), you may automatically recognize your child's tendencies. In the research I've conducted, I've found that each of the four Types of children express similar patterns in all areas of their life. Certain activities may look a little different depending on age or gender, but the movement is still the same. Keep reading and you'll see what I mean.

Don't get discouraged if you feel confused or unsure about your child's Type! Depending on your situation, your child might not currently be living true to his or her nature. Any number of situations at school, with friends, or family can compromise a child's true nature. We'll talk about some of those situations later—and what you can do about them.

For now, consider these three essential keys to discovering your child's Energy Profile as you read about each of the 4 Types.

1. *Live true to your own nature.*

This is more important than you might realize. In fact, it is huge. As parents, we too often try to change or shape our children into something they are not, often in an attempt to line their behavior up with the priorities of our own Energy Type. We don't even realize we are doing it!

Until you live true to your own nature, you won't be able to get the clarity and intuition you need to read your children. Energy Profiling is an intuitive system and you definitely need intuition as a parent. If you're not living true to yourself 100 percent, that's okay. Self-awareness is the first step to living true to your nature.

If you've already identified your Energy Profile, then good for you. If you don't know your own Type yet, try to identify it as you read through the following sections. You were probably living most true to yourself as a child. You may recognize your tendencies and desires as a child in some of these pages, which will help you discover your own Energy Profile. I can't stress this enough: *You will get clear intuitive hits as a parent when your own true self is honored and whole.*

You may be asking yourself where Energy Profiling even comes from and how I've identified these four Types of movement. I have studied the energetics and movement of human nature in the field of energy psychology for over 20 years. In that time, I have discovered that these four elements are the building blocks of our biology and the four Types: nitrogen, oxygen, hydrogen and carbon. (For a broader look and more information about the science behind Energy Profiling, I recommend the resources you can find in Appendix B in the back of this book).

2. *Look at movement, not personality.*

Energy is a movement that begins in the womb—before your child ever develops a personality. So many factors and expectations influence your child's expression of personality. But natural movement and the basic design of facial features do not change.

In my discussion of each of the Energy Types, I describe typical patterns in physical development, body language, and physical characteristics that can be a more reliable indicator of a child's Type than their personality.

Some of the descriptions or stories for each of the Types may remind you of your interaction with your child or your parents' interaction with you. To varying degrees, every person carries all four Types within them. But your child leads with the expression of only *one* dominant Type that will stay consistent throughout his or her life.

Something to remember: All children are naturally gifted and capable. The only difference between them is that they each move through life experiences with a different quality of movement. When you identify their dominant movement, you can better honor children to move at their own pace and in their own way.

3. *Get your child in on the conversation.*

Unless your children are very young, don't Type them without talking about it with them! They know themselves well and will be the best source for knowing their own Type. You can definitely become familiar with this material before sharing with them. However, you shouldn't expect them to just accept the Type you've chosen for them. Children don't like being told who they are any more than adults do.

Energy Profiling is a process of self-discovery that empowers children to recognize and own their strengths and abilities. Don't rob them of that opportunity for self-reflection and fulfillment.

Children are naturally drawn to experiences that honor their true natures, so they may naturally be drawn to learning about Energy Profiling along with you. If they aren't interested, consider the possibility that your child has a reason. Ask yourself which patterns in your family create resistance to understanding their true nature. Which expectations have been placed on your children that pressure them to deny their true natures?

Children younger than three to four years old are not yet capable of being included in this conversation. That doesn't mean you should wait to learn their Type! You can still identify your young child's Energy Profile through the information and stories shared in the next few sections. When you honor your child's nature from a very young age, you will find that they act more naturally cooperative and happy (and you'll avoid those twos that are supposedly so terrible!).

. . . .

JAKE AND MAX'S STORY
What Changes When You Know Their Type

Eight-year-old Jake had a hard time with his younger brother, Max. He expressed a lot of anger and blamed Max for things, even though four-year-old Max was always trying to get his approval. His parents experienced a challenge in trying to help their boys have positive interactions.

When their mother discovered Energy Profiling, she soon learned that both Jake and Max identified with a dominant Type 4 expression. They both have naturally structured, exact natures. They both felt very strongly—even from a young age—about being their own authority. You can imagine how they could push each other's emotional buttons.

One night, Jake's mom was tucking him into bed after reading about Energy Profiling. She told Jake that he and Max were lucky to have each other because they thought the same and understood each other. She shared some of their tendencies that were similar.

Since that night, Jake's mom says, "It has been night and day. Seriously. I thought I had to do something more drastic, or bigger than that. All I did was talk to them. It has helped Jake more. I think he feels that he now has somebody in the family that gets him."

A few days later, she took her boys to the local library. Jake was using the self-scanner to check out their books when one of the books wouldn't scan. Max grabbed the book from his brother and his mom says, "I was ready for the meltdown and the fit." But Jake just let Max help him with the book. Then he took the book down and put it in the pile. Max grabbed the other books, put them on the scanner, and Jake took them off. They worked together.

His mother says she hasn't done one thing different besides talk to them. Just understanding each other's natures helped both parents and siblings to support and cooperate with each other.

. . . .

One last note before we look at the four Types. All children—no matter their Type—have certain basic needs and traits in common. All children are innocent and active. They all possess childlike curiosity, imagination, and a desire to explore this world. Every child needs to be validated by their parents.

Most importantly, children *need* to be loved and accepted for who they are. Meeting that need is the most important reason you could read this book, for both yourself and your children.

It's time to discover your child's unique Energy Profile and use that knowledge to become a Child Whisperer.

The 4 Types of Children

Before you take an in-depth look at each of the four Types, let me introduce you briefly to all of them.

What follows here is just an overview. It is not meant to serve as your only assessment tool. If one of these brief explanations looks like it may describe your child, you may want to skip to that section to read it at length.

While children express all four Energy Types to varying degrees, each child will always lead with a dominant natural expression, followed by a secondary Energy Type.

Type 1: The Fun-loving Child

- Primary Connection to the World: *Social*
- Primary Movement: *Bouncy and random*
- Primary Need: *To have fun and happy parents*

May be described as: *animated, fun, bright, light-hearted, friendly*
May be negatively judged as: *flighty, hyperactive, unreliable*

Type 2: The Sensitive Child

- Primary Connection to the World: *Emotional*

- Primary Movement: *Subtle and thoughtful*
- Primary Need: *To have feelings honored and everyone in the family feel loved and connected*

May be described as: *tender, gentle, kind, thoughtful*
May be negatively judged as: *wimpy, shy, hyper-sensitive*

Type 3: The Determined Child

- Primary Connection to the World: *Physical*
- Primary Movement: *Active and determined*
- Primary Need: *To be challenged and have new experiences with support of their parents*

May be described as: *Strong, active, persistent, energetic*
May be negatively judged as: *Pushy, loud, demanding, rambunctious*

Type 4: The More Serious Child

- Primary Connection to the World: *Intellectual*
- Primary Movement: *Straightforward and exact*
- Primary Need: *To be respected by their parents and family members and respect them in return*

May be described as: *Thorough, efficient, responsible, analytical*
May be negatively judged as: *Critical, judgmental, know-it-all*

Your child is a gift, no matter which dominant Energy Type they express. As you now look at each of the Types in depth, I encourage you to read with the intent to identify your child's Type and to honor their true nature more every day.

Type 1: The Fun-Loving Child

Primary Connection to the World: *Social*
Primary Movement: *Bouncy and random*
Primary Need: *To have fun and happy parents*

The Type 1 expression comes from the element of nitrogen/ air, and its natural primary movement is upward and light. A child with a dominant Type 1 movement will be naturally fun-loving, spontaneous, and cheerful. These children move upward and out to create in this world. They have the highest level of natural movement of all the Types.

Other words that describe the movement of the energy in a dominant Type 1 child: animated, bubbly, brilliant, light-hearted, and unstructured. Adults often describe a child with a dominant Type 1 energy as a "ray of sunshine." When I meet a Type 1 child, I always notice the twinkle in their eye and the sparkle in their energy.

Keeping life light and fun is one of the primary motives for a Type 1 child. Many cultures worldwide value this kind of energy in children, but expect these kids to "grow up" and stop playing games at some point. Treating a Type 1s buoyant, playful movement as a strength will give them powerful permission to live true to themselves. Dominant Type 1 children who are supported to live true to their natures maintain their youthful energy and love for fun, even as they grow into adulthood.

Natural Gifts and Talents: Ideas and Hope

Type 1s naturally offer some unique gifts to the world without even trying: *lots of new ideas matched with the hope that they are possible.*

They initiate the cycle of wholeness by coming up with new ideas and truly believing those ideas can come true. Their animated quality brings new life to everything. The Type 1 catchphrase is: *"I have a new idea, and we can do it!"*

Ideas come easily and readily for Type 1 children. They are naturally brimming with new ideas and they truly believe in all of them. Their natural movement of being light and carefree can also mean they do not naturally follow through. Since they thrive with new experiences and ideas, these children face the challenge of choosing an idea and carrying it to the end.

• • • •

JENS' STORY
Lots of Ideas!

Jens' mother appreciates his endless ideas, but observes that some of them can result in a costly mess. The object of one of his ideas? A game to see how many juice box drinks he could pop with his bike tires before his friends hit him with a roll of wet toilet paper! Eight boys, a case of juice boxes from Costco, an economy pack of toilet paper, and a hose make for a lot of fun—and a lot of mess!

Type 1 children are full of creative ideas. While they grow, they need both direction and space to make mistakes, so they can learn which of their ideas might be best to act on, and which are best to just appreciate as fun ideas and then let go.

• • • •

◯ **Child Whisperer Tip:** As a parent, you do not have to take responsibility for following through on every idea your Type 1 child has. It's just not possible! Nor is it helpful for your child. In an attempt to teach them responsibility, you might insist that they carry out an idea that was just that—an idea. You might try to shut down the endless ideas because they overwhelm you. Let go of your anxiety about all their ideas and just appreciate how many of them your child has!

My oldest daughter, Jenny, is a bright and cheery Type 1. She is full of ideas. As her mother, I used to think that she needed to learn to follow through on every idea she came up with. The day I realized that all her ideas did not have to turn into results—and that the idea alone was valuable for her—we had a lot more fun celebrating her ideas. Try acknowledging your child's ideas as good and fun. Sometimes, that's all a Type 1 child needs to feel validated and move to the next new thing.

Fun-loving Type 1 children are socially oriented. Their gift for living in the present and being naturally optimistic means they make friends easily, with everyone! As they grow, Type 1 children become very devoted to their friends. Other people and children are drawn to them because their energy makes things more carefree and light wherever they go. They are natural experts at cheering people up. For a Type 1 child, life's meant to be fun and happy!

◯ **Child Whisperer Tip:** A mom shared with me that she used to say to her six-year-old, "Everything doesn't need to be a game!" Then she realized that for a Type 1 child, it does! Type 1 children have a natural orientation to the light, the playful, and the animated in life. They love surprises, games, and pretending. That's a *good* thing. Honor your Type 1 child's orientation to keep things light and playful by making little games out of ordinary tasks (getting dressed, grocery shopping, getting the mail) and you will find that your child brightens up.

How can you make your own family's daily activities a little more fun for your Type 1 child? List some ideas here:

_____

_____

_____

_____

Personality Traits: Social and Fun

When Type 1 children are honored in living true to themselves, their personalities shine. Other people often describe them as cheerful, friendly, charismatic, outgoing, funny, or cute. Their animated nature bubbles over into everything they do and say. A Type 1 child's personality engages other people in a fun, social and entertaining way, which often makes them the center of attention. They are little social butterflies, even as babies and toddlers—a quality of being that helps them make friends easily throughout their entire lives.

. . . .

HENRY'S STORY
Making Friends With Everyone!

Henry started speaking at 10 months and hasn't stopped since. When he learned his address he started telling it to everyone—including complete strangers at the store. His parents had to tell him to stop inviting everyone over to their house!

. . . .

Your Type 1 child's naturally bright, bubbly personality might be judged as a weakness in certain situations—sometimes even by you. These children might be labeled hyperactive, flighty, or irresponsible. Your Type 1 child will not be naturally structured or serious, and demanding that they become so will only make them doubt their natural spontaneity and cheeriness.

It is your job as a parent to help your child to recognize that their natural movement is valuable. Acknowledge the strength in your Type 1 child's natural tendencies before trying to teach them how to manage those tendencies better.

Thought and Feeling Process: Quick and Random

Thoughts for a Type 1 child are quick and spontaneous. They jump from one idea to another quickly and randomly. If you parent a Type 1 child, you may wonder if there are connections between the ideas they share in rapid succession. The connections are there, but they are random and they come in spurts.

Parents of these children often observe that they act "without thinking things through." But Type 1 children often just think things through too quickly for their parents or others to notice. They may seem scattered or thoughtless, but they are jumping from idea to idea, mentally organizing quickly, and juggling many things at once. They seem to instantly know what they want and then jump to the next idea just as easily.

⌒ **Child Whisperer Tip:** Their quick movement from idea to idea often earns these children the label of "child-ish" or "silly." So Type 1 children *long* to be respected as they grow up. In order to be taken seriously, they commonly attempt to slow down their energy and change who they are. Take your Type 1 child's thought process seriously and listen to what they have to say, no matter how scattered it may appear at times. Their brains work quickly and their language has a hard time keeping up with how quickly thoughts move through their mind. Be willing to just try to make the jump from thought to thought with them sometimes.

When it comes to a Type 1's feelings, everything is larger than life. Little joys are huge delights. Hurt feelings can lead to bursts of emotion. Both expressions may sound quite loud, as they express their emotions vocally, especially as young children. Type 1 toddlers are either screaming in delight or screaming in frustration. The highest squeal you hear from teenage girls is most likely to come from a Type 1.

. . . .

ADRIA'S STORY
Celebrating Every Day

Little Adria was playing by herself outside one day, not realizing that her mom was watching. She went down the slide and at the bottom, she shouted, "Ta da!" Even when she was playing by herself, and she thought nobody else was around, she still enjoyed herself enough to celebrate and shout out loud to congratulate herself for a fun accomplishment. This is just how cute a little Type 1 child thinks and feels. What a delight!

. . . .

Type 1s process emotion very quickly when given permission to feel their feelings. They feel it and move on. They do not feel emotion deeply. Feelings are light and are meant to stay that way. Just like Type 1 children go from sunny to tears in a second, they often go back to their naturally cheerful disposition just as quickly after being validated and heard. Just because a Type 1 child moves through their emotions in what might look like a disorganized or disconnected way, that does not make their feelings any less valid or real.

A Type 1 child can get emotionally explosive at times, but when acknowledged and honored for their feelings they let go of them easily and then often feel guilty for getting so upset. As their natural expression is designed to help lift the mood and energy of others, these children can be very hard on themselves if they feel their emotions have done just the opposite.

Child Whisperer Tip: Help your Type 1 child by inviting them to express their feelings before they build up and turn into explosive expressions. Your child may shy away from expressing uncomfortable emotions, as they do not want to add anything they perceive as negative or unhappy to stressful family situations. But you do not want your Type 1 child to learn to repress emotions. I have met many Type 1 adults who started doing this in their childhood in an effort to make mom or dad happy. This pattern only turns the child into a depressed, overweight, Type 1 adult.

Encourage emotional expression and be patient with any outbursts. Type 1 energy is like a geyser—it erupts randomly, goes off big and then suddenly, it's over! After the outburst, reassure your Type 1 child that it is okay to express feelings and everyone is fine and happy. They need to know their feelings do not disrupt the family's general state of happiness.

If you parent a Type 1 child, notice the little things they do every day with the intent to put a smile on your face. Remember, they are more random and don't always think things through. I am certain your Type 1 child has gotten into trouble sometimes for doing something that was designed in their mind to cheer you up. When this happens, they are really not sure why they are in trouble, when their intent was to bring you joy.

Type 1 children dislike situations in which others get upset about relatively small issues. These children will experience serious punishment or a mistake blown out of proportion as a bigger emotional downer than their parents may realize. In the words of my Type 1 son, Mario, "It makes me feel like life is wrong when people bring their worries to where we are having fun." If your Type 1 child is not expressing their naturally light energy effortlessly, consider which situations around them might weigh their feelings down.

Child Whisperer Tip: Having happy parents is a big priority for Type 1 children. If they perceive that their parents are unhappy with them, these children will often adapt to try and cheer their parents up. This is not a child's responsibility, but a Type 1 will try to take it on, especially if they feel unhappiness is directed at them personally. If you are upset or sad, reassure your Type 1 child that everyone is sad sometimes, that you will be happy again, and that they are okay. Never use disappointment or an expression of unhappiness to coerce or manipulate your Type 1 child into behavior that you want.

When my Type 1 daughter, Jenny, was only 8 years old, I noticed she would pull out the vacuum and start vacuuming the house when I was upset. I figured out that her reason for doing this was to try and make me happy. I made sure I let her know that my happiness was not her job and that I appreciated her doing something to make me happy. My job as her parent was to turn my mood around so she would not feel stressed about her unhappy mother.

How can you help your Type 1 receive the gift of having a happy parent? List some things you want to focus on here:

_____

_____

_____

_____

If you don't feel emotionally connected to your Type 1 child, there's a reason. Consider the possibility that your child has one of these experiences with you:

- They are not having fun with you.
- They feel everything is heavy and serious when they are with you.
- They feel controlled, like they have no room to breathe and express their random nature.
- They feel judged or unimportant because of their light, airy nature.
- They are confused about who they are because their true expression is in conflict with what has been judged by their parent as a weakness.

Having things light and playful is not a preference or a wish for a Type 1 child. They *need* fun. They *need* spontaneity. Imagine telling the wind to just calm down and be more responsible. When you honor your Type 1 child's true nature, you will see them become happier and more emotionally responsive to you.

◯ **Child Whisperer Tip:** Keeping things light and fun doesn't mean you have to come up with activities and games constantly. Light and fun is a mood, an energy. Notice the tone of your voice and the mood of your home. Do you speak in a friendly, loving voice? Do you let you Type 1 child run and bounce at home? Allow them to create their own fun and express their naturally light energy.

. . . .

MARIO'S STORY
Type 1s Respond to Support!

I met our Type 1 son, Mario, when he was an 11-year-old boy. He came into our family when he was 15 and we officially adopted him when he was 17. Mario came from an abusive background, and his Type 1 nature had been judged most of his life as irresponsible. This led him to believe he was incompetent—which was another, more subtle layer of abuse that needed to be healed in his life. He had many limiting beliefs that he could not succeed in school and that his animated nature was immature.

He had already started to overdevelop his secondary Type 4 nature by the time he was 15, as he no longer felt he could trust his true nature to help him succeed in life. Knowing his true nature made all the difference in understanding how to parent him and help heal his past wounds. I was very mindful to make things light for Mario and to support him in developing his gift for ideas and his love for people and having fun.

We had many difficult challenges that we needed to overcome, and it was not easy. I have to say that knowing about his Type 1 nature made all the difference in knowing how to better parent him. Today he is a successful young man who embraces his playful, animated nature and has learned to use his brilliant mind to succeed in life. He puts a smile on my face every time I am with him.

. . . .

Communication: Enthusiastic

These kids are chatty! Even from a young age, Type 1 children are verbal and motivated by social interaction. They love talking to anyone and their communication patterns are often friendly and inviting.

Type 1 children enjoy chit-chat, jumping from one idea to the next in a random way, and they prefer conversations that are light and uplifting. They often say what they think as soon as it comes to mind, even if that means that they interrupt someone else with the thought that just popped in their head.

Child Whisperer Tip: Your Type 1 child will probably interrupt you at times. Rather than shush your child when this happens, acknowledge them and let them know you will listen in a moment. If they persist, remind them that they do not need to interrupt you to be heard, and that you think that what they say is important. Make sure you really do ask them to wait only a moment before giving your attention—otherwise their quickly moving thought will be lost. Type 1 children only need a moment, as their ability to connect and disconnect quickly is an attribute that allows them to get their needs met very quickly.

Type 1 children get excited about what seems like the littlest thing—and parents may think they need to quiet down this excitement, thinking that some things are not worth getting that excited about. For a Type 1 child, they are.

♡ **Child Whisperer Tip:** Admire and acknowledge your Type 1 child's excitement and enthusiasm with simple compliments like these: "I am so glad you are having so much fun with that." "That is so wonderful how much fun you are having." "I love how much enthusiasm you have." Your approval of their natural enthusiasm will mean so much to them, and it will also help them to naturally find a healthy balance of how much enthusiasm they express.

. . . .

JENS' STORY
Saying Whatever Comes to Mind

Nine-year-old Jens will say whatever he's thinking, right when he thinks it. He and his mother were talking in the car one day about what they wanted to do during summer vacation. In that moment, Jens saw a Burger King he'd never seen before. He disconnected immediately from talking about summer vacation and just lit up at the surprise of that Burger King he'd never noticed. He sounded as excited about that Burger King as he did about Christmas morning! That's a Type 1 child.

. . . .

Communication for a Type 1 child is often loud and animated. They move their bodies and hands to communicate. Imagination even applies to language. They often make up their own words and silly phrases, just to make communicating that much more fun.

◯ **Child Whisperer Tip:** Because a Type 1's natural movement is random, they may expect you to keep up and follow their train of thought, which might not look like it has any connections. If you get lost about what your Type 1 child is talking about, don't make them retrace their steps. Just express your desire to understand what they're talking about and celebrate with them.

Behavioral Tendencies

Family Relationships: *Need play to feel loved.*

Type 1 children are fun to be with. They are generally affectionate and cheery. Even older Type 1 children will not have difficulty engaging in playful behavior with younger siblings. They often notice if someone in the family is sad, taking it as their personal goal to cheer that person up. They create fun with whichever member of the family they are with.

In order to feel loved in the family, these children need to be played with, rather than merely told they are loved. When you play with your Type 1 child and take time to have fun with them, *you* will put a smile on *their* face.

• • • •

BRIDGER'S STORY
Playing with Siblings

As the oldest of five siblings, Bridger's fun-loving nature makes it easy for him to play with and relate to his younger brothers and sisters—even though he's a teenager. He'll play Legos with his younger brothers, and can make them laugh easily by being goofy. On top of that, he's a fun babysitter to all of his younger siblings. The only challenge? Instead of putting them to bed on time, he gets them all riled up at bedtime. So much fun!

Because Type 1 children want everyone in the family to be happy, they may tend to become a people pleaser or a helper. This can turn into a pattern of compromising their true nature or needs in order to please others.

I had to be careful with this possibility with my son Mario. He was always so willing to lend a helping hand that I learned I could take advantage of it if I was not aware. Since a Type 1's energy easily connects and disconnects from one activity to another, I knew Mario would drop pretty much whatever he was doing (even if it was something important to him) in order to help me out. So I tended to call on Mario more often than maybe I should have, until I realized it was not honoring to take advantage of his random, spontaneous nature.

If a Type 1's random nature ever gets on the nerves of a more structured child, make sure to support both children in living true to themselves. Don't let a Type 1 compromise their light nature just to please others.

We experienced this with our two sons, Mark and Mario. Mario often sat at the kitchen table, eating a snack, tapping his fingers on the tabletop, and humming a tune all at the same time. Mark, with his more structured Type 4 nature, became irritated if he was doing something in the same area. I noticed this becoming a problem when Mark often told Mario to stop making so much noise and to stop moving so much. These incidents usually occurred in the general family areas of our home, which meant that Mario was being shut down in the space where family members should feel free to be themselves.

I spoke with Mark about the situation. I shared with him that he needed a different solution than to tell Mario not to be himself! I asked Mark to come up with another solution—which he did. He decided that if Mario was getting on his nerves, it was better for him to leave the space rather than shame his younger brother by telling him he was annoying and getting mad about it. Mark honored his brother and himself this way from that point forward.

Friends and Social Settings: *Naturally friendly*

Type 1 children make friends readily and they naturally thrive in social settings. As a Type 1 child grows, he or she will always want to engage with new people in new situations. It can be a challenge for these children to stay entertained and amused all by themselves. They need regular interaction with people around them, hugging, laughing, and smiling. They will often bring out the playful side of their friends.

For example, I often asked Mario what Type his friends were in high school and he would tell me they were Type 1s, just like him. Then I would meet them and see that they were not Type 1s, but another Type! I finally figured out that his friends became more playful and fun-loving with him around, so they came off like Type 1s because of his energetic influence! Mario brought out his friends' Type 1 nature, which is part of all of us, though it may be hidden from view until someone who leads with Type 1 gives us permission to bring it forward.

Because others sometimes judge Type 1s as shallow, a Type 1 child may become concerned about superficial friends. You can reassure a Type 1 child that having many friends comes naturally to them, and it's never a problem unless they keep creating friendships that compromise their animated, optimistic nature.

· · · ·

CLAIRE'S STORY
Type 1s Need Friends

Claire was two years old when she moved out of state with her family. Her parents understood her random, playful, Type 1 nature, so they planned fun activities for her and thought she would love experiencing all the new sights of an unfamiliar place. But by the end of the first week in their new home, Claire was cranky, irritable, and unusually whiny. Her parents wondered what they were doing wrong. In a flash of child-whisperer inspiration, they got the answer. Fun activities alone were not enough— Claire needed friends.

Her parents immediately went looking for play groups and social settings where many young children would be present. After three days of activities that involved groups of other young children, Claire's naturally cheery demeanor returned. She started singing to herself again and rarely whined, even when doing activities with just Mom or Dad.

. . . .

Type 1s are so socially oriented that they have a hard time when isolated—even if there are plenty of new things to see and do. They thrive on the social aspect of those experiences.

⌒ **Child Whisperer Tip:** Facilitate opportunities for your Type 1 child to interact with various people. As long as the opportunity is there, they'll make friends with whomever they meet!

Timeliness: *Unstructured*

As you might imagine, a Type 1's unstructured nature shows up in the way they manage time. The Type 1 children I know often run late for school or getting out the door. They sometimes forget plans they've made with friends. And they often rush at the last minute.

Remember, these children are not *trying* to be late. Most of them want to be on time, but they get distracted while getting ready. Their minds move so quickly that they actually get distracted by several things at a time.

♡ **Child Whisperer Tip:** Treating Type 1s like they need to fix a flaw in themselves will not help them become punctual. Every time you fight against a child's true nature, you actually increase the tendency for the very problem you want to avoid.

Helping your Type 1 child have fun along the way as they prepare to go somewhere will help them get out the door easier.

♡ **Child Whisperer Tip:** You could invite your child to make up a silly get-ready-for-school song (just start singing and they'll probably make up more words), you could play follow-the-leader out to the car, or if you're going somewhere fun, just surprise them with the news of where you're going close to the time you're leaving. If it sounds like a good idea, they'll want to go right when you mention it.

What are you doing to make your Type 1 child's get-ready-for-school routine just a little bit more fun? How could you turn it into a game?

_____

_____

_____

_____

Jobs and Household Chores: *Make chores a game*

Giving a Type 1 child a long chore list just will not work. They appreciate ideas and newness, but follow-through is not their natural strength. One look at a long, boring list and they will lose focus and motivation. You will end up feeling frustrated, like you have to hold their hand every step of the way. Even then, they may only do chores quickly and not thoroughly.

Type 1 children do love to be helpful. They want to put a smile on your face, but they would obviously rather play than clean up. So why not transform work into play? Turn a chore into a game or an opportunity to pretend and you will find the best Type 1 helper on the planet. "Cinderella, mop the floor!" or "Quick! Let's see if we can make all the toys in the front room fly into their box!"

Even very young Type 1 children like to join the fun. I know of one sweet mom who gives her two-year-old the weekly job of pushing her basket of clothes to the laundry room and back to her room when they are clean. It's amusing, simple, and her daughter is already learning to help.

Money Management: *Motivated by fun*

Type 1 children usually spend their money on what seems most amusing to them. Some children spend the money they have freely on whatever seems most fun at the moment, while other (usually older) children might save a little longer to get an item they've had their eye on.

Whatever a Type 1 buys is motivated by fun. Most Type 1 children are naturally generous with money, either loaning it to siblings or buying little gifts to make others happy. Their generosity is a wonderful gift that can be encouraged. Make sure to help your Type 1 child to recognize that money isn't the best or only means to put a smile on someone's face.

◯ **Child Whisperer Tip:** Consider taking your Type 1 child to a store that carries inexpensive items. Give them some money (or they can bring money that they've earned) to purchase a simple gift for a sibling or friend. The activity will be fun *and the fun continues as they anticipate sharing their gift!*

Recreational Activities: *Imagination is key*

Type 1 children will engage happily in most any activity, as long as it feels amusing and free to them. They are often active and prefer social settings. Dance classes, pretending, running, jumping, riding bikes, playing sports or games outside are common activities enjoyable for a Type 1 child.

Even in quieter situations, they usually prefer activities that allow for creativity, originality, and imagination. For example, they might prefer reading fantasy fiction to other genres. If your Type 1 child likes video games, you may find they prefer the kind where they can create their own characters and levels. I know of a nine-year-old whose preferred quieter activity is planning parties for her friends—including menus, décor, and food. So social!

Activities to Help a Type 1 Child Develop Natural Gifts

As a parent, you can create opportunities for your children to develop their natural gifts. Remember that Type 1 children are socially oriented and express the highest level of movement. Consider involving them in high-energy activities that offer a significant amount of interaction with peers and friends.

Type 1s enjoy making and moving to music. As very young children, they may even sing and dance as a way of getting around the house. Learning and performing in a group may be very supportive to their desire to entertain and delight others.

⌒ **Child Whisperer Tip:** Always consider the movement! When it comes to dancing, ballet may be too structured for a Type 1 child to enjoy for very long. You can find so many other kinds of dance or other movement to engage your Type 1 child more quickly and help them have more fun. Think: tap, jazz, tumbling, etc.

If you want to encourage your child to play a musical instrument, make it socially engaging. Consider an instrument they could play in a group or a band, not for hours of isolated practice at a keyboard.

• • • •

EMILY'S STORY
The Right Movement

Emily has always loved dance. At age three, her mother signed her up for ballet. Emily loved ballet for those first few years because they involved creative movement and the visual imagery of being a princess. She enjoyed pretending and performing on stage.

But as she got older, the class became less about expressive dancing and more about technique. By the age of eight, Emily was begging her mom to quit. Her mom worried about letting her quit, thinking she should learn muscle control. And because Emily didn't want to disappoint her mother, she kept learning and trying beautifully, even though it caused her a lot of stress and anxiety. At this time, she started the nervous habit of pulling out her eyelashes and eyebrows.

Her mother knew something needed to change, so she enrolled her in jazz dance classes. But Emily missed her friends from ballet and asked to go back just so she could experience social time in the carpool. She endured the actual ballet class so that she could be with her friends.

As soon as Emily's mother learned that Emily was a Type 1, she let Emily quit ballet immediately. She realized that Emily needed social opportunities in order to make her activities fun and they started exploring other options, including drama. Emily is much happier and so is her mother, knowing that she is supporting her daughter's true self.

. . . .

Type 1 children love games, so they may enjoy sports. But be aware of the environment they play in. Fun-loving children value experiences with light moods, and they value the game more for the fun they have while playing it, rather than the end result. Sports in a demanding, competitive environment can be too stressful for some Type 1 children. I have found that competitive sports for Type 1 children work if their experience is fun first and competitive second. If too much pressure is placed on them to perform at high levels and they are not having fun, they will not be as drawn to competition.

Whichever activities you choose to encourage or provide your Type 1 child, give them time and tools to cultivate their imaginative experience! These children have vast imaginations and endless ideas. This means that you don't need to come up with nearly as many activities to entertain these children as you may think. Allow your child's natural energy to be expressed and they will naturally just make everything they do more fun.

Supporting them is the key! Rather than taking on the job of fun, just make sure you are not stopping them from expressing what is natural to them. Even chores around the house can be imaginative play for a Type 1 child. I know one mother who encourages her Type 1 daughter to wave her magic fairy wand (the feather duster) all over the house. The dusting gets done and the Type 1 daughter loves how her mother helps her reframe a chore as fun.

♡ **Child Whisperer Tip:** Remember that Type 1 children love newness. They love new ideas, new possibilities, new experiences. They enjoy the optimism and hope that comes at the beginning of a project. You may find them wanting to jump from activity to activity, or starting something only to be distracted about the next new thing they get excited about. Demanding that they stick with one activity or sport or talent for an extended period of time will make that activity drudgery for a Type 1. Type 1 children will stick with what they start if it's important to them and they are free to express their true nature in the experience. So before signing them up for a long class or activity, help them to identify what is most important to them.

Because their energy is light, and they are often misjudged, Type 1 children may take on the belief that they can't accomplish much. Please tell your Type 1 child that their energy is a powerful, creative force that blesses everyone around them.

Which activities can you think of that would honor the movement of your Type 1, fun-loving child? List a few here:

_____

_____

_____

_____

Learning Tendencies

Learning Style: *Visuals matter*

Type 1 children generally prefer visual and hands-on learning over written instruction. It's faster and much more creative. They love learning new concepts and enjoy applying them immediately with hands-on activities. They would rather just get started with a fun project than to sit and listen to instructions.

. . . .

MELISSA'S STORY
Making Homeschool Fun

Melissa homeschools her Type 1 daughter and she discovered a way to bring fun and surprise into every single day. She filled a jar with slips of paper with all the learning activities she felt they needed to accomplish that day. She made sure to include some slips for free play time. Then, she allowed her daughter to draw out one of the slips and they did the activity.

One by one, they went through the slips of paper throughout the day. And every time, the activity was a surprise! It created just the sort of randomness that her Type 1 daughter needed and she couldn't wait to have school the very next day.

. . . .

Classroom Behavior: *Teacher's pet, class clown?*

The classroom experience for these children is split, depending on the nature of the classroom they're in. In an environment supportive to their creative nature, Type 1 children are beloved by teachers and classmates. They offer lots of good ideas and they cheer on their peers. In these classroom situations, they are described as happy, confident, and always willing to participate.

On the other hand, classrooms that demand too much structure or isolated quiet time will bore them and they will get distracted and have trouble completing their work. In these cases, a Type 1 might be labeled as loud, disruptive, or bad. Or they may take on a "teacher's pet" role to try and make a grumpy teacher happy. Be aware of the energy in your Type 1 child's classroom setting so you can know how to best support them in having fun with learning.

Some may say that Type 1 children need to learn to sit still, and that allowing them the kind of random freedom that Type 1s value just teaches them to be disrespectful. It is important to put this idea in perspective. Let's look at the unfortunate label used to classify many Type 1 children.

Unfortunately, due to a Type 1's need for a higher movement, many Type 1 children have been labeled hyperactive and ADHD. When you put a Type 1 child in a very still and structured learning environment, they will create more movement in their experience naturally. They get very bored sitting still and are not able to maintain long periods of focus. So they will talk to their neighbor, start playing games with the items in their desk, fidget and squirm in their chair, drift off in their imagination, or otherwise appear that they cannot settle down and pay attention.

The truth is, they are stifled by the stillness. They can learn much faster in a more interactive environment, as they have very quick thought processes and brilliant minds. The more hands-on and multi-sensory the learning, the more successful they will be. So can they ever learn to sit still?

I believe all children and adults benefit from learning to sit still and pay attention. These are valuable behaviors that we all need to exercise in various settings. Every Type of child is capable of learning to sit still for appropriate amounts of time. However, Type 1 children have too often been expected to sit still and stay focused for unreasonable amounts of time in respect to their natural movement, especially when it comes to our traditional model of learning.

I have met many Type 1 adults who were labeled hyperactive and ADHD only to find out they were just high movement, creative, brilliant children who were not given the chance to learn and move according to their natural gifts and tendencies. Type 1 children *can* learn to sit still, but demanding that they do so all day long actually hinders them in their ability to learn.

Study Habits: *Always changing focus*

A Type 1 child will often move through homework assignments randomly, completing answers that look quickest or tasks that look most fun. They like variety and creativity, so the same routine will weigh them down. They work best with a group or someone there to support them. Solitary work can feel like punishment to a Type 1.

Type 1 children have a hard time with a single focus. Expecting a Type 1 child to sit for long periods of time focusing on one school subject is a challenge for them. You may find them drifting off in their imagination or drawing or doodling on their paper. Type 1 children do better when they can change their focus often or have more going on at once in their study environment. For example, while they are doing their homework, they could be eating a snack and even have the TV on in the background. Also, support them in working on one subject for only 10-15 minutes, changing to another for the same amount of time, then a third subject, then returning to the first. Their natural energy connects and disconnects easily and needs to change focus in order to keep them from losing interest in what they are doing.

Just because they don't focus methodically for long periods of time doesn't mean that Type 1 children aren't bright or excited to learn. They just learn best when their natural movement is honored. When teaching a Type 1 child or helping with homework, enjoy learning with them!

. . . .

JASMINE'S STORY
Making Homework Fun

Nine-year-old Jasmine's grandmother did her homework with her and realized that she just couldn't sit and focus for a long time. So they answered a few questions together and then ran around the table together before doing more. You know what? It worked!

Homework became something fun and active. It was a big game that she got to play with her grandmother, and so with the help of her creative grandmother, Jasmine completed much more than she would have been able to on her own.

. . . .

How do you feel inspired to make your own Type 1 child's learning and study experiences more light-hearted, random, and fun? List your ideas:

_____

_____

_____

_____

Physical Development

Learning to Walk: *Give them time*

Type 1 children engage with the world socially from a very early age. If walking means they can interact better socially, they'll go for it.

Child Whisperer Tip: Don't push your Type 1 child to walk too early. Give them plenty of time to crawl. Studies show that crawling helps connect the right and left brain hemispheres, which Type 1 children need. We made the mistake of encouraging our daughter, Jenny, to start walking at a young nine months old. A few years later when she was learning to read and do math, she had a difficult time. Type 1s are naturally more right-brained (the creative side of the brain), and need to be allowed to crawl to make those strong neural connections to their left brain so their learning of more analytical subjects comes more easily to them.

Learning to Talk: *So social!*

Type 1 children love to talk and interact. They can develop their language skills early, but will not be as clear in their speech. Most Type 1 children are very verbal and love to chatter. The Type 1 brain thinks in whole concepts, so the ability to break those ideas and thoughts into specific words takes more time for a Type 1 child to develop. They try to engage in adult conversation patterns long before they can form words, even laughing when everyone else laughs. They may make up silly words and talk to imaginary friends.

Potty Training: *Occasional accidents*

The biggest potty-training challenge for these kids is the occasional accident that happens when they get distracted or don't want to stop playing. Keep the experience light. The minute you make it serious and unhappy, your Type 1 child will pull away. I'll say it again. . . .Type 1s *need* fun and creativity. Make potty training a game! Show some exuberance with each success. Clap your hands. Be delighted with your child whenever they succeed!

. . . .

ELLIE'S STORY
Make Potty Training Fun

Little Ellie was potty trained in a few days and did great wearing her underwear. However, for the next few weeks, she didn't always get to the potty on time by herself. She worried about the problem of peeing on the floor and often did a little dance to help her hold it.

She did better going potty if she got to play a little game. Together, she and her mom pointed to things and her mom asked her if each thing was the potty. It was a silly game that didn't really have rules or a winner, but it made things fun. If her mom tried to get around the game and took Ellie straight to the bathroom and pulled down her pants, Ellie screamed on the potty. It seemed too serious and it stressed her out. She did fine as long as mom put some effort into making it fun!

. . . .

Child Whisperer Tip: Type 1 children may not learn to potty train in one intense, short time period. It may take several months of interest and then a lack of interest. I recommend you wait a little longer until they show a lot of interest. If you start too early, you will have a lot of trial and error and a very stressed-out fun-loving child.

Sleeping: *Don't want to miss the fun*

Type 1s don't want to miss out on all the fun, so they can have a tough time falling asleep. I love the story of six-year-old Elyce who had such a hard time going to bed that her parents found her in the morning, asleep in her dress-up clothes, with all her toys arranged around her where she'd stayed up playing the night before! Many parents have noticed that their Type 1 children don't like being put to sleep alone in their own room. It's tough for a Type 1 to feel socially cut off.

Type 1 children have usually been so active during the day that they will sleep through the night, but don't expect their schedule to be consistent. There's nothing wrong with your Type 1 child if they don't have a consistent bedtime. They are just naturally more random. Trying to get them to conform to a bedtime that stays the same to the minute may lead to frustrating bedtime experiences for both of you. Give them a little leeway time on when they go to sleep.

⌒ **Child Whisperer Tip:** Turn off the TV, and keep the noise very low in the home if you want your Type 1 child to be able to disengage from the activities going on outside their bedroom and fall asleep more easily.

I learned this with my daughter, Jenny. She came into this world bright-eyed and very alert. She never laid her little head on my shoulder, as she never wanted to miss out on anything! As a baby, she did not want to go to sleep. One solution we found was to have her fall asleep in her swing. The only problem? When we carefully took her out, she too often woke up again, eyes wide and bright as could be! I learned to turn the TV off and not have any noise, which helped her think, "The party's over—go to sleep!"

Going to Pre-school and School: *New friends are a plus*

Type 1 children love to see and meet new friends. Some Type 1 children are a little nervous the first time they attend a preschool setting, but they always come home happy. Any tears don't last long as soon as they see all the fun everyone is having. Most Type

1 children see toys and other kids and don't even bother to say goodbye to Mom and Dad. If they are having trouble parting from you, make sure you're not treating your goodbye like a serious event.

Being Left with a Babysitter: *They warm up*

A babysitter is a fun, new person to play with. As long as the sitter is willing to play and have fun, most Type 1 children will warm right up. Some Type 1 kids will even flirt! If they don't feel comfortable, consider what you're doing in the process of dropping off your child with a babysitter. Do they feel like leaving them with someone is a serious situation? If so, it will create stress and discomfort. Also consider the possibility that your child doesn't feel like disconnecting from you the second the sitter arrives. They will. Just give them a moment and show them something fun to do.

Dating: *So many possibilities*

Type 1s love possibilities, so they may change up boyfriends or girlfriends often to experience lots of different options. This connected-then-disconnected process is natural for a Type 1 teenager. Their relationships may not last very long or look very deep. This doesn't mean that Type 1s do not invest in relationships. They can best create meaningful, lasting relationships when they feel mutually supported in living true to their bright, hopeful nature.

· · · ·

BRIDGER'S STORY
First Girlfriend

When Bridger had his first girlfriend, he spent hours talking to her on the phone. He mentioned to his mother that his girlfriend's mother had died. She asked when that had happened. Bridger didn't know. How did it happen? He didn't know. How many brothers and sisters does she have? He didn't know. Bridger's mother was confused that he spent hours talking on the phone with this girl and in her words, "knows nothing about her."

Bridger's mother asked another question: "What do you talk about?"

"Nothing," he said. "Chit-chat."

That's not unusual, nor is it a problem for a Type 1 relationship—especially in high school. In fact, Bridger's ability to keep things light may have been one of the reasons his first girlfriend was drawn to him!

. . . .

High school experience: *Social, with a catch*

Type 1 teenagers enjoy the social aspect of high school, but they have to be careful not to adapt or take on the negative energy of their friends. These children face the challenge of being expert chameleons, adapting in whatever way they feel necessary in order to lighten others' moods. As your Type 1 child goes through their high school experience, watch for signs that they feel weighed down and give them permission to be themselves.

. . . .

SUMMER'S STORY
Adapting to Others

Summer loves soccer—and she got the bad news that her high school would not be able to have a soccer team unless enough girls played basketball. So Summer joined the basketball team, but she soon became overwhelmed and depressed because it wasn't fun for her and made her schedule too full and structured.

She chose to quit the basketball team and has decided to be more careful in the future to recognize her tendency to try pleasing and adapting to others' demands, particularly when those demands don't support her natural movement.

. . . .

Type 1 children will excel in school when they are able to engage in activities that feel fun to them, whether it be through classes they have fun in, extracurricular activities, or otherwise.

 Child Whisperer Tip: If your Type 1 child has to take classes they deem less fun, support them in finding a way to make the subject they are bored with more entertaining and engaging for them.

My son, Mario, learned to do this in high school classes he was not as engaged by. Mario used to say he did not have a good memory for test taking in subjects like math, science and history. Yet, he could recall movie lines flawlessly, and sing every word to every popular song. When I noticed how great his recall was with movies and songs, it made total sense—the movies and songs were more entertaining and fun, and his brain more easily engaged. So memory was not an issue for him in learning; it was the lack of fun in more left-brain subjects and style of teaching that lost his interest. He was very successful in creating ways to make these subjects more interesting and engaging for himself. Once he understood this about himself, he sat up front, got more involved in the discussions and even imagined he was watching a movie, which helped him do much better on his tests.

Driving: *Quick-minded, maybe distracted*

Parents get a little worried about their Type 1 teens as drivers because these teens seem so distracted much of the time. Yet, these teens are very quick-minded and can be aware of numerous things going on at once and make very quick decisions. The key is not adding extra distractions in their first few months of learning to drive. Keeping the radio and cell phone off and the side conversations to a minimum will keep them from getting distracted and keep their eyes and attention on the road.

After reading through this section about the development of a Type 1 child, what inspiration do you have about supporting your Type 1 child in living true to their nature? Make note of your thoughts here:

_____

_____

_____

_____

Physical Characteristics

At first glance at the 4 Energy Types, most every parent may think their child is a Type 1! This is because we tend to refer to all babies and children as cute and playful. One of the most telling ways to determine your child's true Energy Type is to look at his or her facial features and body language. Your child's physical characteristics are often more accurate than personality, which can be altered by situation or expectation. The overall quality of a Type 1's physical expression is animated, youthful and cute. Their bone structure creates circles and points of a star with features being asymmetrical or random.

Something to remember: Learning facial profiling for babies and children in a book without pictures or illustrations can be difficult! That is why I have created a library of videos on my website called, "How to Profile Babies, Children, and Teens!" To access this library visit www.thechildwhisperer.com.

Face shape: *Circular or heart shaped*
Very high, rounded forehead that may look even higher than normal in infants before hair grows in.

Skin/skin texture: *Clear, fresh, smooth skin, with random freckles or moles*
Type 1 skin often features a soft golden or rosy glow. Babies can have tendency for rosacea, or baby acne.

Cheeks: *Circles*
What we call "apple cheeks." Cheeks look round and dimples will often be found around the smile.

Nose: *Turned up, button nose*
Often small and round. Cute. LIttle.

Eyes: *Sparkly, bright, wide-eyed, and often round*
Their eyes appear to be "smiling eyes," which means their whole face smiles with an upward movement. Even the lines on the sides of their eyes move upward when they smile.

Eyebrows: *Come to a point right over the eye, or half circle, shorter in length*

Lips: *Plump lips or fuller bottom lip*

Ears: *Disconnected ear lobe, pointy at the top of the ear, ears that poke out*

Hands: *Little cherub hands, chubby, very childlike*
Short, circular nail bed.

Your Type 1 child may not express all of these physical features in their face—and some features may not fully express themselves while your child is still growing. One common tendency that most all Type 1 children express is their animated facial expressions.

People may comment on the wide variety of facial expressions your Type 1 child makes, or say that they make faces that look like a cartoon. These children are definitely animated. They will probably continue to make these faces as they grow because they often draw a laugh or a smile from others.

Body Language

Body language is an excellent clue to your child's Energy Type. Since Energy Profiling is an assessment of our natural expression of movement, pay attention to the way your child moves. Do any of these movements describe your child?

Crawling: Type 1 children crawl very fast. Some may prefer to roll toward whatever they want to get closer to, putting crawling off for a little while longer.

Walking: Type 1 children have a bounce in their step. Sometimes, their walk looks more like a skip, a dance, or a run. They are bouncy, energetic, and light on their feet. They skip through life with quick steps and their heads up.

Sitting/Standing: These kids just don't sit still. When they sit, it's often on the edge of their seat. They change positions often and they usually fidget, bouncing their leg or otherwise. Standing still—especially to wait in a line—is just not an option. Younger Type 1 children love to twirl and fill up as much space as they have with their energy.

Child Whisperer Tip: PLEASE do not tell your Type 1 child to, "Settle down and stop moving around so much!" This is probably the most common phrase Type 1s hear! This is damaging to your child as it tells them to be the opposite of who they are, and that who they are is not acceptable. The dominant movement of a Type 1 is upward and light. Tell a Type 1 child to stop being upward and light time after time and they will begin to no longer trust their natural movement—they will start to believe that it just gets them in trouble. Rather than tell them to settle down or stop moving, come up with some clever phrases like, "It's time to see how long you can sit and pretend you are a statue!" or, "It's time to get the wiggles out and sit like a doll."

Voice/Language: A Type 1 child is often a giggle-talker. These children like to laugh. They often shriek or squeal when excited. They can also be loud. They enjoy using goofy words for fun and their voices are very expressive and animated.

Child Whisperer Tip: Your Type 1 child may shriek loudly or get very loud and animated in public places. Rather than shush them, ask them to use their indoor voice and/or to make a game out of whispering to them and having them whisper back to you.

Personal Space: Organization to a Type 1 often looks like disorganization to the rest of us. So a Type 1 child's room might look like a disaster, but they will think it's clean. In fact, Type 1 children often feel uncomfortable if everything is organized and put away. These kids prefer their possessions to be visible, meaning that they are out and around. For that reason, don't let a Type 1 child own a lot of stuff. Keep the possession count low, or rotate their items in and out of hiding regularly, and you'll be tripping over a lot fewer things.

♡ **Child Whisperer Tip:** Make it easy for your Type 1 child to clean their room by only having enough belongings out and available so they can clean up a messy room fast. One mom I know of a Type 1 child rotates toys. This is a brilliant idea, as Type 1s love variety and new possibilities. Changing which toys are out once a week not only keeps it easy to clean up, but also keeps play creative for your child.

Consider how you help your Type 1 child organize their room. For example, a Type 4 mom called in to my Child Whisperer radio show looking for help with her Type 1 four-year-old daughter. She was not having any success teaching her daughter to clean up her room.

I asked her what she was expecting of her daughter. She was trying to teach her to fold her clothes and put them in her drawers. This experience usually ended with an unhappy four-year-old who spent a lot of time sitting in her room until she finished this task. I told her that folding clothes was too tedious and slow for a Type 1 child. Plus, this girl had absolutely no fun having to do it by herself.

I suggested this mother get some bins that could hold all the clothes to put under her daughter's bed, and then to put on some music and have her daughter do a silly dance while she tossed her clothes into the bin. Then I suggested that this mom have her daughter call for her and hide in her room when she was finished and jump out when her mother came to find her.

What was a grueling battle of wills and hours of frustration for both mom and daughter could become a light and happy bonding moment that resulted in a clean room and big smiles on both their faces!

What can you do to make your Type 1 child's personal space simple and easy for them to maintain? Is their personal space bright and cheery in its décor? How could you help them create that? List your ideas here:

_____

_____

_____

_____

Challenges as a Parent: Lack of Focus, Not Enough Fun

Parents of Type 1s face specific challenges in raising these children true to their natures. True to their nature, Type 1 children can bring out an animated level of their parents' frustration. The biggest challenge parents often express about these children is keeping a Type 1 child focused or on task. These kids can get distracted easily and do not follow through on everything they begin.

Most parents think the solution to this lack of follow-through is to create more structure in their Type 1 child's life. It's an obvious conclusion: What we see as unstructured we think will be fixed by more structure. This will actually create more difficulty, more of what you are trying to change. Consider the possibility that your Type 1 child already is being subjected to too much structure, and their tendency to get distracted and off track is due to their need to create random, spontaneous movement in their experience. This is their natural movement and they will find a way to express it. If you see this natural expression as something that needs to be disciplined by adding more structure, you will either wound your Type 1 child or cause them to act out more randomly, even to the point of rebelling in their teens.

♡ **Child Whisperer Tip:** Don't demand that your Type 1 child focus on one thing at a time. They won't! If they try to in order to please you, they will feel flawed, inadequate, and frustrated. It will only lead to conflict in your relationship. Instead, help them decide which of their ideas they value enough to pursue and then support them in creating a fun, socially engaged process that they can maintain all the way through the experience.

The second major challenge is creating enough fun! Parents of Type 1 children may start to feel that their child expects them to be an entertainment director, always creating new and exciting adventures. Trying to keep up with this can feel downright exhausting, especially if you're not a Type 1 parent. What do you do?

♡ **Child Whisperer Tip:** Remember that your Type 1 child is an expert at creating fun wherever they go. Fun does not have to mean a specific activity or something that you *do*; think of it as an expression, an energy that feels light and free. We tend to classify certain activities as fun and other activities as not so fun. With a Type 1, though, anything can be more fun when they are supported in being themselves. Even cleaning the garage can be fun with a Type 1! They naturally bring the energy of lightness, spontaneity, creativity, and cheeriness to everything they are a part of—it's this energy they naturally express that makes us all feel lighter. We identify that as fun! Their natural expression of this energy is effortless and makes everything they are part of more enjoyable for everyone who is around them.

Tune into the ways your Type 1 child is pretending and celebrating wherever you are—the grocery store line, in the car, during dinner—and encourage it. Are they laughing, smiling, or imagining? Then they are having fun. You are not responsible to create all the fun for them. Many times, all you need to do is stop shutting down the fun your child is already creating.

Type 1s also naturally have the gift of ideas. Rather than be the director of their fun, ask them what ideas *they* have to make life more fun. A great question to ask a Type 1 who is stressed, whiny, frustrated, or resistant is, "How can we make this more fun?" or, "What are your ideas right now?"

Child Whisperer Tip: You cannot be your Type 1 child's sole social outlet. They love newness and will engage with a variety of friends. If your child is small, create a play group that meets regularly, go with other parents and children to the park, or hire some added help to come and play with your child. As your Type 1 child grows, listen to the activities and friends they want to participate with. They will let you know how social they need to be.

What offsets these challenges? The joys.

Fun-loving, Type 1 children truly are joys. They are naturally happy and optimistic and they forgive easily. If you worry that you have shut down your Type 1 child's bright, happy nature, you can do something about it today. Type 1 children naturally forgive quickly. They will likely light up when you express your intention to help them have fun and move through life with their light, buoyant movement.

When a parent understands their Type 1 child's natural gift for keeping things uplifting, they recognize the beautiful gift that child is to their family, especially in a world where there is so much focus on negativity. These children truly are rays of sunshine that brighten every day! What a blessing to have a Type 1 child in your family. In fact, put down this book and go tell them that right now! All children yearn to be recognized for who they are. All too often, Type 1s are seen as problems or as too much energy to handle. They need to know what a brilliant gift they are to this world.

The Type 1 Fun-loving Daughter

Type 1 daughters are joyful and caring. Their energy tends to be recognized more readily as a feminine expression, due to its lighter nature. Type 1 daughters like to express their creativity by playing dress-up and pretending at a very early age. Our Type 1 daughter, Jenny, loved putting on shows. From an early age, she loved organizing and directing her younger siblings in creating plays and dramas. She was always at the center of the stage and cast the others in supporting roles.

Type 1 daughters are seen as cute and adorable when they are young, but may begin to struggle with being called cute and adorable as they grow. This is unfortunate, as these words truly represent their nature. They struggle with those labels because they want to be taken seriously and feel recognized for their brilliant minds and talents as they grow into young women. Being called cute and adorable suggests they are still little children.

⌒ **Child Whisperer Tip:** Encourage your Type 1 daughter to embrace the power of her cuteness and understand that her natural energy is not something she will grow out of. Help her feel and believe that she can be a force to be reckoned with by staying true to herself and continually developing her natural gifts and talents to make a difference in the world.

The Type 1 Fun-loving Son

Type 1 sons are engaging and uplifting. They easily live true to their natures in the younger years of their life, as we tend to recognize Type 1 energy as childlike and youthful. We don't necessarily think of this energy as gender specific when Type 1 boys are so young.

When a Type 1 male starts to mature and move into his teenage years, though, he may begin to question and try to alter his true nature. This is due to the cultural imprint of what we believe is male energy. We have created the belief and the perception that male energy as it matures needs to be stronger, bolder, and more serious. The whole idea of this belief is captured in the phrase: "It's time to grow up and be a man!" I have met many Type 1 men who live in conflict with their Type 1 energy because they think they cannot be successful if they live true to it. This is completely false. Many successful Type 1 men have contributed to humanity with their ideas and optimism. Nelson Mandela is one example of many.

⌒ **Child Whisper er Tip:** Make sure you do not send the message to your Type 1 son that he needs to "grow up and be a man!" He just needs to grow up living true to himself and when he does, success is guaranteed. Honor his random, buoyant nature as he grows and help him to honor it himself.

Our son, Mario, struggled with his true nature in his early 20s, until one day I recognized what he was doing. He believed he could not live true to his nature *and* be successful. All this belief did was keep him from progressing. I pointed this out to him and told him he needed to stop shaming and doubting his true self and start loving and trusting it. He grasped onto this quickly (true to his Type!), and his life started to shift. Since then, he has created one successful outcome after another.

Two areas where this lesson helped Mario experience success were work and sports. While he worked for a barricade company, setting up and staging barricades on highway construction sites, he learned to use his Type 1 energy to think quickly, to keep things light and fun for other co-workers, and to use his gift for ideas to come up with creative solutions to flow the traffic. His secondary Type 4 energy supported his dominant gifts by keeping him focused in a high-risk environment and maintaining the structure he needed to work long hours into the night. In his college sports career as a rugby player, Mario's Type 4 tendencies sometimes took over and he berated himself if he didn't play to an optimum level, which took all the fun out of it for him. He learned to make sure he was having fun first and executing at high levels second. This actually supported him in playing even better during his games, as he lived true to his nature rather than repressing it.

The Type 1 Child Through the Years

The following are some examples of the many ways Type 1 children express their true nature from birth to age 18 as they mature and develop. They express many general tendencies in these first 18 years. I noted here those I have seen most commonly. These examples may surprise you by how well they describe your Type 1 child.

At each developmental stage, your child has a specific emotional need. This is true for all Types of children. I share some specific phrases to share with your Type 1 child to help meet each need. Use these phrases in words, or consider how you could express these phrases in action to help your child feel loved and wanted in each stage of their life.

When your child is supported in living true to their nature, they can more easily enter their adult experience ready and able to create emotionally healthy relationships. You can meet your child's developmental emotional needs in many ways—just use my examples as a way to get you thinking.

Baby 0 to 18 months

Primary Emotional Need: *To be validated for their bright, fun-loving nature and to be supported in starting to explore and sense the world around them.*

The Type 1 baby is delightful. All Type 1s start their life experience with a primary connection to the social experience of this world. These little ones draw attention to themselves wherever they go as people feel their cheeriness. Around them, others have a feeling of, "I like you and want to connect with your energy!" You may hear a lot of people comment that your little Type 1 is very friendly. These kids truly do start to put a smile on people's faces from the very beginnings of their life.

Messages your Type 1 child needs to hear in this stage of life:

- Welcome to the world; we've been eagerly waiting for your bright energy.
- We have a special place prepared for you.
- All your needs are important to us. You can grow at your own rate, and we are here for you.
- We love your bright, animated nature—you are a gift to the family.
- It's okay to bounce and run and play; we will make it safe for you to explore.
- You can be you and we will always love you.
- It's okay for you to be different from Mom and Dad. We will work out our differences.

♡ Child Whisperer Tips to support this stage: Type 1 babies love to be played with and they enjoy a variety of people to connect with. Talking to your Type 1 baby in fun, animated ways that get them to laugh is very nurturing to them. Too much stillness in a home will not provide the necessary movement for a Type 1 baby. Playing music with light and playful beats will also support them.

Avoid wrapping your baby too tightly in blankets and carriers. They need to feel light and free in their clothes, as well. This will be true for the rest of their lives, so if you notice your Type 1 kicking off their shoes whenever they can, it's because they feel a bit confined.

As your baby becomes more interactive, choose toys that have a lot of movement and variety. Colors, lights, sounds, and music are all good. Just don't give them to your baby right before you want them to go to sleep! Type 1s love to sit up and see their world, so baby seats tilted up, walkers, and Johnny Jump-ups are great options.

We all need balance, so make sure to weave in other movements to nurture your baby. Softer movements and moments of stillness can support a Type 1 baby at appropriate times.

Toddler 18 months to 3 years

Primary Emotional Need: *Support in sensing, exploring and doing in the world.*

The Type 1 toddler is very excited when they learn to crawl and walk. There is a big, wide world to run around in and this is when you start to see them move as a Type 1 with the bounce in their step, the twirls and the jumps. Their engaging personality emerges as they begin to talk to pretty much anyone.

Language skills develop in this stage, and as I said earlier, your Type 1's language skills may come more slowly than the other Types. It will vary from child to child—as is true for everything in the Type 1 world, where there is a lot more variety and randomness. This randomness shows up in levels of Type 1 movement. You may notice that your Type 1 child has very high and bouncy movement or lesser degrees of bounciness. Your child's secondary Type factors into what that may look like for your child (we'll get to that in a few chapters).

Messages your Type 1 child needs to hear in this stage of life:
- It's okay to be curious, to move, to bounce, and to touch and explore this world.
- We want you to explore. We will make it safe for you.
- You can be you and we will always love you.

- You can try out new things and find your own way of doing things.
- It's okay for you to make noise and laugh and play.
- You are so creative and imaginative.
- You are so friendly and eager to please others. We are here to take care of you.
- You put a smile on my face.
- I love you just the way you are.

◠ **Child Whisperer Tips to support this stage:**
Make sure your home environment supports your child's active nature as they begin to crawl and move around. Type 1 children need to feel like they can move randomly and explore in their own way without getting in trouble or being told *no* all the time.

Pre-school 3 to 6 years

Primary Emotional Need: *Coming into their own identity and power.*

In this stage, the one behavior that may begin to stand out for your Type 1 is their tendency to be a bit bossy! You may wonder why your fun-loving child would express their nature this way. Their bossiness comes from their need to be heard and seen just like everyone else. It seems that they know they can at times not be taken as seriously as the rest of humanity, due to their more light, airy nature. Bossiness is their way of putting their foot down and saying, "Listen to me! I have something worth saying."

In this important stage, recognize your child's bright and animated nature and make sure you say *yes* to it! Type 1 children can hear more *no's* than any other Type of child, due to their higher movement and the way they explore the world.

Messages your Type 1 child needs to hear in this stage of life:

- It's okay for you to start things and then change your mind.
- You are learning what is right for you—trust your instincts.
- We are glad you are starting to think for yourself.
- We love to have fun with you.
- Your light and animated nature is powerful. Trust it!
- You have great ideas; thank you for always sharing them.
- Thank you for the positive energy you so willingly share with our family.
- You are an important member of the family. Your natural gifts and talents are a blessing to all of us.

Child Whisperer Tips to support this stage: Since Type 1s experience the world socially, give them the opportunity to meet other little children. Their natural ability to make friends has no minimum age. They will enjoy the social interaction—and you will enjoy how happy and cooperative your Type 1 child is as a result!

School Age 6 to 12 years

Primary Emotional Need: *Fitting in, working with structure, knowing and learning*

I have talked a lot about how a Type 1 naturally moves through this world with less need for structure. This is not to suggest that they cannot adapt to structure. Adapting is one of their greatest gifts and you will find that they are often *too* willing to adapt to what everybody else wants in order to make sure they are happy.

This is an important stage to watch for their tendency to be too adaptive. Are they sacrificing their true nature in too many situations to please others? This is the stage that a Type 1 can be conditioned to become a people-pleaser, which they then carry into their adult lives.

Your Type 1 child is very capable of adapting to structured environments for short periods of time and learning to sit still and pay attention. The question to ask yourself as their parent is, "Are they being asked to do too much of this, which denies them of their need for more movement and variety in their life?" Your Type 1 child will let you know by how happy they are. When they feel sad for a reason you can't easily identify, look for places in your child's life where they are being compromised by too much structure.

Messages your Type 1 child needs to hear in this stage of life:

- You are smart and brilliant, and you learn so quickly.
- You are able to create whatever structure works for you.
- You can succeed at anything that feels right and honoring of you.
- Trust your ideas; they are brilliant.
- You deserve to succeed.
- Follow what is right for you. You don't have to do things that are not honoring of you.
- It is not your job to make sure everyone in the family is happy. We are in charge of our own happiness.
- Thanks for being so adaptable and easy to get along with.
- You never have to adapt to others if it is not right for you.
- You have a right to have boundaries and know what is important to you.

⌒ **Child Whisperer Tips to support this stage:** This is the phase when Type 1 children enter school. Our traditional school system at large does not honor the learning style of a Type 1 child. If your Type 1 child is fortunate, they may have Type 1 teachers (or intuitive teachers of other Types) through the years who just naturally make learning more fun. If they happen to have teachers who demand rigid structure, stillness, or linear learning processes, your Type 1 child's learning potential will be compromised.

In this stage, it is very important to understand your Type 1 child's learning style and work with both your child and their teachers to make sure they are free to develop their brilliant, quick-thinking minds and are not mislabeled in negative ways. I wonder what amazing ideas this world would be experiencing at this time of humanity if all the Type 1s who have already grown up had been taught how brilliant they are and how important and valid their ideas are.

Talk to your Type 1 child and learn about how he or she feels about their life. Read them this section of the book or share this information in a way they will relate to. If you have not been parenting your Type 1 true to their nature by this stage of their life, you will be seeing signs of stress in their behavior and feelings. This is easily remedied by your being honest and accountable with them by sharing that you have not been honoring of them and you want to change that. This is true for the next stage as well! Type 1 children forgive quickly and adapt easily to make changes that allow them to start living their lives with a natural bounce and optimism.

High School 12 to 18 years

Primary Emotional Need: *Separating and creating independence from the family.*

In this stage of a Type 1 child's life, friends take on a high level of importance. Due to their natural social orientation, they will make and enjoy friends fairly effortlessly. They are usually considered a friend to many more people than they even know. Their peers love their friendly energy and love being with them as they make things more fun and enjoyable for the friends they hang out with.

Messages your Type 1 child needs to hear in this stage of life:

- You can have as many friends as you want.
- You can change your friends any time you want to.
- You do not need to please others to be loved.
- You do not have to adapt to others in order to be a friend.
- You can take all the time you need to grow up.
- We are happy with your choices.
- It is okay to make mistakes.
- It is okay to change your mind.
- You can follow through on the things that are most important to you.
- You don't have to act on all your ideas, but we appreciate you sharing them.
- Good for you to think things through before you take action.
- You can develop your own relationships, interests and causes.
- You can learn about sex and be responsible for your needs, feelings, and behaviors.

⌒ **Child Whisperer Tips to support this stage:** Being with their friends takes on a priority at this stage of life—and at times, parents and siblings may feel offended that a Type 1 would rather be with friends than family. Choosing friends over family will not happen if a Type 1 is supported and honored for living their true nature in the home.

The main reason a Type 1 teenager wants to be with friends over family is they are supported and appreciated for their fun-loving nature by their friends and they may feel compromised in being able to be their true selves in their home. If this is true for your child, you can turn this around so your Type 1 teenager feels their fun-loving nature is welcomed and appreciated in their own home.

It's Never Too Late!

Please note that even if your Type 1 child has grown past any of these stages, it is never too late to validate and meet their emotional needs.

Right now, we are all every age we have ever been. If we have unmet emotional needs, we carry them with us into the next stage of our lives. If you have a Type 1 16-year-old daughter, it's not too late to validate and affirm all the previous stages of her development. For that matter, if your son is a Type 1 40-year-old, it's not too late for him, either! And if you are a Type 1 parent yourself, I hope this section has helped you recognize and heal some of your own inner child's unmet needs to help you feel much happier now, too!

Most of my work in the field of Energy Psychology helps adults heal their inner child's unmet needs. What a gift it is when a parent shows up and meets the needs of an older child once and for all! Like I said, it's never too late to become a better parent!

The Child Whisperer's Top 10 Things
A Type 1 Child Needs From You!

In summary, this short list includes some of the most important things to remember when parenting a Type 1 fun-loving child. This general list will be supportive to all Type 1 children. After reading this section, please add your own inspirations to this list. I aim to initiate your Child Whisperer gifts as a parent. As a Child Whisperer, you will receive your *own* inspirations and aha's, specific to your Type 1 child. Write them down!

1. *Happiness*
Your Type 1 child wants and needs you to be happy as often as possible. You will certainly experience stress and down days, but make sure you reassure your Type 1 child that he or she is not responsible for your happiness. Make an effort to be happy in spite of your challenges. Your Type 1 child will certainly try to help you smile a lot more about life.

2. *Freedom*
Type 1 children need the freedom to move, to create, to explore, to interact and to adapt. Too much structure boxes them in and represses their true nature.

3. *Praise for their ideas and creativity*
Remember, you don't have to make sure your Type 1 child follows through on every idea they come up with, but help them learn to follow through on the ones they feel are most important to them.

4. *Encouragement to live true to who they are*
Since it is so easy for Type 1s to adapt to family and friends,

make sure to support them in checking in with themselves to see if they are living true to themselves.

5. *Change*

Type 1 children grow tired of things being the same. Give them the chance to change things up in their life—like their room, their hairstyle, their toys, or friends. Respect them when they change their mind on things.

6. *Time to have fun together and let your hair down!*

Schedule regular times to have fun with your Type 1 child. Even to this day, I make sure I have fun with my adult Type 1 children.

7. *Laughter*

What brings laughter to your family? Funny movies, YouTube videos, jokes and stories, reminiscing about funny memories? Engage your Type 1 child in sharing experiences that help everyone laugh!

8. *Take them seriously*

Even though they have a light and animated nature, this nature wants to be taken seriously and acknowledged without having to become serious! Take their ideas seriously, their lighter feelings seriously, their glass-is-half-full outlook on life seriously! Don't try and get them to take life more seriously by becoming more serious!

9. *Don't sweat the small stuff*

You will experience plenty of times to easily get upset at your Type 1 child for dropping the ball on things, being late, letting their rooms get messy, not turning in homework.

Pick and choose what you need to discipline them for and how you discipline them. Reevaluate how much structure they are trying to adapt to and failing at. Make necessary adjustments so they can create success consistently in their own natural movement.

10. *Avoid these phrases and judgments:*
- Settle down.
- Grow up.
- You're too silly.
- When are you going to become responsible?
- Okay, that's enough fun.
- Everything doesn't have to be a game.

After reading this section, add to this list by writing the inspirations and aha's you have received regarding what your Type 1 child needs from you. Make your notes here:

_____

_____

_____

_____

Type 1 Child Word Portrait

Refer to this word portrait list often as a quick reminder of the nature of your Type 1 child. Compare your child's mood and disposition to this list. Is your Type 1 child expressing these movements and qualities on a consistent basis? If not, what do you need to change in your parenting approach to support them in living true to their nature?

Type 1 children are often described as:

Active

Agreeable

Animated

Amusing

Bouncy

Bubbly

Busy

Charismatic

Cheerful

Cute

Cute as a button

Energetic

Engaging

Friendly

Frolicking

Fun-loving

Funny

Happy

Light-hearted

Likes to be the
    center of attention

Little actor

Little ray of sunshine

Never sits still

Outgoing

Pixie

Positive

Random

Smiley

Social

Social butterfly

Smiles at everyone

Talkative

Negative labels that are not honoring of Type 1 children:

Attention deficit

Daydreamer

Flighty

Hyperactive

Idealist

Irresponsible

Lack of follow through

Messy

Mischievous

Type 2: The Sensitive Child

Primary Connection to the World: *Emotional*
Primary Movement: *Subtle and flowing*
Primary Need: *To have feelings honored and everyone in the family feel loved and connected*

The Type 2 expression comes from the element of oxygen/water, and its natural primary movement is fluid and flowing. A child with a dominant Type 2 movement will be naturally calming, subdued, and sensitive. These children move in a subtle, connected flow to create in this world. They naturally express a medium to medium-low level of movement. Keeping life comfortable for themselves and others—both emotionally and physically—is one of the primary motives for a Type 2 child.

Other words that describe the movement of energy in a dominant Type 2 child are: soft, steady, easy-going, relaxed, and tender. Adults often describe babies with a dominant Type 2 energy as the most easy-going babies they've ever seen. When I meet a Type 2 child, I notice their gentle nature and naturally calming energy.

Many adults value the lower level of movement in Type 2 children, as these children are generally quieter and have the natural capacity to sit still for longer periods of time. But their lower movement, which expresses itself calmly, also means that many Type 2 children are often told throughout their childhoods to, "Talk louder!" and "Hurry up!" Honoring a Type 2's lower energy and need to take their time will give them powerful permission to live true to themselves. Dominant Type 2 children who feel supported in living true to their nature grow up knowing that their steady pace and need for comfort are strengths.

Natural Gifts and Talents: Peace and Plans

Type 2s naturally offer some unique gifts to the world without even trying: *Lots of questions matched with the ability to use details they gather to make life peaceful for all.*

Once an idea has been created (initiated by the natural gift of a Type 1), Type 2 energy becomes the next phase in the cycle of wholeness by asking questions to gather details, and then using those details to create a plan that will flow easily. These children do not have to learn to be detail-oriented planners—it just comes naturally to them. The Type 2 catchphrase is: *"What do we need to know and plan for to make the idea possible?"*

Type 2 energy moves like a deep, steady river. When given the time they need, these children are deliberate and methodical in their approach to life. Parents can rest assured that their Type 2 child will think things through before acting.

Questions come readily and constantly for a Type 2 child. In every situation, they naturally have questions and truly feel they need the answers to all of them. Since they can think of questions indefinitely, these children face the challenge of proceeding through their question phase and just moving forward into action with their plan. They will often question themselves after they've made a decision and started to act. Recognize that this will always be their natural tendency. Help them understand that trying to shut down their questions would be contrary to their nature—they should just let their questions flow, even if they do not find the answers to all of them.

⟨ **Child Whisperer Tip:** Sometimes, you may wish that your Type 2 child's questions would stop! But these children will continue asking questions and gathering details their entire lives. If you try to shut down that part of their process, you are basically demanding that they not be themselves! Instead of telling them to stop asking questions, encourage and empower your Type 2 child to consider places to look for answers. It is important for you to remember you don't have to be the one to have all the answers! If they have questions about a particular topic, you can show them how to find experts, books, online resources, and other references. If you reach your question limit for the day, consider encouraging your Type 2 child to call someone they feel comfortable with, like a grandparent, uncle, or aunt. These children will enjoy forming stronger connections with those they love while learning that they can turn to various people for answers.

Type 2 children relate emotionally to the details they gather. Even as young children, they often use what they have learned to make life comfortable and flow more easily for others. When my Type 2 daughter, Anne, was still in diapers, she would gather all of the supplies when she needed to have her diaper changed—the new diaper, the wipes and her blanket to lie on—and then would come to me to have her diaper changed. She started doing this at about 15 months. Even before she could talk, she was already paying attention to the details and putting together a plan to make it easier for me to change her diaper! Just like Anne did in her diaper-changing experience, you may notice that your Type 2 child enjoys making plans that they think will please others.

Type 2 children often notice and remember others' preferences without ever being told what they are directly. As these children grow, they tend to give thoughtful gifts that they prepare well in advance for birthdays and other holidays.

Child Whisperer Tip: Since they go to so much thought and planning for others, Type 2 children feel especially loved and honored when you put in more thought and planning to their special days: birthdays, graduations, and other celebrations. Birthdays in particular tend to be very important for Type 2s. We always joked that my daughter Anne would love it if we arranged for a band to march down our street on her birthday, playing the Happy Birthday song! Type 2 children love being doted on. They are so conscientious about doing nice things for others on their birthdays that they hope to experience the same. Your child will recognize when you take time to plan ahead, which will make them feel special. My own Type 2 children love it when I have put a lot of thought and attention into their family birthday parties!

Child Whisperer Tip: Type 2 children also need time to think about what they want for their birthdays or for Christmas. They are planners and they want to feel their plan has been heard. So ask your child to make a list in advance! A month in advance, I ask both of my Type 2 children to make a list and let me know which things on it they want the most. I also give them a budget so they can plan accordingly, as they put more thought into it than any of our other children, and appreciate receiving just what they want.

Because Type 2 children's primary connection to the world is emotional, they are naturally sensitive to others' feelings. They empathize readily with children who feel left out, family members who are having a bad day, or anyone else in their world they sense is unhappy. They value the comfort of everyone around them, which they often facilitate with their naturally soothing energy. This sensitivity also relates to themselves; they are more easily offended and can more readily have their feelings hurt.

. . . .

MAISY'S STORY
So Sensitive to Others!

Three-year-old Maisy was sitting on her mother's bed when she noticed her mother put a clean pillowcase on a pillow. Maisy questioned where it came from. Her mother said it was a pillowcase that her own mother had made before she died. When she got a little teary-eyed talking about her mother, a concerned look appeared immediately on Maisy's face and Maisy started to cry. She patted her mother's arm and told her that it would be okay. Even eight months later, Maisy asks every now and then if her mother still misses her mom.

. . . .

Child Whisperer Tip: In an effort to bring peace and comfort to those they love, Type 2 children sometimes take on too much emotional responsibility for others—especially their parents. You can appreciate and honor your Type 2 child's natural gift of bringing peace into your home, but if you ever find yourself depending on it to resolve family conflict or your own personal issues, stop immediately. Recognize your Type 2 child for their loving nature and the strong emotional connections they feel. And then reassure them that they are not responsible for anyone's feelings but their own.

Just like Maisy and her mother shared an authentic emotional experience, your Type 2 child appreciates connecting with you on a deep, emotional level. They are able to do this best when they feel welcome to comfort you, but not responsible to do so. Share your emotions freely with these children and appreciate their comforting energy, but reassure them frequently that their job is to be a child. Tell them that your job as a parent is to make sure their needs are met, especially their emotional needs. Take full responsibility in resolving any of your own uncomfortable feelings.

One of the best ways you can meet these needs is by maintaining a physical connection with your Type 2 child throughout the years. Frequent touch occurs naturally when Type 2s are little because babies are held often and toddlers reach out for hugs and cuddles. But touch continues to be important for Type 2s as they grow. They need to be held and comforted. They enjoy sitting close to people they feel comfortable with. Touch reassures them of their connection with you. Reach out and make a physical connection when you are speaking to your Type 2 child. They will appreciate it.

What are some ways you can make your Type 2 child's current experience feel more safe and comfortable? Write down some ideas:

_____

_____

_____

_____

Personality Traits: Steady and Connected

When they are honored in living true to themselves, Type 2 children express an easy-going personality that invites others to relax and feel comfortable. They have an innate ability to help people feel connected due to their sensitivity to others' feelings. Others describe them as responsive, sensitive, concerned, low-key, gentle and emotionally aware. A Type 2 child's energy is like a soothing sunset at the end of the day. People are naturally drawn to these children and their calming natures.

Although Type 2 children can move steadily through life with quiet determination, they tend to hold back if they feel pushed too hard by others. If they experience an interaction that feels too intense to them, they retreat internally, thinking and feeling without sharing, often blaming themselves for causing an aggressive response in another person. Type 2 children have a greater tendency to blame themselves for plans gone wrong than any of the other Types.

. . . .

CALEB'S STORY
A Type 2 Retreats

When Caleb was five years old, he told a lie. His mother could tell that his story didn't add up, but even when she started to gently coax him to tell her what really happened, he picked up on her upset energy and he withdrew. The more intense and demanding she became, the more he closed down. Since they were driving in the car together, Caleb's mother pulled over to the side of the road to wait him out. Even that did not convince him to open up and talk!

. . . .

The tender nature of a Type 2 might be judged as a weakness by certain people, sometimes even by you. These children might receive labels like wishy-washy, wimpy, or hyper-sensitive. But their natural sensitivity can develop into a great strength with your support. Reassure your Type 2 child that their emotions are valid and they can take as much time to process and express those feelings as they need.

What can you do to help your child feel like you appreciate their natural sensitivity? List some things you want to focus on here:

_____

_____

_____

_____

Thought and Feeling Processes: Planners and Worriers

A Type 2 thought process is all about connections—which means that these children are both expert planners and potential worriers. They can often recall detailed memories. And they think far into the future, connecting present details with future events. As emotional thinkers, they require lots of details so they can make connections that lead them to calm and safe decisions.

. . . .

SAM'S STORY
Making Plans

Twelve-year-old Sam is a Type 2 planner and his mom knows it. So to honor his natural gift, she asked him if he had any plans for the upcoming summer—even though there were three more months still left in the school year. "No," he said. "I am trying to decide which elective classes I should take in high school." A planner, indeed.

. . . .

These children experience a continuous process of interconnected thought, thinking things through from beginning to what they foresee as the end. They spend a lot of time gathering details and making plans, and they like those plans to follow a steady flow. For this reason, these children have a hard time disconnecting from their current plan to follow a new plan. They are sensitive to abrupt or unexpected changes.

〇 **Child Whisperer Tip:** Help your Type 2 child feel like they have a plan each day. You may even want to talk about it a day in advance. Let your child know what to expect from you and get input on their own preferred plans (believe me, they've thought about it already). You will avoid emotional breakdowns later on in the day if you're clear on what your Type 2 child expects and you follow through with plans you both agree on. If your family's plans need to change as the day goes on, communicate these changes with your Type 2 child as soon as you can. Explain the details and acknowledge that accepting this change may take them a moment. Give them time to process how they feel about it. Even if the new plans are exciting and fun, change can feel jarring or disappointing for these children. Allow for tears without negative judgment from you.

A Type 2 child can obviously never answer every question and gather every single detail. But they might try anyway. When they do, they can become preoccupied with future unknowns. Of all four Types of children, these are the worriers.

〇 **Child Whisperer Tip:** Planning together with your Type 2 child will lower their anxiety level before upcoming changes: starting a new school year, moving to a new city, meeting a group of new people. These children need to feel like they've thought through enough details to enter a new situation safely and comfortably. Your participation in this process can add support and perspective that helps them avoid spinning downward into worry. You do not need to create the plan yourself—only offer the opportunity for it to happen. All you need to ask your Type 2 child about an upcoming change is, "How can I help you plan and feel comfortable for this?" Listen closely to the answer.

Feelings are a big deal for Type 2 children—after all, their primary connection to the world is emotional. They value emotional connection and are amazingly sensitive to the emotional state of relationships they cherish. With their sensitive demeanor, these children need time and validation from you to explain how they feel and to occasionally cry. Sometimes they need to cry for no apparent reason, only to realize afterward what the crying was about. In other words, they need to feel the emotion first before they can always articulate what it is. If they start crying, don't demand that they explain immediately what is wrong—they might not know how to tell you yet!

Type 2 children often feel things without revealing them to others. They usually want to share how they feel, but may not know how. They may also worry about sharing feelings that make you feel uncomfortable. So they wait for you to notice their subtle emotional cues and start the conversation. If you've ever found your Type 2 child crying quietly alone somewhere, waiting for someone to come find and comfort them, you know what I mean. These children will share their own feelings openly if they are asked and do not feel rushed.

Child Whisperer Tip: Even though they have a strong emotional orientation, these children need to be encouraged to share their feelings. Take a tip from your Type 2 child and ask some questions! Try one of these examples: *How are you feeling? Are you okay? Do you need help? Would you like to share something with me?* And then think of some of your own. Asking questions like these on a fairly regular basis will help you check in emotionally with your child.

What are some more questions you thought of that will help you emotionally check in with your Type 2 child? List them here:

_____

_____

_____

_____

♡ **Child Whisperer Tip:** Type 2 children appreciate reassurance. Reassure them with phrases like, "Your feelings are important. You can feel whatever you are feeling and share your feelings with me at any time." Once they open up, make sure you don't judge their feelings as inappropriate or weak by telling them to "get over it." Sharing their feelings allows them to start working through emotions so they can move through them rather than get stuck in them and feel depressed and sad. By making sure your Type 2 child feels heard, you can help them with any unresolved feelings under the surface.

You can tell when a Type 2 child is not supported in feeling their feelings and working through them when they start to seem very needy, clingy, and whiny. Type 2s who are not offered the opportunity to work through these feelings develop into children and teens who lack self confidence and start to believe the #1 limiting belief Type 2s create about themselves, which is that their emotional orientation makes them weak and they need to "toughen up." This limiting belief only disconnects them from one of their greatest natural gifts that is meant to be a blessing to them and others.

Since their movement is naturally more subdued, Type 2 children sometimes get talked over. They will stop sharing their emotional experience if they feel they're not being listened to—sometimes even in mid-sentence. Do not demand that they start sharing again.

A Type 2 child who believes his or her feelings are not being heard may become very stressed. In young children, this can look like whining, pouting, or a tantrum. In an older child, it may look more like sulking, excessive silence, or withdrawal. Give them your full attention, express that you genuinely want to hear them, and emphasize that they can take their time in telling you whatever they want to. You will find that your child's gentle and sensitive demeanor returns.

A Type 2 child's natural sensitivity also makes them responsive to contention. A lot of yelling and fighting in your home will damage a Type 2's emotional state more quickly than you realize. And nobody even needs to yell for Type 2 children of any age to sense underlying tension. Because they want everyone to feel comfortable, these children might even compromise their own needs and desires in order to keep the peace. Hold everyone in your family accountable for resolving their own conflicts and don't allow your Type 2 child to become the regular middleman or sole peacemaker in your house.

Although I think it's best not to yell at any Type of child, try not to raise your voice with Type 2 children especially. Type 2s are the most sensitive to extreme emotional expressions and it can really jolt their energetic alignment.

. . . .

KAELA'S STORY
Bothered by Contention

Sometimes, Type 2 children react negatively to what they simply perceive as contention. For example, six-year-old Kaela often became very agitated by the direct communication style between her parents who expressed dominant Type 3 and Type 4 energies (strong expressions that you'll learn about in the next two sections of this book). For them, their direct, blunt manner of discussing things did not cause hurt feelings, but to Kaela, it felt like fighting—and it bothered her. Her parents decided to tone down their conversations in her presence and wait until Kaela was asleep to discuss hot topics so that she felt more comfortable in her family.

. . . .

A Type 2 child's sensitivity may lead to assumptions about others that aren't quite right. For example, one twelve-year-old boy got a call from a friend, who asked him to come over to play. He thought his friend sounded sad, so he took some treats with him to cheer her up. When he got home, his mom asked what was wrong with the friend, but there was nothing wrong. He had just assumed that there was.

Incorrect assumptions can sometimes lead to your Type 2 feeling hurt about unintended offenses. If you notice your Type 2 child making assumptions about what others think or feel, help them recognize that they can usually clear up any misunderstandings by just asking the other person a question!

If you don't feel emotionally connected to your Type 2 child, there's a reason! Consider the possibility that your child has one of these experiences with you:

- They do not feel they can speak up around you.
- They feel rushed or pushed when they are with you.
- They feel like you dismiss the details that matter to them.
- They do not feel like they can count on you to follow through with plans.
- They feel required to take emotional responsibility for you.
- They are confused about who they are because their naturally emotional expression has been judged by their parent as a weakness.

Type 2 children *need* comfortable moments and spaces in which they feel safe to express their emotions to their parents. Ignoring this need is like telling a river to just stop flowing! When you honor your Type 2 child's true nature, you will see your child become more peaceful and emotionally responsive to you.

• • • •

SUZETTE'S STORY
Picking Up On Subtle Clues

Suzette is a Type 1 mom with a Type 2 daughter. Her daughter participated in a children's performance at their church one Sunday. Suzette planned to take her daughter and drop her off in the children's Sunday School class immediately after the service and the performance. But because of what she learned from Energy Profiling, Suzette could tell that her Type 2 daughter was not feeling quite right in her energy.

Here is what Suzette said about the experience: "I was just about to take her and drop her off at her Sunday School class, but I had the thought to stop and take some quiet time with just her. I explained to her what I felt was happening and that I wanted to take some time to be with her until she felt calm and comfortable again. We went outside and walked around the church for a few minutes and she totally shifted. She was calm and happy again. We connected and the rest of the day [was] very peaceful and pleasant with her."

As a Child Whisperer, Suzette has learned to take her daughter's subtle cues as opportunities to stop and think about what her daughter wants or needs. By emotionally validating and comforting her daughter, she did something meaningful that honored her daughter's gentle nature.

. . . .

Communication: Soft-Spoken and Emotionally Aware

A Type 2 child's lower level of movement shows up in their communication tendencies. They prefer comfortable conversations and may withdraw, worry, or cry if they feel things get too heated. Talking through details is enjoyable for them, so some Type 2 teenagers like to debate issues, but only as long as everyone feels heard and the conversation ends on a positive note.

Because their thought process involves so many details, these children take their time telling a story and they often respond slower when asked a question. If they are called on to answer quickly or feel put on the spot, they may mumble. If someone gets too pushy in a conversation, they will often get quieter, more subdued, and want to leave the situation.

. . . .

CALEB'S STORY
They Need to Think About It

Seventeen year-old Caleb and his parents were discussing his college plans one evening. His parents told him that they would help in any way they could—he just needed to tell them what he wanted. All they got was a long pause. His father, who has a more swift, determined energy, jumped in and told him, "You've got to decide." Another long pause. After they waited for what seemed a long while, Caleb said, "I'm thinking." Like his fellow Type 2s, Caleb was probably thinking through details, making connections, putting together what he already knew and questioning what he didn't know before putting anything into words.

You can teach your Type 2 child this excellent phrase they can use that will help them in moments when they feel rushed to make a decision: "I heard what you said and I need to think about it and see how I feel about it." Then have them communicate a deadline for talking about the matter again after they've had time to think through the details and get in touch with their feelings.

· · · ·

Type 2 children are naturally more soft-spoken, which means they are told on a regular basis to "speak up!" I have met so many adult Type 2s who were told as children that they were too quiet. They feel like they can never speak loudly enough!

Parents need to be careful not to overlook Type 2 children because they will not demand as much attention. Instead of saying what they want, they give subtle clues—like the Type 2 child who sits and waits quietly by the door when she wants to go outside. Other clues are not so subtle, like pouting, whining, sulking, or yelling. Type 2 children often don't understand that they can speak up and ask directly for what they need.

Child Whisperer Tip: These children need to be invited to speak up and articulate their needs. Here are some ideas of phrases you can use to encourage and teach them: "Your needs are important." "I want you to tell mommy or daddy what you want." "Say what you need and I will hear you." Tell your Type 2 child on a regular basis that they can come to you if they need help.

One of the reasons Type 2 children give such subtle clues is their own intuitive ability. They are so sensitive that they naturally intuit others' needs and assume that everyone can and should do the same for them. You may need to explain to your Type 2 child that you do not relate to the world in the same way they do, and unless they tell you what they need, you will not always know that they need help.

Because they are so concerned with people's feelings, Type 2 children may try to avoid communicating things they think will make others uncomfortable. Acknowledge your child's natural ability to be diplomatic and kind. Let them know that they never need to cloud or hide the truth in order to live true to their sensitive nature. Help them understand that they can communicate openly and honestly while still maintaining their soft approach.

. . . .

SYDNEY'S STORY
Communicating Tough Things

As a teenager, Sydney manages a fast-food restaurant and has to discipline employees frequently. Instead of being harsh, she often tries to find something nice to say about the person and offer suggestions for improvement. If she has to give a warning she says something like this: "I'd really like to keep you on, but the owner was upset when he heard about employees reading on the clock.

You'll need to do better." Her concern for others' feelings helps her to be an empathetic manager.

. . . .

These children are naturally good listeners. They notice and remember others' emotional cues, along with their words. And they often expect others to pay the same careful attention to them and their needs. Type 2 children may get particularly frustrated when asked to repeat themselves—they assume they are not being listened to as attentively as they listen to others. But they probably just spoke too softly to be heard!

⌒ **Child Whisperer Tip:** When you ask your child to repeat something they said, change your demeanor. Stop what you're doing, make eye contact, tell them that you didn't hear what they said but that you want to. Type 2 children will feel less flustered about repeating themselves if they can see that you are invested in them and prepared to really hear them the second time.

Behavioral Tendencies

Family Relationships: *Enjoy feeling connected*

Ever sensitive, Type 2 children are attuned to the details that make everyone in the family comfortable. They want everyone to feel part of the group and may try to make plans to bring the whole family together. They want to feel connected to something bigger and often enjoy the added connections that grandparents, cousins, and other extended family members offer to their life.

They truly want everyone to get along and quickly withdraw from heated family conflict. When things have cooled down, they are naturally able to listen to everyone's side of the story and empathize. They value harmony in the family and may try to facilitate it.

> ☾ **Child Whisperer Tip:** Your Type 2 child naturally brings peace to the world—and they are meant to be the first recipient of that gift. Remind your child that they cannot offer peace to the family if they do not feel it themselves. If they feel stressed or anxious about helping everyone get along, they have probably tried to take on emotional responsibility that belongs to others. Your Type 2 child's own inner sense of peace can serve as an excellent guide for them throughout their life.

Fairness is important to Type 2 children, especially in their families. They are so aware of the details of what everyone receives in the family—whether it's time, attention, or money spent on birthday gifts. They perceive who is getting what and can take on a "poor me" attitude when they feel they are not being treated as fairly as everyone else. Don't get sucked into this pity party. Acknowledge and validate their feelings and then support them in learning how to communicate what they need and want.

Friends and Social Settings: *Take their time*

These children take a moment to warm up in new situations. They hold back, observing details, until they feel comfortable or are engaged by another child. This more subtle, gradual approach to social situations leads some adults to label these children as shy. They are not shy. They have an introverted energy that expresses itself as an inward flow rather than an outward one. In other words, they need to internalize the details of the new situation before moving forward. Do not rush them! When allowed to take the time they need, Type 2 children make new friends just fine, though often not as quickly as other Types.

Because they take their time and value connection, Type 2 children often make and maintain close friends throughout the years. They are reliable friends, they remember details, and they intuitively help others feel comfortable if they feel comfortable themselves. In social experiences, these children value connecting with others and being heard. They thrive if given the opportunity to interact one-on-one, rather than in large groups where they may feel ignored or overwhelmed. Sensitive to others' needs, they may reach out to children who might feel left out.

· · · ·

SYDNEY'S STORY
Reaching Out

When Sydney was in the fifth grade, a new girl arrived at school. The new girl was from Japan and she didn't speak a word of English. Many kids at school were distant and unfriendly, but Sydney instantly felt sad for this lost little girl. She began sitting by her at lunch and drawing pictures during class to help her understand what was going on.

After about six months, it became "cool" for kids to be friends with this girl who had been an outcast when she first moved in. Sydney felt angry that these kids were so mean to the new girl at the beginning of the year, but all wanted to be her friend as soon as it became popular. What Sydney didn't realize at the time was that her gentle attention and encouragement probably contributed to all the other kids feeling comfortable enough to connect with this new friend.

· · · ·

Because they are natural peacemakers, Type 2 children may tend to create a pattern of being in the middle of their friends' dramas. They may allow themselves to become the middleman who makes everyone feel comfortable and safe. Type 2 children may compromise their true nature and wear themselves out emotionally if they try to single-handedly create harmony within their group of friends. Help your child feel like they deserve friends who are as supportive to them as they are to others.

❤ **Child Whisperer Tip:** Type 2 children need opportunities to recharge on their own. Do not tightly pack your Type 2 child's schedule with social experiences or they will start feeling drained and overwhelmed. Allow your child chances to relax and spend quiet time alone.

Timeliness: *Always making plans*

Their plans keep these children fairly punctual, especially for events they care about. But as they grow, they are still learning how to manage all the details required to get out the door, and this means they might move more slowly than you prefer—especially when you are in a rush. As one mother explained, her Type 2 child is rarely late according to the clock, but usually just barely makes it.

❤ **Child Whisperer Tip:** The word *hurry* will turn your Type 2 child into a turtle (and set up a pattern of feeling that they can never catch up). Don't even say it. Without an end in mind, your Type 2 child could take all day. So instead of pushing your child to move faster, communicate the timing of your plans. Use your own variation of this phrase one parent used with her six-year-old Type 2 daughter: "I know you would rather think about this, but right now I want you to put on your shoes so we can be on time." Then trust your child to move fast enough, even if their movement doesn't look like it matches your pace.

If your Type 2 child has been rushed in the past, consider giving them some words to counteract the message that they are too slow. When they feel stressed about timing, suggest that they say this out loud to themselves: "I have plenty of time to move at my own pace."

It is important for young Type 2 children to experience pleasant transitions. Time spent before bed or before leaving for school have a great impact on how smoothly (and how quickly) they move to the next activity. If they experience those transition times as negative and stressful, they may drag their feet the next time, making everybody late. Keep things positive and flowing at a steady pace.

Jobs and Household Chores: *Organize the details*

These children want to make their home comfortable for the family, so they are great helpers. Once a Type 2 child learns how to do a particular household task, they usually do it well. In fact, with their attention to detail, they sometimes do certain household chores more carefully than their parents. But they may drag their feet when getting started, especially for jobs they don't enjoy.

Type 2s might take more time to complete chores than children of other Types, but they generally do them with great attention to detail. They will follow through to the end if they don't feel overloaded, so plan out in advance which chores need to be done and in what order. Support your child in tackling only one task at a time.

◯ **Child Whisperer Tip:** Service-oriented chores are high on a Type 2 child's priority list. In other words, they enjoy (and will be more likely to finish) jobs that will make others feel more comfortable at home. Here are just a few of the endless examples: making their parents' bed, arranging décor on a table or counter in an attractive way, or helping make a yummy dessert for the family. I know of a Type 2 little girl who prefers to eat dinner at a table with a full setting, flowers, and candles. Why not put your Type 2 in charge of making things nice around the house?

Money Management: *Plan, plan, plan*

Type 2 children plan when it comes to money and how they want to spend it. Even Type 2 children who are just learning about the concept of money have this tendency. One mom told me that her five-year-old, Type 2 son is just learning about money and tells her often, "I'm going to save my money for that," or "I'm going to buy that for you." He doesn't have any money, but he's already planning what he'll do with it when he does.

• • • •

SARAH'S STORY
Saving and Spending

When Sarah was 12 years old, she saved her money and bought a horse. Using her natural gift to research all the details and think about every aspect of her plan, she also made all the arrangements for its board and feeding long before the horse ever arrived.

• • • •

Type 2 children want to feel comfortable with their decisions, so they gather details and compare as many possible options as they can before spending money. As you've already learned, questioning, and considering answers to those questions, is a large part of a Type 2 child's life experience. So even after they've made a choice of what to spend their money on, they may even continue to question their decision. This will be a life-long experience for them. Rather than rush them to decide, honor their tendency— and then take another turn around the store with them so they can look at their options one more time. Help them see that this tendency will help them spend money wisely as an adult.

⌒ **Child Whisperer Tip:** A Type 2 child may allow their financial plans to paralyze them in the present moment. As they grow, help them consider setting aside a small amount of "it-doesn't-matter" money that they can spend on spontaneous items without feeling anxious that they are deviating from their plan.

Recreational Activities: *At their own pace*

Type 2 children will engage in most any activity as long as they feel comfortable to take it at their own pace. They do particularly well in social situations that offer one-on-one or small group interactions. They also enjoy activities that they can do on their own to relax and unwind. Some common activities that Type 2 children enjoy include dancing, riding bikes, playing house, storytelling, and pretending with friends. A simple activity most Type 2 children enjoy is going on a walk with someone they feel comfortable with.

Even in large social settings, they prefer activities that allow them to feel comfortable. They may excel at competitive sports as long as they feel comfortable with their skill level and they are not expected to act aggressively. For example, one mom told me that her seven-year-old Type 2 son is too polite to steal the ball while playing soccer!

Activities to Help a Type 2 Child Develop Natural Gifts

As you facilitate opportunities for your Type 2 child to develop their natural gifts, remember that these children are emotionally oriented and express a medium-low level of movement. Consider involving them in activities that offer enough time for them to think things through, practice on their own, and enjoy details along the way.

Most Type 2s enjoy walking and hiking. These activities allow them to take in all the details of the world around them, while simultaneously connecting with whomever is walking with them. Type 2 children love connections and they will be especially open to activities that bring their family together. Extended family gatherings and outings often appeal to them.

Type 2 children experience connections everywhere, including connections to tastes and smells. You can involve them in cooking and eating comforting food. They like to gather the details of a new skill, so you could encourage your child to research recipes and ideas for a comfortable family meal and then help them assemble all the ingredients.

Consider other activities that involve gathering details, planning and then creating. Some ideas include painting, Legos, sewing, sculpting, writing stories, taking pictures, planning parties or decorating. I'm sure you can think of many more that your Type 2 child is naturally drawn to.

Music and entertainment are also good options. These children have the patience to practice piano or other instruments. And they enjoy being part of a group, so choir may be a good choice. Drama or dance can give them the satisfaction of using their natural gifts to connect with an audience.

Consider involving them in personal sports like swimming, karate, track, or golf. These kinds of sports allow for an inner focus that Type 2 children enjoy. Before signing them up for a class or activity, always give your Type 2 child enough details about what to expect and let them tell you how they feel about it.

⌒ **Child Whisperer Tip:** Remember that these children need quiet time to recharge. They especially need time to just sit and connect with you—both emotionally and physically. Give your Type 2 child regular (preferably scheduled) "alone time" with you when you ask, "How are you feeling?" Use this time to listen patiently as your child expresses the answer, even if it takes them a while to respond. Reach out to your Type 2 and touch them while you are talking to them. Sit close, put your arm around them, or hold and comfort them. Reaching out and making a physical connection while you make an emotional connection is very powerful for a Type 2 child.

Which activities can you think of that would honor the movement of your Type 2 sensitive child? List a few here:

_____

_____

_____

Learning Tendencies

Learning Style: *Gathering details*

Type 2 children enjoy doing research (just another form of gathering details), as long as they are interested in the subject. The older they get, the more hours they can spend discovering detail after detail. Some of their best learning happens when they are free to meander through a topic with plenty of resources available to explore and answer their questions.

They also tend to learn best from stories and examples. I know of a Type 2 kindergartener who doesn't want to solve 2 + 2. But she does just fine when asked, "If I have two Barbies and my friend gives me two more, how many Barbies is that?"

Classroom Behavior: *Sensitive to the environment*

Teachers generally love Type 2 energy in their classroom. Our current school system values quiet children who sit still and follow directions. This behavior comes naturally to a Type 2, especially if they have been given the opportunity to ask clarifying questions before being left alone to work on a task.

Because classroom learning generally involves a large group of children, and Type 2s are more subdued, they may sometimes feel overlooked or even invisible. They do not jump into group discussions loudly or quickly, so by the time they feel comfortable enough to speak, the opportunity may have already come and gone. Reassure your Type 2 child that they do not have to speak out, act up, or mimic their higher energy classmates in order to be recognized and valued.

Type 2 children are sensitive to their classroom's emotional environment—how they perceive that the teacher feels about them, how other children treat each other, and any classmates who might feel left out or sad. If your Type 2 child is reluctant to go to school, ask first about the emotional aspects of their experience: how comfortable they feel at school, how they feel about the other children, or how their teacher makes them feel.

. . . .

CHRIS' STORY
Type 2s in the School System

Even though Type 2 children can naturally be successful
in the traditional school system, not all Type 2s are drawn

to it. I have two Type 2 children, Chris and Anne. They both had very different experiences in school.

Anne used her natural gift for details and planning to create a very interesting and easy educational experience that she was very successful with. She received a college scholarship, graduated at the young age of 20 from college, and was involved in many leadership and volunteer activities. You may find that your Type 2 child follows a similar path. But if they don't, don't worry.

My son, Chris, was not that interested in school. He did fine in elementary and middle school. But in high school, he was old enough to feel he had an opinion about what he valued. And he decided he didn't care that much about what was taught in school. We ran into many power struggles trying to get him to care more and invest more effort, without any success. Every attempt turned into a fight and he disconnected from us more and more until he felt he couldn't trust us when it came to this experience in his life.

Things changed when we finally backed off and allowed him to do it his way and trust that he knew what he was doing. Even though it appeared he didn't have a plan, he had thought about it. His plan was to do just what he needed to pass his classes and no more—and he followed his plan to a T! In his senior year of high school, we received a notice from the school that he may not pass all of his classes and not be eligible for graduation. I talked to him about it, and he very confidently told me, "Don't worry about it, Mom. I know what I have to do and I'll do it." Which he did! So Type 2 planning may not always look the way we parents think it needs to look.

Chris is a natural entrepreneur and the traditional

school system did not allow him to pursue and develop his natural interests. He went to college for two years to study business. But once again, he felt that what he was learning did not meet his plan to become a successful entrepreneur. So he left college after earning his Associate Degree, gave himself an honorary four-year diploma and set out on his path to study the minds and methods of the most successful entrepreneurs of our day.

We hired Chris when he was 25 to lead our company as our CEO. We realized that Chris did not shy away from learning—what he wanted to learn just had to fit into his bigger plan for his life and career. To this day, I have never met anyone who spends more time reading, studying, and observing the online business and marketing world than my Type 2 son. I truly believe the methodical, planned-out nature that he brought to our company at a pivotal time set us on a path for growth and success. True to his nature, he prioritizes everyone feeling honored in their work environment and our customers feeling connected and supported by our company. I am so proud of him.

Whatever learning experience feels most honoring and supportive of your Type 2 child's nature and natural gifts is the experience you should support them in.

· · · ·

Study Habits: *Detail gatherers*

These children love learning new things and they complete homework successfully if they feel they have enough time and don't feel pushed. At a younger age, they may enjoy working on homework with parental support. As they get older, they usually prefer to work on their own, sometimes checking in with you to ask questions.

Type 2 children usually follow through on homework and projects, but many of them (as early as elementary school, all the way up to high school) tend to put things off until the last minute. High school students may try to stay up all night right before a big project is due. Because of their sensitive nature, this pattern of stress can lead a Type 2 to sickness. Help your child recognize their tendency to stay in a detail-gathering phase until the last minute. Ask how you can help them move into the action phase of their plan a little earlier on the next project.

How do you feel inspired to make your own Type 2 child's learning and study experiences more supportive and move at a steady pace? List your ideas here:

_____

_____

_____

_____

Physical Development

Learning to Walk: *Cautious and comfortable*

There is no consistent pattern to how early or late a Type 2 child begins to walk. Some start well before their first birthday, while others only attempt walking many months afterward. But the Type 2 keyword for learning to walk—no matter when it happens—is *cautious*! They want to feel safe and comfortable, so they will take fewer risks than other Types of children.

⌒ **Child Whisperer Tip:** Create a space in your home where your Type 2 child feels comfortable to move around. As in all things, honor your child in learning to try this new skill at their own pace. The harder you push, the longer they will take.

Learning to Talk: *Quieter, but still verbal*

Even though they are naturally quieter, Type 2 children are verbal and many are fairly early talkers. They observe the details of speech and then use them to create connections with others. You may find that they use polite language like *please* and *thank you* without much prompting.

Potty Training: *A methodical experience*

Once a Type 2 child shows a desire to stop using diapers, potty-training may be finished in just a few days. These children are more methodical and gentle and respond best to a comfortable experience.

⌒ **Child Whisperer Tip:** Make a plan with your child and get all the supplies you need ahead of time. Get supplies that make the experience comfortable, including a small potty seat. Don't make your Type 2 child climb up on the adult toilet. And make sure to offer praise that is more private between the two of you—not with the whole family present.

If potty-training your Type 2 child feels like it's taking too long, this is an indication that something in the experience is not comfortable for your child. It might be something as simple as the kind of potty seat they are being asked to use, or not feeling involved in the potty-training plan. Even the toilet paper may make a difference. Have them pick out the toilet paper with you, choosing a nice soft brand. My Type 2 daughter, Anne, jokes that she never knew that soft toilet paper existed, as I never paid any attention to this detail. I went for the cheap brands that were usually much rougher in texture! Ask your child to identify what would make them feel more comfortable. Resolve the issue and your Type 2 child will be potty-trained in no time.

Sleeping: *Need comfy, cozy spaces*

At a young age, these children generally sleep well. They also cry so quietly during the night that their parents often don't hear them. In fact, one mom said that she got up more than her newborn did for the first several months because she could never tell when her Type 2 baby was awake and crying—so she'd get up to check all night long! If an infant Type 2 sleeps in a different room from his or her parents, a baby monitor might be a good idea.

These children also love cozy connections, so as they become more mobile, parents may find Type 2 visitors in their bed who want to cuddle. Make sure you slow down long enough to give your Type 2 child time to connect with you during the day so they don't try to make up for it at night!

Type 2 children may take a long time to fall asleep because their minds get going with details and potential plans. While every child needs adequate sleep, a Type 2's naturally sensitive physical composition is particularly vulnerable to lack of sleep or interruptions to their sleep patterns. Help them settle their minds with a predictable bedtime routine that helps them to wind down.

♡ **Child Whisperer Tip:** It's a jarring experience for a Type 2 to be in the middle of something and suddenly be told it's time for bed. They feel like they need 10 more minutes to process what seemed to come out of nowhere. Give them notice that bedtime is coming up so they can prepare and plan. Also make sure that they have comfortable pajamas, sheets, blankets, and pillow. If they have a comfy bed that feels warm and inviting to them, they will want to get into it more readily!

. . . .

CHRIS' STORY
Comfort, Comfort, Comfort!

I cannot stress the word comfort enough when it comes to a Type 2 child's experience. At a very young age, my Type 2 son Chris whined and fussed about his socks. He was only three years old and when it came to putting on socks and shoes, he fought me, kicking and screaming while saying, "I hate my socks!"

I tried everything I knew, like making sure they lined up on his toes properly, that the heel was in the right position, being firm and telling him it didn't matter. I even resorted to telling him that everybody hated socks and we all just learned to live with it! I tried everything except the one thing that I now know would have fixed it.

If I had the chance to do that over, I would validate that his socks did not feel comfortable to him. Then I would take him to the store and let him feel all the socks until we found and bought the comfiest socks. What was a five-month daily battle would have ended in one shopping trip. To this day, he still is very picky about his socks feeling very comfortable and I honor him for that, as that is just one more reminder that his nature is a gift!

. . . .

Going to Pre-school and School: *Hesitant*

These children can be hesitant on the first day—or even first few days of going to school. They need some time to acclimate and observe before getting involved. And they may hold back until another child comes to engage them or they finally feel comfortable. This may happen with or without parents present.

◯ **Child Whisperer Tip:** Your child will do best if you can help them plan ahead to know what to expect (what they'll do, who will be there, how long it will last, what you will do together after you come to pick them up). As soon as Type 2 children feel comfortable and connected with the people, the space, and the experience at the school, they will have no problem going after that. Take the time to go to the school, meet the teacher, see their classroom, walk around the playground a couple weeks before school starts so they can start to connect with their future experience there.

Being Left with a Babysitter: *Need feelings validated*

Many Type 2 children would rather go with their parents than stay with a babysitter, but they usually do fine with sitters they know and feel comfortable with. Even if they know a sitter, they may cry when their parent is about to leave. Rather than trying to make them stop crying, validate their feelings. Tell your Type 2 child that it's fine to be sad that you're going away, but that you'll come back soon.

◯ **Child Whisperer Tip:** Again, planning is key here. Communicate the time frame that you'll be gone, what your child and the babysitter will do while you're gone, and the time they can expect you to be back. If your child is still too young to understand this, just make sure you connect with them through eye contact and a little snuggle before you rush off.

Dating: *Prefer comfortable experiences*

As Type 2 children mature, they continue to value comfortable experiences. When they start dating, they may only want to go on dates with people they already know fairly well. They will plan activities and timing carefully for dates that they initiated. And for dates they were asked on, they will likely choose what to wear well in advance and even mentally plan some topics they will discuss or questions they might ask. Having an outfit prepared and set out ahead of time will be supportive to a stress-free experience before a Type 2's date.

> ♡ **Child Whisperer Tip:** Type 2 teenagers value being liked and making things comfortable for others. Make sure your Type 2 child knows that their own comfort is just as important as their date's. Tell them that if they ever feel uncomfortable about how their date treats them, they have the right to speak up, rather than just go along with something. And if someone asks them out on a date or to an activity, they have a right to say no if they feel uncomfortable about going. This tip goes for both Type 2 daughters and sons.

High School Experience: *Need to connect in advance*
Because they prefer low-key situations, the bustle of a large high school with many different classes, teachers, and classrooms full of people they don't know can feel overwhelming to a Type 2. In looking forward to their high school experience, they may worry about feeling invisible or left out. But Type 2s can have a fun, supportive experience in any school.

> ♡ **Child Whisperer Tip:** Help your child set an intention to find a group of friends they genuinely connect with. If your child focuses on finding like-minded friends they feel comfortable around, they will find them. Remind your child of their gift to put others at ease, which natu-

rally brings out the best in the people they meet. Getting involved in clubs and extra-curricular activities they are drawn to allows them to meet other students in smaller settings, where they tend to make connections more easily.

. . . .

CALEB'S STORY
High School Blues

Caleb's first year of high school was tough. Even though he was well-known and well-liked enough to become the sophomore class president, many of his friends experienced a lot of drama in their lives. This was stressful for his more sensitive nature.

The next year, he switched schools and found a new group of friends that did not pull him into the middle of their drama and expect him to resolve it. Because of those new friends, his high school experience became much more positive and supportive.

. . . .

Another option for a Type 2 who feels overwhelmed is to look into schools of different sizes. One 16-year-old who moved to a significantly smaller school felt much more supported in her ability to make connections and learn at her own pace.

Driving: *Responsible and cautious*

Type 2 teenage drivers are generally responsible and aware. When they first start learning to drive, they may be almost too cautious. Answer their questions and give them the time they need to practice. Once they have enough experience, they will generally be responsive drivers.

After reading through this section, what *aha's* do you have about supporting your Type 2 child in living true to their nature in their current experience? List a few of your thoughts:

_____

_____

_____

_____

Physical Characteristics

You may think your child is a Type 2 because your child is emotional. But all four Types express emotion. They just do so with a unique movement. One of the most telling ways to identify which movement your child dominantly expresses is to look at facial features and their body language. Your child's physical characteristics are often more accurate than personality, which can be altered by situation or expectation.

Contrasts in a Type 2 child's features are low and subtle, and their bone structure creates elongated S-curves and ovals. The most noticeable overall characteristic I see in all Type 2 babies and children is their softened, blended features that all move in a downward movement on their face.

Something to remember: Learning facial profiling for babies and children in a book without pictures or illustrations can be difficult! That is why I have created a library of free videos on my website called, "How to Profile Babies, Children, and Teens!" To access this library visit www.thechildwhisperer.com.

Face Shape: *Oval*
Their hairline often makes an S-curve.

Skin/Skin Texture: *Soft, supple, with blended skin tones*

You may notice that your Type 2 child has particularly sensitive skin. As babies, they may get diaper rashes and other rashes on their face if exposed to harsh chemicals. As they hit puberty, harsh products or too much movement on their face (through washing too often or through other irritants) can lead to blemishes that become inflamed. Type 2 skin responds well to water-based products with soothing components like aloe or lavender.

Cheeks: *Elongated cheek, S-curve cheek, or "jowls"*
No obvious cheekbones or jawline, as cheeks blend in with everything else. There is a downward, softened movement to their cheeks.

Nose: *Soft on top, S-curve on the sides and in the nostrils, medium size, slight bump on the bridge*

Eyes: *Almond-shaped eyes, heavy or drooping lids*
May be described as doe eyes. When you follow the line of their eyelids from the inside of the eye to the outside, it always follows a downward sloping movement.

Eyebrows: *Half an oval, long S-curve, low arch, no angles*
Often blends with skin tone. Eyebrow ends have an obvious downward movement.

Hands: *Long, soft, graceful fingers (and toes), fingers taper toward nail, oval nail bed*

Your Type 2 child will not express every one of these physical features in their face—and some features may not fully express themselves while your child is still growing. Most all Type 2 children express the common trait of downward motion in their features, almost as if parts of their face are melting or moving downward. Whatever features they do have will be very blended in quality.

Body Language

Since Energy Profiling is an assessment of our natural expression of movement, body language is an excellent clue to your child's Energy Type. Your child may not express all of the following movements, but if they are a dominant Type 2, you may recognize many of them in your child if you pay attention. Do any of these movements describe your child?

Crawling: Type 2 children scoot around before they start to crawl. Since they are a lower movement, they don't have a need to move around quite as much, so crawling will be less noticeable in their world. They generally start to crawl around six to eight months and do just enough of it to get to where they want.

Walking: Type 2 children generally walk with a smooth, fluid movement. They keep their feet close to the ground and adults might get after them for literally dragging their feet. They like to stroll, which will be especially apparent if you prefer to powerwalk.

Sitting/Standing: A dominant Type 2 movement is an elongated S-curve, which you may see in your child's posture. They may stand in a relaxed bend, holding their head to one side. When they sit, they often lie back, looking for the most relaxed position they can find. They like leaning on other people they feel comfortable with. *Lounging* is a good word to describe how these children sit.

Voice/Language: These children often have a softer voice with a medium pitch. Because they speak more softly, they may feel like others often talk over them.

⌒ **Child Whisperer Tip:** It's fine to ask a Type 2 child to speak a little louder if you do it in an honoring way. But the next time your child speaks quietly, try something different. Stop what you're doing and lean in until you can hear, even if you need to get down on your child's level. The more attentively you listen, the more you may find that your child naturally finds a more confident voice. Help your Type 2 child understand that when they relax into their subdued nature, instead of fighting it, others may actually hear them even better.

Personal Space: *Type 2 children like their space to feel cozy and they enjoy details like pictures, flowers, or decorations.*
Because your Type 2 child is so detail-oriented, you may find that they are expert organizers. They like to keep track of details and they may keep their rooms very tidy and comfortable.

That description may sound confusing if your Type 2 child's room is pretty messy. But look carefully at the quality of the mess. If your child is a dominant Type 2, a large amount of the clutter will be sentimental. They tend to keep mementos like cards, letters, gifts, knick-knacks, photos, or tickets to movies or concerts that were meaningful to them. These items help them feel a sense of connection to comforting, pleasant memories and people they love. Without support to help them sort through the details, they may pack their closet or shelves full of stuff they don't understand they can let go of.

Type 2 children also tend to organize things in piles. All their piles have a connection and they have an ongoing plan to go through all of them. But when they finally do, it doesn't take them long to create new ones! Even if the pile looks like a mess to you, each pile has meaning and an intention for your child.

⌒ **Child Whisperer Tip:** Your Type 2 child will function best in a clean space. There are many ways you can help your Type 2 child manage their tendency to hang onto items and create piles. Warning: Throwing things away while your child is gone is *not* the best solution. Even if you do clear things out, your child will not learn the process of choosing what to keep and what to let go— and the clutter will build right back up.

Instead, help them identify a designated place to create each one of their piles: a pile for dirty clothes, a pile of papers to go through, or a pile of projects they want to finish. If the pile grows beyond that border, it's time for them to go through it.

Add another pile to their room: a "maybe-let-go" pile. In this space, they can place items they're considering letting go of, but are still questioning. This gives them time to just consider the possibility that they can let go of it, without actually having to make the decision yet. Once they see how long some of those items sit in that pile, they may be more willing to donate them or throw them away. I know a grown Type 2 who actually uses a recycle bin to trick himself into believing he can get papers back if he really wants them. This is a great option for a Type 2 to start young.

Scrapbooks can be a good gathering place for cards, tickets, and other mostly flat memorabilia. Consider helping your child take pictures of other sentimental items that take up lots of space in their room. Always give them the final decision in which items are deemed important enough to keep. Put the rest of them in the "maybe-let-go" pile so your child has time to think about it.

What can you do to make your Type 2 child's personal space more comfortable? Is their room cozy and calming? How could you help them create that sort of environment? List your ideas here:

_____

_____

_____

_____

Challenges as a Parent: Communication and a Slower Pace

I've heard some parents with other Types of children say that they want a Type 2 child because they must be so easy. And they are! These children truly do bring a gentle peace to their families.

But they also face their own unique challenges—however subtle they may be—that parents need to be aware of so they can empower their Type 2 children to live true to themselves and create the peace in their homes that these sensitive children crave.

The first challenge for parents of Type 2 children is often figuring out if and why something is wrong. Type 2 children give subtle signals from day one, and they can be tricky to pick up on if you're not paying attention. Because these children do not express their needs or feelings very loudly, a parent may think everything is fine until their Type 2 child's suppressed anger bursts or the child gets sick. If these children do not feel safe or invited to speak up, they may go along with everyone else, even when they don't want to. This can lead to whining and moping that parents often don't understand.

⌒ **Child Whisperer Tip:** When your child is very young, you'll just need to pay more attention to pick up on their subtle cues. As your child grows, ask and invite them to share their feelings. They might not come out and say what they really want at first, but they will learn as you encourage them to say what they really want. Don't cut them off or tell them that what they are feeling isn't true or real. They need to feel safe in expressing themselves or they will shut down.

Don't let whining be the only time you respond to your Type 2 child's needs. By the time they begin whining, they already feel ignored and looked over. If they whine, tell them you want to hear them and you will listen as soon as they use a normal tone. Reassure them regularly that it's safe to speak up.

Parents of Type 2 children may also wonder how to motivate their child to move forward and act. To parents who express a different dominant Energy Type, their Type 2 child may look like they just sit around thinking about plans, but never making a decision and moving forward. The truth is, Type 2 children do have a hard time making decisions when they don't know what to expect. You can do something to help them.

⌒ **Child Whisperer Tip:** If your Type 2 child feels like they've stalled in the detail-gathering phase of their plan, you can help them by asking questions, rather than pushing them forward. Here are some ideas: "I notice you've wanted to do this for a long time, but haven't done it yet. What's keeping you stuck?" "What else do you need to know in order to start working on this?" "What would help you feel more comfortable about making this decision?" Also reassure them that their plan is good enough and it's safe to move forward. Share with them: "Trust yourself. You can always modify your plan once you get started." "You can get going on it now. You've done a good job planning and preparing—it will be fun for you to move into the activity phase." And sometimes they just need a gentle push. In those moments, share this: "You are ready. Go for it. You can do it!"

. . . .

CALEB'S STORY
Making Decisions

As a teenager, Type 2 Caleb was offered a summer job in Arizona. He didn't give an immediate reply and was trying to figure out whether or not he wanted to take it. His mother asked him a question so perfect for his Type 2 nature: "What would help you feel more comfortable about making a decision?"

He explained that he just didn't know what to expect. So they called an aunt who had worked in the same place for the same people. She shared her experience and Caleb got to ask her questions. Learning what to expect helped Caleb feel comfortable enough to accept the position.

. . . .

One of the biggest challenges that parents of Type 2 children face is knowing how to handle their child's seemingly slower pace. Life moves so quickly that a parent may feel daunted by the idea that they need to slow down and give one of their children all this extra time. Here's a Child Whisperer tip that I want you to read twice:

⌒ **Child Whisperer Tip:** Type 2 children are not slow. They need time. I'll say that again. Type 2s aren't slow. They just need time—both for planning and breaks. When Type 2s are engaged, their flow is steady and strong. When they're living true to themselves, they get things done and they create successful outcomes. The slow, dawdling movement happens when experiences in their life get too pushy or aggressive. If your Type 2 child is shutting down, look at which areas of their life feel out of control and plan a way to change it with them. Then give them a break to just relax and unwind. You will find that your Type 2 child accomplishes plenty and feels much happier if they have time to unwind.

. . . .

CHRIS AND ANNE'S STORIES
Ambitious Type 2s!

My Type 2 son Christopher rode his bike across the country when he was 15 years old. While he served a volunteer mission in Thailand for two years, he was given serious responsibilities to lead 200 other volunteers serving all over Thailand, which allowed him to travel to all parts of that country at the young age of 20. He is now the CEO of our company and was entrusted with that role at age 25.

My Type 2 daughter, Anne, studied abroad in France, served as her senior class president, and finished her college degree by age 20. She served an 18-month volunteer mission in Bulgaria at age 21, and speaks three languages fluently. As an Expert at our company, she plays a pivotal role in helping women all over the world feel inspired and connected to our message.

Because we seem to expect ambition to be expressed in a much higher movement, Type 2 children can be perceived as less ambitious. But this is not true! Both of my Type 2 children have proven this wrong with their many pursuits and accomplishments at a very young age. They each achieved their ambitious goals with a lot of planning and follow through—and a lot of belief from their dad and me that they could do it.

Whatever activities your Type 2 child pursues, trust that their more subtle, methodical nature is their natural movement, even when being ambitious!

. . . .

These challenges seem like easy issues to work with when you look at the great joys these children are. Their easy-going nature makes them mellow, snuggly babies. And as they grow, they are pleasant and affectionate—especially when they are allowed to just be themselves. If you worry that you have pushed your Type 2 child too intensely, you can change that pattern right now. Type 2 children want their parents to both hear and honor their feelings; they will respond to your genuine intention to do just that, no matter how old they are.

Your Type 2 child's naturally peaceful energy invites everyone to slow down and connect emotionally. These children have a genuine concern for the feelings of others and an innate ability to put others at ease. Your Type 2 child is truly a great gift for your family to have received—take a moment to tell them that today in a quiet moment between the two of you. All children yearn to be recognized for who they are. And too often, Type 2s feel overlooked or invisible. They need to know that you see them as an immense gift to your family and to the world.

The Type 2 Sensitive Daughter

Type 2 daughters are sweet and kind. Their energy is soft, gentle, and sensitive—what our culture generally recognizes and values as a feminine expression. In fact, women of other Types often try to mimic this quality of energy in order to be seen as more feminine. Type 2 daughters like to make things pretty, decorating their rooms and their home. They are thoughtful and often share sweet notes or little gifts to make others feel special and connected.

As they grow, they may worry about being too soft, too nice, or unable to stand their ground and share their feelings. These girls want to show up in the world and be heard, so they may try to take on a tougher outer exterior. But it backfires—they actually end up feeling more invisible than ever! Share the information you have learned in this book and tell your daughter that she can offer great peace to this world when she lives true to her sensitive nature.

The opposite can also happen. A Type 2 daughter may become *so* concerned about others' feelings and comfort that she doesn't acknowledge or speak up for her own needs at all. Constantly giving without receiving takes an emotional and physical toll on these sensitive girls. They may state their needs in a way that seems less urgent than they actually feel. When your Type 2 daughter says what she needs or wants, listen up.

As I have come to better understand my Type 2 daughter Anne's nature, the more I have been able to support her in staying true to herself and to trust her gentle power. I started to develop this information about Types when Anne was a teenager. My sense is if I had not come to these understandings of what Type 2 energy is and recognized it in her, she would have been more likely to model her life after me and my Energy Type. Due to her more sensitive composition, I believe it would have put a tremendous amount of stress on her body and caused unnecessary illness and health problems. I am grateful to have a daughter who recognizes the value of her more subtle nature and is a role model for other Type 2 females.

⌒ **Child Whisperer Tip:** Whatever you do, honor your Type 2 daughter's sensitivity as strong and beautiful. Teach her that her gentle, elegant nature is a gift.

The Type 2 Sensitive Son

Type 2 sons are gentle and considerate. Naturally attentive, easy-going, and attuned to details, they have great strengths that can create success for them from childhood to adulthood. But Type 2 energy is not typically valued in most cultures as masculine. We expect our sons to be more aggressive, rambunctious, and noisy than a Type 2 boy usually feels comfortable being. They are naturally more sensitive and connected. But from a young age, Type 2 boys are often sent messages—both directly and indirectly—that they need to toughen up and act more manly.

I have met many grown Type 2 men who consistently received these messages as they grew up. These men struggled with feelings of being weak and incompetent. My husband is a Type 2 who was raised by a Type 2 dad. Even though his dad offered him a more gentle expression of masculinity, Jonathan was living in conflict with who he was by the time he hit his teens, due to the cultural expectation for him to be more aggressive in order to be a true man. He has healed a lot of false expectations of himself that he could never achieve naturally and is very comfortable with his more subtle masculine nature.

I am grateful to have a Type 2 son who, at a much younger age than his father, learned to value his true nature. Chris is a kind man with great strengths and attributes that support him in all areas of his life. I respect his nature and mindfully support and acknowledge it as his mother. As I look back at Chris's early years, he was more subdued and quiet in his presence in the family, but he was very aware of every little detail that was going on. When we reminisce, I am always surprised by how much Chris was paying attention to the details of our day-to-day life, and how much he took in without letting on!

Child Whisperer Tip: Allow your Type 2 son to be emotionally expressive in your presence without negative judgment. Recognize that he may need to be given time to cry and be validated for his steady, flowing energy that is his greatest strength.

The Type 2 Child Through the Years

Type 2 children express their true nature from birth to adulthood in many ways. The following will give you some of the most common general tendencies they may express in their first 18 years of life.

At each developmental stage, your child has a specific emotional need. This is true for all Types of children. I offer some specific phrases to share with your Type 2 child to help meet each need. Use these phrases in words, or consider how you could express these phrases in action to help your child feel loved and wanted in each stage of their life. When your child is supported in living true to their nature, they can more easily enter their adult experience ready and able to create emotionally healthy relationships. You can meet your child's developmental emotional needs in many ways—just use my examples as a way to get you thinking.

Baby 0 to 18 months

Primary Emotional Need: *To be validated for their gentle, sensitive nature and to be supported in starting to explore and sense the world around them.*

The Type 2 baby is easy-going. All Type 2s start their life experience with a primary connection to the emotional experience of this world. People around these babies can sense their soothing, sensitive nature. You may hear people comment that your Type 2 baby is so calm. These children truly do express their natural gift to calm and connect others from the very beginnings of their life. A characteristic very typical of all Type 2 babies is their desire to cuddle and even burrow into their moms.

Type 2s are also very attentive babies. They notice and respond to changes and items that are different or out of place. Notice what your baby is noticing—they may draw your attention to beautiful details you hadn't even seen. In one mom's words about her Type 2 son, "The first snowfall with him was a blast."

Messages your Type 2 child needs to hear in this stage of life:

- Welcome to the world; we've been eagerly waiting for your peaceful energy.
- We planned and prepared a special place for you.
- All your needs are important to us. You can grow at your own pace and we are here for you.
- We love your soft, subtle energy—you are a gift to our family.
- It's okay to play; we will make it safe and comfortable for you to explore.
- You can be just who you are, and we will always love you.

- It's okay for you to be different from Mom and Dad. We will work out our differences in a way that supports you in feeling heard.

◠ **Child Whisperer Tips to support this stage:** Type 2 babies need to feel comfortable and safe. They felt very safe and connected to their moms in the womb, so make sure you give your Type 2 infant a little more time to separate from you once they are born. These little cuddlers feel safe and comfortable when swaddled or wrapped up tightly. Consider buying a cozy swaddling wrap for your Type 2 baby.

These babies can also become fussy if their environment feels too harsh or if anything they're wearing (like clothing, diapers, or blankets) feels irritating. Use fabrics next to their skin that feel plush and soft, and make sure your baby has a soothing, cozy space to just be quiet. This will be a need for the rest of their lives, so if you notice your Type 2 child getting fussy or cranky, move with them to a comfortable space and let them connect with you and express their feelings.

As your baby becomes more interactive, choose toys with textures that feel comfortable to your baby. And be sure to give them plenty of snuggle time with you.

Toddler 18 months to 3 years

Primary Emotional Need: *Support in sensing, exploring, and doing in the world*

The Type 2 toddler can begin to gather more details about their world as they become more mobile crawling and walking. They want to connect with others, and this shows up in their speech patterns. Language skills develop in this stage and Type 2s start asking questions as soon as they can form the words.

A child's diet usually includes a lot more variety in this stage of life. It is important to remember that Type 2s have the most sensitive nature of the Types in all aspects of their lives. Even certain foods can be too harsh for some Type 2s. I experienced this with my son, Chris. By 18 months old, he had eaten numerous food items that I had introduced into his diet, including cow's milk, wheat and other allergy-prone foods. Chris developed numerous ear infections for several months, all treated by antibiotics that weakened his immune system. After much study, I discovered that his ear infections could be related to food allergies. I found a pediatrician who worked with me to clean up Chris' diet and strengthen his immune system using natural interventions. Within six months, Chris was healthy and vital and I slowly reintroduced these foods into his diet. As I look back, I am sure that his more sensitive Type 2 nature definitely played a part in those early health problems.

Messages your Type 2 child needs to hear in this stage of life:

- It's okay to be curious, to move, to touch, explore, and gather details about this world.
- We will make it safe for you to explore.
- You can be you and we will always love you.
- You can try out new things and find your own way of doing things.
- It's okay for you to have questions and trust that your parents will have answers.
- You are so sensitive and kind.
- You are so pleasant and eager to make others comfortable; we are here to take care of you and make sure you are safe and comfortable.

- You bring peace to our family.
- I love you just the way you are.

♡ **Child Whisperer Tips to support this stage:**
Type 2 children need to feel like they can move through the world comfortably and safely. Make sure your home environment supports them in moving freely. Consider that your Type 2 child will feel more comfortable and connected if they can see you while they play. Also make sure your Type 2 child has a quiet space where they can safely go by themselves to unwind and recharge.

Also pay attention to how your child's sensitive nature responds to anything that may cause them discomfort from foods, environments, TV shows, and music that may cause them undue stress.

Pre-school 3 to 6 years

Primary Emotional Need: *Coming into their own identity and power.*

You may find at this stage that your calm little Type 2 begins to get whiny, mopey, and grumpy. You may wonder where your calm, peaceful child went. These children get pouty and moody when they feel their feelings are not being heard, that they haven't received enough attention, or that they are being pushed too hard.

They often come to realize that their soft-spoken nature doesn't receive quite as much attention. Their whininess is just their misguided attempt to try and change that pattern. This is an important stage to recognize your child's gentle voice and to make sure that they know you can hear it loud and clear. With how often these children hear the phrase, "Speak up," a Type 2 child would do well to hear you say "I hear you" just a little more often.

Messages your Type 2 child needs to hear in this stage of life:

- It's okay for you to take your time and think things through.
- You are learning what is right for you—trust your instincts.
- We are glad you are starting to think for yourself.
- We love to spend quiet time together with you.
- Your subtle and gentle energy is powerful. Trust it.
- You have great questions; thank you for always asking.
- Thank you for the peaceful energy you so willingly share with our family.
- You are an important member of the family. Your natural gifts and talents are a blessing to all of us.

♡ **Child Whisperer Tip to support this stage:** Since Type 2s experience the world emotionally, invite them frequently to share their feelings with you. Even if their language is not yet sophisticated enough to convey exactly what they want, this open invitation from you will lay a foundation of trust and openness. No matter how young they are, sometimes a Type 2 child just needs to be held and comforted while they process their feelings.

School Age 6 to 12 Years

Primary Emotional Need: *Fitting in, working with structure, knowing and learning*

This is an important stage to watch for a child's tendency to be *too* well-behaved. Are they sacrificing their true nature in order to feel liked or recognized in a group? Are they being too nice to so-called friends who take advantage of them? Are they always the peacemaker and the connector, getting caught in the middle of drama between friends?

During this stage, a Type 2 child might take on the belief that in order to fit in and have value, they need to take on and resolve others' emotional problems. Help them clear this lie from their lives so they do not carry it into adulthood. How peaceful does your Type 2 child seem during quiet moments at home? That's usually a good indicator of how well they feel their feelings are being heard and their needs are being met.

Messages your Type 2 child needs to hear in this stage of life:

- You are smart and brilliant, and you learn so intuitively.
- You are able to take whatever time works best for you.
- You can succeed at anything that feels right and honoring of you.
- Trust your emotional intuition.
- You deserve to succeed.
- Follow what is right for you. You don't have to do things that do not honor you—and you can speak up about them.
- It is not your job to make sure everyone in the family gets along. We are in charge of our own happiness. We are in charge of our own feelings.
- Thanks for being so sensitive and easy to get along with.
- You never have to go along with something if it is not right for you.
- You have a right to have boundaries and know what

is important to you.

⌒ **Child Whisperer Tips to support this stage:** In this phase, Type 2 children enter school. Your Type 2 child will generally work well within structures presented to them. They are most likely to be polite, quiet, and well-behaved in classrooms. But don't let that throw you off the trail of identifying your Type 2 child's Energy Type correctly if they get a little rowdy in class or loud with their friends. Their movement is fluid and flowing, but that doesn't mean these children are quiet all the time. In fact, some of them might even get a little *too* rowdy in social settings, especially when they're trying to gain attention they feel they are not getting enough of.

Ask your Type 2 child often how he or she feels about their life. Read them the Type 2 section of this book or share this information in a way they will relate to. If you have not been parenting your sensitive child true to their nature by this stage of life, you will likely see signs of stress in their behavior and feelings, including emotional withdrawal and moodiness. You can easily heal this pattern together with your child by being honest and accountable as a parent.

High School 12 to 18 Years

Primary Emotional Need: *Separating and creating independence from the family*

In this stage of a Type 2 child's life, friends become very important. Due to their natural need for connection, they will form close friendships that they cherish deeply. Their peers enjoy their relaxing energy and often feel safe to confide in them.

Messages your Type 2 child needs to hear in this stage of life:

- You can connect with friends however it feels most comfortable to you.
- You do not need to please others to be loved.
- You can take all the time you need to grow up.
- We are happy with your choices.
- It is okay to make mistakes.
- You can take your time to make a plan.
- You can gather all the details that you feel are important to you.
- You don't have to answer all the questions that come to your mind.
- Good for you to move forward with a plan you've made.
- You can develop your own relationships, interests, and causes.
- You can learn about sex and be responsible for your needs, feelings, and behaviors.

♡ **Child Whisperer Tips to support this stage:** In this stage you may notice a push-pull process going on with your Type 2 child. Their emotional development is encouraging them to become more independent from you and to learn to operate more autonomously in the world. With their nature being so oriented to connection with others, this can feel a bit awkward and scary to them at times. Be patient as your Type 2 moves through this emotional development reassuring them along the way that you are always there for them no matter what and you will always maintain a deep and lasting connection with them.

It's Never Too Late!

Even if your Type 2 child has grown past any of these stages, you can still validate and meet their emotional needs. We are all every age we have ever been and we still carry our earlier unmet emotional needs with us. If your Type 2 daughter is 16 years old, you can still validate and affirm all the previous stages of her development. Even if your son is in his 30s or 40s, he would benefit from the messages in this book that he has not yet received from you as his parent. Your Type 2 child is sensitive at any age and will respond to your earnest attempts for connection. If you are a Type 2 adult, you can tell yourself the messages you did not receive during your childhood to heal some of your own inner child's unmet needs.

Most of my work in the field of Energy Psychology helps adults heal their inner child's unmet needs. What a gift when a parent shows up and meets their needs at any age! It's never to late to become a better parent.

The Child Whisperer's Top 10 Things A Type 2 Child Needs From You!

To summarize, I've put together a brief list of what I feel are some of the most important points to remember when parenting a Sensitive Type 2 child. This general list will be supportive to all Type 2 children. My goal with this list (and this book) is to bring out your own Child Whisperer gifts. As a Child Whisperer, you will receive your *own* inspiration, specific to your particular child. Make sure you write down those aha's!

1. *Comfort*

   Remember the importance of all things comfort in the Type 2 world! Your baby may be fussy because the outfit they're wearing is uncomfortable. Soft clothes, blankets, and bedding are very supportive to a Type 2 child. Other places to think about comfort in your Type 2 child's life: bedrooms, study areas, towels, food, and a mood of peace and comfort in the home.

2. *Reassurance*

   Take a few extra minutes and a few extra words to reassure your Type 2 child. Help them limit their tendency to worry and fret by supporting them with encouragement. Even if you correct them gently, make sure to tell them that they are still okay with you. It may be obvious to you, but it doesn't feel that way to them.

3. *Validation for their feelings*

   With a strong emotional connection to the world, Type 2s thrive when they are validated for their feelings and supported in feeling them. Your permission and validation for their feelings will support them in staying very emotionally balanced and stable.

4. *Encouragement to live true to who they are*

   Refer to the phrases in each of the developmental stages in earlier sections to continue to validate and encourage your Type 2 child to live true to their nature throughout all the phases of their childhood.

5. *Answers to their questions*

   Whether you have the answers or can refer your child to

other resources for answers, support their questioning nature. Recognize it as part of their process of gathering details to make a mental plan on how to move forward in all aspects of their life.

6. *Time to be quiet and connect with you*

It's possible you could be giving your Type 2 child lots of attention—just not the kind they need. Take time to sit and connect physically with your Type 2 child. They appreciate a physical connection like a hug, an arm around them, or a hand on their back. They will continue to cuddle and sit close to you even up through their teens, which will be very nurturing to you as well.

7. *Attention*

Your Type 2 child is very aware of the amount of attention other children in the family receive and they want to be treated fairly in receiving the same amount of attention. They will not speak up for it, but will give you subtle clues they need more attention. Rather than wait for the clues, just make sure they get the same amount of attention as their siblings.

8. *To be heard*

Encourage your Type 2 child to speak up and share themselves with you and others—including their feelings, their interests, their hopes, their dreams and their plans!

9. *Don't sweat the small stuff*

You'll experience plenty of opportunities to get frustrated

over the endless questions, the apparent dawdling, and the constant piles of clutter in your Type 2 child's room. Decide today to let go of some of that frustration and focus on the calming energy that your child creates when they are honored and validated for who they are.

10. *Avoid these phrases and judgments*:
- Hurry up.
- You're too slow.
- You're too quiet.
- Stop worrying so much.
- Don't be shy.
- You're too picky.
- You're a little awkward.
- When will you finally finish?

After reading this section, add to this list by writing the inspirations and ideas you received regarding what your Type 2 child needs from you. Make your notes here:

_____

_____

_____

_____

The Type 2 Child Word Portrait

Refer to this word portrait list often as a quick reminder of the nature of your Type 2 child. Compare your child's mood and disposition to this list. Is your Type 2 child expressing these movements and qualities on a consistent basis? If not, what do you need to change in your parenting approach to support them in living true to their nature? Type 2 children are often described as:

Agreeable	Loving
Calm	Low-key
Careful	Pleasant
Cautious	Pleasing
Comforting	Quiet
Concerned	Relaxed
Cuddly	Reserved
Detailed	Sensitive
Easy going	Soothing
Feels for others	Subdued
Gentle	Sweet
Graceful	Tender-hearted
Kind	Thoughtful

Negative labels that are not honoring of Type 2 children:

Cry-baby	Slow
Overly sensitive	Timid
Pouty	Whiny
Shy	

Type 3: The Determined Child

Primary Connection to the World: *Physical*
Primary Movement: *Active and determined*
Primary Need: *To be challenged and have new experiences with support of their parents*

The Type 3 expression comes from the element of hydrogen/ fire, and its natural primary movement is active and reactive. A child with a dominant Type 3 movement will be naturally determined, purposeful, and persistent. These children move forward with intensity to create in this world. They express a medium to medium-high level of movement in relation to the other three Types.

Other words that describe the movement of this energy in a dominant Type 3 child: independent, adventurous, and self-motivated. Adults often describe a child with a dominant Type 3 energy as "busy" or "rambunctious." When I meet a Type 3 child, I always notice their forward movement to get their hands on things. And as they grow, I notice their drive to get things done!

Getting out or getting into things in order to physically explore their world is a huge priority for the Type 3 child. Some adults may feel pushed or irritated by a Type 3 child's constant forward movement and judge it as a flaw. A Type 3 child might be told too often that they need to calm down and stop being so demanding. If you recognize your Type 3 child's swift, determined energy for the strength that it is, you will give your child powerful permission to live true to him or herself. Dominant Type 3 children who experience support in expressing their dynamic, powerhouse movement as children grow up with even greater confidence and determination to make big things happen. Some of the most well-known athletes are Type 3s who must have been raised true to their natures. Michael Phelps and Serena Williams are just a couple examples.

Natural Gifts and Talents: Encouragement and Results

Type 3 children naturally offer some unique gifts to the world without even trying: *Determination to create results, which encourages everyone around them.*

Let's revisit the cycle of wholeness again. Type 1 energy initiates the cycle with new ideas and hope. Type 2 energy gathers the details by asking questions and making plans. Then Type 3 energy moves those ideas and plans into action! Without even trying, Type 3 children push forward from the very beginning of their lives, taking action in order to create results. The hardest thing for the parent of a Type 3 child to learn is that those results don't always look the way parents expect them to—your Type 3 three-year-old emptying out the dishwasher onto the floor, for example. You do not need to instill determination and drive into your Type 3 child. Just help them set their course appropriately, get out of the way, and they'll naturally go big. To put this natural gift into a catchphrase, *"Let's get to work and get it done!"*

When a Type 3 child has their mind set on a certain result, they do whatever it takes to reach it—at any age. As an infant, they might crawl early, just so they can reach the toys they want. As a child, they might start a business on the front lawn to raise money for something they want to buy. As a teenager, the possibilities of what they can dream up and go for are truly endless. Type 3s always have an end in mind: action, reaction.

In fact, since they're so determined and they think so big, they'll probably pursue several big goals at the same time!

Type 3 energy moves like the strong, dynamic push of Niagara Falls. When supported to pursue the goals they value most, these children are driven, persistent, and independent. Encourage those natural tendencies in your child—those traits will serve them well throughout their entire life.

Type 3 children also like to appreciate their results after they have attained a certain end. I am an active, determined Type 3 myself—and as I joke with my Type 3 daughter-in-law, Sarah, we both write tasks on our to-do lists that we've already accomplished, just for the satisfaction of checking them off the list. As it turns out, this starts early for Type 3 children.

. . . .

ANNIE'S STORY
The Gift of Getting Things Done!

Nine-year-old Annie has a big calendar on the wall of her room to write down events, practices, and other activities. When she finishes something that she didn't write down earlier, she still writes it on her calendar later—even weeks after the fact. One day, her mother told her that she didn't need to go back and write down activities that had already passed. Annie said to her mother, "But I like to see what I've done!" Her mother smiled, happy that her Type 3 daughter was living true to her nature and desired to see her results.

. . . .

Type 3s truly do enjoy standing back to see what they've accomplished and the results they've created. The sooner you acknowledge and celebrate your Type 3 child's results with them, the more love and understanding they will feel from you.

These children bring forward momentum into the lives of those they interact with. They move swiftly when they see what needs to be done, and sometimes wonder why everyone else doesn't jump up to do the same. They push many things forward quickly and powerfully. Rather than moving forward through life on one linear track, they move forward along three or more tracks at a time, completing projects simultaneously and keeping a lot of things going.

Child Whisperer Tip: At times, your Type 3 child's forward movement may feel pushy to you, especially if you are not a Type 3 yourself. Do not tell your Type 3 child to stop being so pushy! Just as you don't like to feel pushed, your Type 3 child does not like to feel blocked or thwarted from the result they are trying to achieve. If you try to calm or shut down their energy, the experience will run contrary to their natural movement. That forward energy needs somewhere to go, and your child will probably just push back harder or even react explosively. If your Type 3 child is pushing for results that will harm them (like running toward a busy street), redirect them rather than stop them altogether—where *can* they run? If they are pushing for results that are bigger than what you want to deal with at the moment, consider the possibility that you can let them go for it without interfering. Why not? They want you to stand aside anyway!

Type 3 energy is an extrovert expression that leads these children to be outgoing, friendly, and self-assured when interacting with people of all ages, even those much older than themselves. Size does not matter to them when talking to older children.

Their tendency to move forward confidently is a characteristic that makes Type 3 children natural leaders, even from a young age. They often take charge when playing with peers and can organize a game or direct a group without hesitation. When sharing toys, your Type 3 child might show others how they work and how to play with them. You may observe your Type 3 teenager making decisions about what their group of friends will do when they all get together. These children move swiftly into action and others often trust and admire their natural confidence.

> **Child Whisperer Tip:** Give your Type 3 child opportunities to take charge. You may not think they are old enough for certain responsibilities, but if you listen to your child, they will always let you know what is appropriate for them. If you allow them to cultivate their gift for leadership in smaller settings, their abilities will keep up with their innate confidence. When they are young, consider letting them take charge of a family outing or dinner—let them make a few decisions for the group. As they grow, help them to move forward as they take on desired leadership positions at school or in the community. They have the confidence that they will succeed and only need to be granted the opportunity. Encourage and honor that confidence and you will see them accomplish great things.

Because Type 3 children's primary connection to the world is physical, they have naturally active and adventurous natures. If you have a Type 3 child, you may have noticed that they are ready to go, to do, and to explore, most any time of day or night. These children get you out of the house and out into the world!

◠ **Child Whisperer Tip:** Tell your young Type 3 child what's going on closer to when it actually happens, rather than far in advance. For example, if you plan to go somewhere with your child, announce it only when you're ready to leave. If it sounds like a good idea, they will just want to go right then, without any waiting. If you still have things to prepare, they will feel frustrated that they have to wait for you—and you'll feel like your child is pushing you out the door! Trust that they'll move into action quickly enough when they hear the news that you're heading out.

Remember that this strategy works best with young children. You will need to modify it as your Type 3 child grows. For example, if you announce to your Type 3 teen that it's time to get in the car, they might push back and tell you no. Why? Because your Type 3 teenager is most likely in the middle of something and a sudden departure would block them from accomplishing their current intended result.

Personality Traits: Passionate and Fiery

Type 3 children express a passionate personality. Their passion and excitement often moves the people around them into action. Others describe them as determined and self-confident. When these children are honored in pursuing what they feel most passionate about, other people experience their fiery energy as encouraging, rather than pushy. Picture a Type 3 child's energy as a little fireball.

If a Type 3 child wants to try something new—as they often do—they will go for it full force. They have no problem acting swiftly and confidently, well before they understand all the details of what they want to do. They go big!

. . . .

KELSEY'S STORY
Thinking Big

Kelsey competed in her middle school track and field team, and in 7th grade, she tied the school's high jump record along with another girl who was in 8th grade. At the track banquet that year, the other girl was recognized, but Kelsey's tied result was forgotten.

After the event, Kelsey climbed into the car with her parents who didn't know how she would react. Rather than get upset about the oversight, she said, "Don't worry. Next year, I'll come back and break the record—not just tie it!"

. . . .

Even though they are motivated by big results, these children are not naturally motivated to impress others with what they do. In fact, what others may think doesn't usually cross their minds while they are in action. Regardless of whether they try or not, a Type 3 child usually leaves a lasting impression wherever they go. Their personalities are naturally big and loud, so it's no effort to make an impression on others.

The loud, dynamic nature of a Type 3 child might be judged as a weakness by certain people, sometimes even by you. Type 3 children might receive labels like these: pushy, aggressive, demanding, or out of control. Labels like these suggest to a child that their natural energy is too big and too much. If they consistently receive these messages, they may take on the lie that their nature is somehow flawed.

In an attempt to fix what they perceive as their flawed nature, Type 3 children may try to alter their natural forward movement or shut it down altogether. However, their naturally forceful energy still needs somewhere to go. A Type 3 child who has been shamed or confused into living contrary to their nature will just exhibit a lot of fiery frustration that can rapidly get out of control. The more they try to contain it, the more it will push back, possibly in other areas of their life.

What's the key to helping your Type 3 child live in balance with their outward energy and fiery personality? Honor them! Recognize your child's dynamic, forward movement as a natural strength that encourages everyone around them—even you!

Pay attention to the times when you might view your child and their energy as too much and clear that judgment from your life. These children are naturally confident, but they don't like others (especially their parents) to judge them for wanting to do something that may seem against the grain. To a Type 3 child, their own energy doesn't feel like too much or too extreme; it's just an expression of who they are. When a Type 3 child feels that their parent just honors that natural expression, their natural confidence remains intact and they don't feel the need to act out or boil over.

Child Whisperer Tip: Parents of Type 3s may try to rein in their children to keep them from getting into things, or doing what the parents perceive as too much. Within obvious boundaries of safety, allow your Type 3 enough space and permission to *do*. They may want to pursue results that are not a high priority for you. If you try to stop them, they will probably find a way around you to do it anyway. If you succeed in stopping them, their frustration may simmer until they act out their frustration in other ways. Both of you will experience much more joy and harmony if you facilitate opportunities for your Type 3 child to actively pursue their dreams, no matter how big. Don't just get out of their way: Cheer them on. Trust that they can do it!

What can you do to help your child feel like you appreciate their natural determination? List some things you want to focus on here:

_____

_____

_____

_____

Thought and Feeling Processes: Quick and Deliberate

The movement in a Type 3 child's thought process is quick and deliberate. Because these children can have a lot going on in their minds, they compartmentalize their thoughts to keep track of everything. They may shift abruptly in focus from one thought to the other, and they return just as abruptly to a thought or project they've already started.

Type 3 children spend time thinking about topics that feel purposeful to them. If an idea or project seems purposeless to them, they won't waste time on it. When they spend time in imaginative thought, the play that accompanies it is very active. The stories they tell tend to be action-oriented, rather than descriptive.

Since a Type 3 child's primary connection to this world is physical, they often move into action as soon as a thought hits them. Their parents sometimes say that they "act without thinking." They do indeed think, but sometimes only after their body has already moved into motion: *Ready, fire, aim!* They can look impulsive, taking action in situations when maybe they should have thought just a moment more.

 Child Whisperer Tip: Your reaction to your child's impulsive behavior will get better results when you remember that their energy is not naturally devious or rebellious. They do not do things to purposely upset you, especially when they are young. Consistently disciplining your Type 3 child for *exploring* (not disobeying) can make your child more and more aggravated, frustrated, angry, and ashamed of who they are. This shame can lead to confusion for them about how they should relate to their world.

For example, a mom of a Type 3 six-year-old called in on my radio show for advice. She felt overwhelmed by her daughter's forward, determined movement. She had labeled her daughter as difficult and unruly. The week prior to our conversation, her daughter had left home and walked half a block down the street to their neighbor's house to play with a friend. Before the mom noticed her daughter's absence, the neighbor mom called to say her daughter was at their home.

I agree that this is a concern and I don't support any Type of young child venturing out on their own without checking in with their parent. I do feel strongly that discipline to punish the girl in this situation would not be helpful, as this child had no ill intent or rebellious drive behind her choice. She honestly felt confident that she could find her friend's house and took the challenge upon herself to prove it.

Here is how I would respond to this Type 3 little girl's choices: "I really admire your adventurous nature. You are such a confident little girl to walk down to your friend's house. Next time you want to do something like that, come and tell Mommy so I know where you are, and I can call your friend's mom and let her know you are on your way. It's not okay to leave the house without talking to Mom or Dad." I would not discipline her unless she chose to do it again without first telling a parent.

Because a Type 3 child's thoughts are accompanied by action, they may come across as impulsive or abrupt. They usually say what they're thinking, and they don't beat around any bushes! They don't usually wait for good timing to add their thoughts to a conversation either—they just go! They may burst into a room to share a joke or story at the wrong time, or barge into conversations loudly with whatever they're currently thinking. This can sometimes get them in trouble because they interrupt or say things they haven't thought through entirely.

Child Whisperer Tip: Let your Type 3 child's experience of sharing their thoughts with you be open and safe. Receive the thoughts that come spilling out of your child's mouth without an immediate negative reaction. If they want to take back something they said hastily, let them.

To handle their constant interruptions, make every effort not to shush them. Rather than shushing, look directly at your child and tell them you will be with them in a moment. Assure them that they can wait to tell you what they want to. And then make sure you honor them by taking a break from your current activity or conversation and switching to focus on them. Let them tell you what they want to share. I promise it will be quick and to the point. When you do this, they will feel heard and honored and then head off to their next activity.

Type 3 children's passionate personalities have a practical side. In fact, a Type 3 child's passion and practicality are closely connected. In order to carry out the results they are so passionate about, they need to move forward in practical ways. Type 3 children have an innate confidence that they can find the practical steps to accomplish the end they have in mind.

• • • •

ROSALIE'S STORY
Oh So Practical

The Christmas right after Rosalie turned two years old, everyone got a kick out of watching her open presents. She gave the paper a single tug, and then if the wrapping didn't immediately come off, she handed it back to the giver to open it for her. She just knew that someone else could get to the prize inside quicker than she could—and they always did!

Even at a young age, Type 3 Rosalie knew the result she wanted and did what her practical nature dictated to get it done. No extended fuss with the wrapping paper— just the quickest path to get to the presents inside.

• • • •

While you may need to help your child recognize times when they need a few more details in place, take care to honor their natural confidence. It is such a tremendous gift that will serve them well. If you question their confidence consistently while they are young, they may take on an inner script of self-doubt that does not actually come naturally to them.

⌒ **Child Whisperer Tip:** Honoring and supporting your Type 3 child's natural confidence is as simple as changing the phrases you use with them. Instead of disciplining or chastising your child when they do something that seems thoughtless, help them learn from it so they can experience more success the next time. Instead of blocking their path when they have already moved into action, help them see additional angles they might consider while in motion. Instead of this: "You never think things through." Try this:

"Tell me what you needed to do to make that happen."

Or instead of this: "Do you really think that will work?" Try this: "I'm excited for you and I'm here to help. Before you start, have you thought of. . . ?"

Better yet, when your Type 3 child has already moved into something, move with them! They move into something, jump in with them! They spring into action for everyone else so easily, and they appreciate it when others do the same for them. You can share your expertise along the way without blocking their path. Your child will know, in a practical way, that you appreciate who they really are.

When it comes to expressing their feelings, Type 3 children process their feelings swiftly. If they scrape a knee, they might rage about it for a second, rub it, and move on. Or if they come to you for a kiss, they'll take off quickly as soon as it's "all better." Extended comfort sessions are not needed. They feel passionately for a brief time, and then they move forward swiftly to the next experience.

Child Whisperer Tip: Pay attention if your Type 3 child ever stops processing their feelings swiftly. Lengthy tantrums or extended struggles with you are a sign that your child feels thwarted or blocked from an activity that they need. If it is truly not possible for them to do what they want, redirect your child to another activity, rather than try to stop them completely.

You will probably never wonder how your Type 3 child feels—because they will tell you. These children actively and loudly vocalize the way they feel. Whether they're happy, sad, excited, or upset, the outward expression of their feelings may seem intense. None of their reactions are overblown. It's just their active/reactive nature showing up!

As mentioned before, some adults may try to tone down a Type 3 child's loud reaction. Negative judgments of them may create a situation in which a Type 3 child does not feel they are allowed to vocalize their feelings. When this happens, these children may *do* something (like scribble on a wall or break a toy) to vent that energy and get attention. Look out for outright destructiveness as a sign that your Type 3 child does not feel allowed to share their feelings at home.

♡ **Child Whisperer Tip:** If your Type 3 feels they need to hold in emotions without expressing them openly, they may explode disproportionately in anger at someone and then feel embarrassed by the intensity of their feelings. If your child explodes at you, do not match their fiery outburst with your own. Don't tell them to calm down—this will only fire them up more! Let them be loud, acknowledge the intensity of their feelings, and recognize that the disproportionate outburst is not all about you. You should always be direct with your Type 3 child. Tell them, "I want you to tell me what you feel," or, "Tell me what you need to do in order to feel better."

If they are misbehaving and not responding to your requests, engage them physically in some way. Rather than just telling your child to stop or to listen, touch your child's shoulder or physically crouch down to talk on their level.

You can also minimize explosive episodes by paying attention to your child's goals and supporting them in accomplishing those goals. These children become most frustrated when something blocks their way and keeps them from moving forward. If you can help them feel a sense of accomplishment and forward movement in the things that matter to them, they will have fewer reasons to explode.

What are some ways you thought of that will help your Type 3 child feel like they are open to express themselves? List them here:

_____

_____

_____

_____

Just because these children are physical, active, and fiery doesn't mean they are not caring. They are actually quite empathetic. You may find that when someone is hurt or sad, your Type 3 child jumps into action to solve it before anyone else. They're the first to run to get the Band-aids or the favorite blanket. They're determined to help. Recognize the active empathy in your child and appreciate it.

. . . .

WALKER'S STORY
Watching Out for Everyone

Four-year-old Walker was out with his family when he saw another family getting into an elevator. The other family's oldest son held the elevator door open for everyone. Walker didn't know how elevator doors worked yet, and became quite concerned that the door would close on the boy. Walker demanded that everyone stop so that someone could take care of the boy holding the door to the elevator.

Even though Walker is much older now, he still approaches other children's parents without hesitation to express concern for the child's safety or to express admiration for a certain behavior. In true Type 3 fashion, he actively looks out for others around him, ready to move into action whenever they need support.

. . . .

⌒ **Child Whisperer Tip:** Because these children are so active and outwardly confident, you might sometimes assume that they don't need reassurance. After all, they already know they are great and they accomplish so much on their own. Because of this assumption, these children tend to hear expressions of love and reassurance the least of all 4 Types of children. Even though they *are* naturally confident, they appreciate your validation. Here are some examples of how to express this in a way that your Type 3 child will appreciate: "Wow, you sure get the job done," "I love how you accomplish so much," or "I am so impressed by you."

If you don't feel emotionally connected to your Type 3 child, there's a reason! Consider the possibility that your child has one of these experiences with you:

- They feel that you always tell them "No."
- They feel too stifled or limited when they are around you.
- They do not experience enough physical activities together with you.

- They feel like you talk about what you will do, but never just do it.
- They are confused about who they are because their natural, physical expression has been judged by their parent as a weakness.

Type 3 children don't just prefer physical outlets for their energy—they NEED them. Telling this Type of child to settle down and stop moving is like telling fire to just cool down a little bit! When you honor your Type 3 child's truly active nature, you will see that child become more content and easy to get along with.

Communication: Loud and Forceful

A Type 3 child's dynamic nature shows up in their communication patterns. These children express themselves loudly, but their loudness does not have the animated quality of a Type 1 child. It's a more forceful, direct expression that gets right to the point. As babies, they may surprise their parents with their powerful scream that sounds louder than the cries of other children. As they grow, they will easily be able to out-yell, out-scream, and out-talk the rest of the family—unless, of course, you are also a Type 3.

Even though these children express themselves loudly, they may actually talk less than other Types of children. They generally answer questions quickly and avoid discussing topics they view as pointless. They may not communicate in words until they feel there is a result worth talking about. Asking for permission or help may feel like an obstacle so they won't bother to do so. They'll often do things themselves without communicating beforehand what they plan to do.

. . . .

LISA'S STORY
Just Do It!

At age six, Lisa's daughter signed up for a talent show as a dance soloist. This talent show was for the entire school, and she was only a kindergartener. She signed up anyway, tried out, was selected—and only then did she tell her parents.

Lisa didn't even know her daughter was thinking about trying out. At six years old, this little Type 3 girl just did what needed to be done and then told her parents to attend the performance. Out of all the children from kindergarten to 5th grade, she was the only one to perform a solo.

She wasn't keeping anything from her parents. She probably just didn't even think of letting them know until there was a result worth talking about.

. . . .

A Type 3's natural confidence also expresses itself as they communicate. They announce their decisions, rather than ask for input. They often state their opinions or plans as facts and expect everyone else to go along. If they want something that a parent or peer won't let them have, they are likely to press or argue for it. When these children are misunderstood, their communication tendencies may sound aggressive or contentious to others. This is not the case. Type 3 children express themselves more forcefully, but they don't necessarily want to fight.

They do, however, like to see a reaction from their actions. If they do not feel allowed to express their substantial energy in a healthy way, they may inadvertently create scenarios where they say or do things just to get a reaction from others. For instance, they might resort to taunting their siblings or friends. They might also persistently poke at their parents or teachers in a subconscious effort to get them to respond, even if their reaction is negative.

⌒ **Child Whisperer Tip:** If your Type 3 child seems to pick a lot of fights with their siblings, friends, or peers at school, consider where in their life your child's energy feels stifled. Where are they not experiencing the healthy reactions and results that they need in order to thrive? You can even ask an older child directly for their feedback: "What do you need to DO right now to feel better and stop fighting?"

When they feel misunderstood or unheard, Type 3 children tend to get even louder than usual. Their voices get bigger and bigger in an attempt to get their point across in a way that makes the other person listen. In these scenarios, they may be told that they never stop hammering the point. They are not trying to badger anyone or hold onto something that's worth letting go. They just won't stop until they feel they've achieved the result of being heard and understood.

⌒ **Child Whisperer Tip:** If your Type 3 child is getting louder and more persistent about a point in a conversation with you, they feel that you're not truly listening to them. You may think you are (how could you not be when they're shouting so loudly?), but something you're doing makes them feel threatened or misunderstood. Don't try to out-shout them or calm them down. You should actually do the exact opposite—be quieter and listen more! Validate their passionate nature: "Wow. I can tell you're really fired up about this. Tell me more about it." When a

Type 3 child feels heard and validated, their volume will naturally come back down to a more reasonable level for you both. They won't shout at you when they feel that they are heard.

♡ **Child Whisperer Tip:** When communicating, it's best to stay practical and to-the-point with a Type 3 of any age. Especially when your child is younger, clearly say what you expect from your child. Stop over-explaining and just pick up and move. Your Type 3 child will value your honest and realistic communication with them and will respond best when you are most direct.

I witnessed firsthand the struggle that over-explaining can create while grocery shopping recently. A Type 3 little girl was pushing her mom to get some candy. True to this girl's determined nature, she kept asking and asking at the checkout stand. Her mom attempted to stay calm and talk things out with her daughter, using a lot of explanation and reasoning why it was not a good time to let her have a candy bar, that it was almost dinner time, etc. I thought to myself, *That child is a Type 3 and she just needs to be told clearly and to the point, "No, we are not going to buy any candy right now. I hear what you want and no matter how hard you push me, it is still not going to happen. I love you and appreciate how determined you are."* So many parents would benefit from knowing they can meet their Type 3 child's requests head-on and actually be more effective that way.

Behavioral Tendencies

Family Relationships: *Love (and fight) with intensity*

Type 3 children love their families intensely. They enjoy doing things together, especially physical activities as a group. These children appreciate physical expressions of love. This can look like hugs, cuddles, high fives, back scratches, or wrestling. As these children are always on the go, let them be affectionate on their own terms. They won't want to sit still and snuggle with you for long periods of time. Expressing your love physically for these children often means doing something with them or helping them to accomplish a goal. A Type 3 child who sees you get up and do something for them will feel more loved and honored than if you just told them you loved them.

Your Type 3 child will often act in order to get reactions out of family members. This can be such a blessing. They'll try to make their baby sister laugh. They'll do something funny to cheer up a grumpy brother. Or they'll help you out, just to make things easier around the house. Explain the result that you want and your Type 3 will move action to help.

The flip side of this tendency? Type 3 children may try to boss the entire family around, make decisions for their siblings, and tell everybody what to do. They may taunt or pinch their siblings in order to get a reaction from them. Remember: The magic word is *redirect*. Instead of telling your child to stop, help them channel that forward movement into something more productive.

. . . .

ANNE'S STORY
What Child Whispering Can Do

My daughter, Anne, came home from her in-laws' family dinner and shared with me that her Type 3 six-year-old nephew had been very rambunctious and rowdy all night. He teased his younger sister, ran up and pushed his cousins, only to irritate the other little children to tears and frustrate the adults. His parents continually scolded him and told him to calm down and stop behaving this way, to no avail. He just continued to get more and more riled up.

Through Anne's "Child Whisperer" eyes, she wisely recognized that he was just trying to get a reaction out of everyone. So she got his attention and invited him to play a game of pushing and shoving, with her on her knees to make the game more equal to his stature. When he shoved her, she made exaggerated sounds to cause the reaction he was looking for. After about 10 minutes of rough-housing with her and experiencing her reactive noises, he became calmer, acted more at ease, and stopped bothering everyone else.

. . . .

Friends and Social Settings: *Natural leaders*

Their extroverted expression leads these children to be friendly and outgoing, and a variety of friends are drawn to their energy and confidence. These children are ready to jump right in and play with children of all ages, and are not intimidated by bigger kids.

They prefer active play, like jumping around on playgrounds, running in the yard, or exploring outside. They wrestle, they run, they tag, they tackle. Even little Type 3 girls may find friends who match their level of energy and wrestle endlessly, giggling the whole time. As they get older, they may not wrestle their friends in the backyard as often (or they might!), but they will always prefer to remain very active, going places, playing sports, or participating in a variety of activities that get them out into the world.

Because Type 3 energy is such a strong expression, and has not been viewed culturally as a particularly feminine energy, Type 3 girls may be labeled tomboys. They can unintentionally come off as too strong for some other little girls. When they are young, they may play best with other girls with strong Type 1 and Type 3 expressions since both of these energies are high movement.

Timeliness: *Going up to the last minute*

These children move abruptly, making them erratic with timing and schedules. Since Type 3 children move many things forward at a time very quickly, they can sometimes make the mistake of trying to accomplish more than what their time allows. As you try to get them going in the direction you need them to go, you might hear your Type 3 child say things like this: "Hang on a second. Just let me finish this real quick." They don't want to stop what they're doing. So these children go, go, go right up to the last minute, which often means they are late and that their movement to get out the door produces a flurry of activity.

⌒ **Child Whisperer Tip:** Because your Type 3 child will always try to accomplish more goals than they have time for, give them quick updates as the time to leave or get ready draws nearer. Given directly (and without nagging), these updates can help your child remember which tasks absolutely need doing. "Be down for breakfast in five minutes." "Get in the car in five minutes."

Recognize that your Type 3 child will not always arrive at places on the dot—but they'll definitely get a lot done all along the way. Don't demand punctuality in every area of their life. Do identify a few situations in which punctuality really matters to you. It might be getting to the school bus on time. It might be coming home at curfew. Communicate which situations matter the most to you and why. Then trust that they will move forward to create the most important result you've both agreed on.

Jobs and Household Chores: *Focused on results*

Chores for chores' sake don't interest a Type 3 child. But they love to help when they feel a job has purpose or is part of a competition. Once they begin a task, they will finish it, especially if given a feeling of accountability about their work. These children move swiftly through their chores—some parents might say a little *too* swiftly. This means that they excel at big tasks, but smaller, more detail-oriented tasks can feel tedious and may not be finished to the standard you prefer.

⌒ **Child Whisperer Tip:** Give your Type 3 child big jobs. Some examples include raking a yard, cleaning up an entire room quickly, moving furniture, or washing the car. When they finish, admire the results of their hard work with them. If you assign your Type 3 child small, detailed tasks like organizing drawers or cleaning all the baseboards, they will not see purpose and put off the task. If you are detail-oriented yourself, you will not see the sort of results you want. Play to your child's strengths and they will accomplish good things around the house.

. . . .

A MOTHER'S STORY
Making Daily Life Easier

One mother shared her delight that she knows exactly how to make day-to-day activities easier and more cooperative with her fiery little Type 3 toddler. She says that her daughter, "may not want to put her shoes on, but if I ask her how fast she can do it, LOOK OUT! It's so wonderful to have these insights and strategies to help us make daily life more fun and peaceful." When you know what motivates and delights your little ones, you can really honor them in every activity throughout the day.

. . . .

 Child Whisperer Tip: Whatever chores your Type 3 children do, make them a challenge. Have a race to do chores around the house. Or tell your child you'll time them while they put something away for you: "Ready, set, go! 1. . .2. . .3. . ." I know one mom who put a dollar on the counter and told her daughter that if she cleaned up her room in a certain amount of time, the dollar was hers. Guess who rushed off to clean her room in a hurry! Because money is an indicator of their ability to create results, Type 3 children will respond readily to a financial incentive to help a little extra around the house. Tell them you'll pay them to do extra chores around the house and they'll ask you how soon they can start.

Money Management: *Natural entrepreneurs*

Type 3 children love making money! It's tangible evidence they can use to measure what they've done and the results they've created. These kids like to go big, so they might save up for a larger item that they really want. I've also heard of some younger Type 3 children who want to earn money, but don't necessarily want to spend it—because then the evidence of their effort would be gone!

While every Type of child can be an entrepreneur, the entrepreneurial experience comes most readily to Type 3 children. They see a challenge in making money and move forward to make it happen. As natural leaders, they have no problem enlisting the neighborhood kids to staff their roadside booth or join their cause. And they are often very successful! When he was 10 years old, my son-in-law, Tanner, built a raft and charged kids 50 cents for rides down the canal behind his house. One nine-year-old Type 3 girl named Annie was always cooking up some business or another at the end of her driveway. She even sold rocks from the family's landscaping to people driving by.

◠ **Child Whisperer Tip:** Support your Type 3 child in their entrepreneurial efforts, without micromanaging them. This might mean that you pay them for some extra jobs around the house or projects you want finished. And if they want to go bigger than that, consider the possibility that even fairly young Type 3 children have an eye for business. Instead of trying to talk them out of it, or managing it for them, just let them try. They will learn so much from small endeavors that they will eventually put those lessons to use on a larger scale in the future. One of the best questions you can ask when your child is moving forward with their plan is, "I want to be here for you. What would you like me to do?"

• • • •

TANNER'S STORY
The Big Games!

My son-in-law, Tanner, is an entrepreneurial Type 3. He is also a big fan of a local university football team, and has been since he was 7 years old. In fact, he has never missed a home game since then!

As a 13-year-old teenager, he hosted away game parties at his home. True to his Type 3 go-big nature, his parties included a lot of fanfare and celebration. He put up hundreds of helium balloons and streamers, built a scoreboard around his TV, bought pizza, soda, and chips.

How did he pay for it? He printed fancy tickets that he sold for $15 a piece that he allowed people to buy by invitation only (they had to be good fans). Average attendance for these game day gatherings was around 25 people. Tanner wanted to have the party, wanted it to be *big, but didn't want to have to pay for it. He threw the party true to his nature!*

. . . .

Recreational Activities: *Prefer competitive action*

Whenever planning activities for your Type 3 child, remember that their primary connection with the world is physical. Make sure they participate in activities with a swift learning curve that they can learn through doing. If they have to sit and wait for extended instructions before jumping in, they will lose interest. Let them dive right in and learn to swim!

Of all the Types, Type 3 children are the most naturally competitive. They love a challenge, especially if it's physical. They also enjoy activities where they can move at their own pace without others telling them they're too fast or too pushy. Give your Type 3 child a lot of opportunities for physical outlets where they can engage in healthy competition. Sports like soccer, basketball, tennis, volleyball, gymnastics, and swimming are good options. Baseball is not always a Type 3 favorite (too much sitting and waiting), unless they play a position that moves things forward, such as pitcher. Dance (hip-hop, jazz, anything with an upbeat tempo, rather than ballet), theater, and other artistic endeavors can all cater to a Type 3 child's movement.

⌒ **Child Whisperer Tip:** Competition doesn't always mean competing against others to win. Although Type 3 children are energetically designed to compete against others in games and sports, it is important for them to learn how to lose gracefully with good sportsmanship. Teaching your Type 3 child that they can always compete against themselves in an effort to improve their skills and timing will help them keep things in perspective and learn that winning isn't everything—although they tend to think it's a lot more fun when they do win!

Activities to Help a Type 3 Child Develop Natural Gifts

As you facilitate opportunities for your Type 3 child to develop their natural gifts, remember that these children are physically oriented and express a medium to medium-high level of movement. They need space and time to run and jump and move without limitations on how hard they play or how much they move. Give them these outlets for release and you will have a happy Type 3 child in your home.

♡ **Child Whisperer Tip:** You do not have to be the sole source of your Type 3 child's energy outlets. It is okay (and I would say it's even necessary) to regularly utilize the help of others, like family members, babysitters, or other people outside the home. If your Type 3 child is still very young, consider hiring a mother's helper—a pre-teen or teenager in the neighborhood who can just come wrestle and play with your child while you are still at home. Several mothers I know who felt they needed to be everything, all the time, for their little ones have expressed relief to me that they do not have to match their Type 3 child's energy all the time. Don't try it— you'll burn out. Give them the activity and movement they need through other outlets and other people and both of you will be happier.

. . . .

KELSEY'S STORY
Jump On In!

At only three years old, Type 3 Kelsey was determined to jump off the high dive at the community pool. She climbed up, jumped off, and did a flip into the water. Her mother wondered what Kelsey's reaction would be to the whole experience. Kelsey came up out of the water with a grin, saying, "I want to do that again!"

. . . .

Competitive sports offer a great opportunity for your Type 3 child to express their natural movement. Team sports are good options because they offer children a chance to interact physically. Plus, they give your Type 3 child a chance to lead. However, don't rule out individual sports. Gymnastics, diving, mountain biking, rock climbing, skateboarding, or skiing all include an element of risk and allow a Type 3 to go at their own pace without anyone to hold them back. They also offer the experience of competing against themselves.

When it comes to activities that are not sports, think about results. Type 3 children want to see where things are going, why they are headed the direction they are. One example of this attribute is their tendency to skip to the back of books or magazines to see where things end up before investing the time in everything that comes before. Consider debate, crafts, or scouting as additional outlets.

When I was a girl, I loved those little kits you could use to make woven potholders. I remember putting them together at age five or six years old. The instructions were easy to follow, the project was quick—and at the end, I had a potholder! I also loved puzzles and when I was old enough (about 12 years old), I asked my mom if I could take sewing lessons and learn how to do needlepoint and cross-stitch. I loved sewing, as it offered me the experience to work on projects and see the results of my efforts. By age 13, I became so skilled at handiwork that I was hired by a local company that produced small needlepoint kits to put together the samples that were displayed in the stores where the kits were sold.

⌒ **Child Whisperer Tip:** Whatever activities you provide for your Type 3 child, allow for variety. They get bored with the same routine and the same activities when they happen every day, unchanged. These children are always willing to jump in and try new things, so let them. Think projects! Type 3 children love a project that offers them a result that they can stand back and admire.

Make sure you take time to admire their results with them. "Look what I did" is an attitude and trait that will be a part of your Type 3 child's nature their entire life. Don't think they are bragging or doing what they do to impress others. Their natural tendencies just create results that make lasting impressions.

I am sure that the mother of Type 3 Michael Phelps, the most decorated Olympic swimmer, is very impressed with her son. It also probably means a lot to Michael to be able to say, "Hey, Mom, look what I did!" Thank goodness that Debbie Phelps raised Michael true to his go-big-or-go-home Type 3 nature or he may have never developed his remarkable talents as a swimmer!

Which activities can you think of that would honor the movement of your Type 3 determined child? List a few here:

_____

_____

_____

_____

Learning Tendencies

Learning Style: *Hands-on works best*

Type 3 children learn best by doing. When they want to learn something, nothing will stop them from doing and trying. If you're teaching your Type 3 child a concept or idea, they'll let you know if you're talking too much by saying, "Just let me do it," or "Just let me try!"

These children move at a swifter pace through life, which might lead you to think they aren't picking up on certain concepts or ideas. They may surprise you with what they know. They learn in passing while moving from one activity to the next. They need fast-paced, flexible learning opportunities in order to stay engaged.

♡ **Child Whisperer Tip:** Waiting around for lots of instructions and minutia—as in a traditional classroom setting—bores Type 3 children. In order to start moving an activity forward, they may act out. If you need to give instructions, do it while your child is already working so they don't feel frustrated.

Classroom Behavior: *Need activity*

Since their primary connection to the world is physical, Type 3 children don't like sitting very long. They appreciate swift-paced learning environments with a variety of activities and tactile experiences. They enjoy projects rather than lectures. Look for hands-on classes with active teachers.

♡ **Child Whisperer Tip:** Sitting for a long time without something to do is torture for a Type 3 child. Talk to their teacher to see if they can be allowed to work on something with their hands during classroom instruction. It can be something as simple as drawing or taking notes, but it needs to be something that creates a result.

One woman who taught a children's class at her church brought a boondoggle keychain for a Type 3 girl to make every week during their lesson. Because that girl had something to work on, she actually listened better.

. . . .

SHIREE'S STORY
In Trouble, But Not With Mom

Shiree's son got in trouble at school for being overly physical and not respecting boundaries set by the teacher. On the way home, Shiree could tell that her son felt pretty badly about getting in trouble. Instead of scolding him for what happened and telling him he needed to change the way he was, she talked together with him about how he could get the movement that he needed while still following the rules.

Validating him empowered him to manage his own behavior so much more than chastising him would have. Shiree is one more beautiful example of the kind of relationships we can experience when we become our own family's Child Whisperers.

. . . .

Because Type 3 children are so results oriented, they may choose to earn high grades and honors. If this is the case, they will be persistent and self-motivated. They juggle several tasks and topics easily on their way to a straight-A report card. This decision is something they must decide for themselves, otherwise they will not have the dedication and interest necessary to make it happen.

A Type 3 child may also approach school as a system they can use in order to get a certain result. This thought process sounds like, "I'm going to do less than I'm being asked and get more from it." These children will be okay with "good enough" grades, rather than straight-A's if it gets them the result they want. If you ever feel like you have to push your Type 3 to get motivated about school, that's a sign that you need to talk with them about the results they aim to achieve and how school fits into that bigger plan for them. Let go of the straight-A ideal and consider other ideas they have in mind.

Study Habits: *Finish what they start*

These children are persistent in trying new things and love to finish what they start. If they are engaged by the subject matter and the work they need to do, they will dive in and concentrate.

Type 3 kids can become fidgety and impatient while they are working. First of all, sitting still for a long time to work on something can be difficult for them. They may need to work on a few things at a time, not finishing assignments in their entirety before moving on to the next. Quick, abrupt breaks are a good way to break up the monotony for a Type 3.

Secondly, impatience with homework can also be a sign that the work they are doing is pointless busy work, or that your child doesn't see the purpose behind the assignment. If you can see a higher purpose in the work they are doing, share it with them. Whatever you can do to help homework to be a challenge that makes sense and is completed swiftly, the easier your child will feel motivated to do it.

Physical Development

Learning to Walk: *On the move in the fastest way*

Type 3 children tend to walk a little later—not because they don't like to move, but because they can't be bothered to stop crawling when they're already cruising around! They like to move quickly, so most Type 3s won't start walking until it becomes a faster mode of transportation for them than crawling is. If they walk early, there's a good chance they'll be running soon after that.

Learning to Talk: *Speaking when it serves*

Type 3 children use speech as soon as they see it as a quick means to get what they want. Until then, they have a loud shout that usually gets the job done. I know of one two-year-old Type 3 who had shown her mother on many occasions that she was capable of speech—and had a lot of words under her belt! Because screaming was easiest and got her the fastest result, she opted for screaming over talking for quite some time. Respond quickly when your Type 3 child attempts to talk so they can see this as an equally speedy alternative to shouting at you. My Type 3 grandson used grunting as a way to communicate to get what he wanted. His mom, my Type 1 daughter Jenny, would politely say to him, "Tell me what you want and I will help you with that," to encourage him to develop his vocabulary and speech abilities.

. . . .

ABRAM'S STORY
So Frustrated!

Around 13 months, Abram developed a habit that left bruises all over his forehead. Whenever he got frustrated at being unable to communicate, he banged his head against something. It didn't matter what was close by: walls, floors, the person holding him. He did it with a lot of force and without warning.

Abram expressed his forceful, determined energy, even if he couldn't put it into words. Such a classic Type 3—when he was frustrated, he just had to do something!

To resolve this, his parents needed to work with him to make sure that he got enough activity and felt like he was allowed to move forward in the ways that mattered to him so he did not take out his frustration on himself. Their support, plus his speech development, helped Abram to grow out of this behavior so that he could communicate what he wanted in a way that felt swift enough for him.

. . . .

Potty Training: *Erratic success*

These children might get a lot going on and not make it to the potty in time. As you train and help them, remember that they are all about results. Emphasize that aspect of their potty-training experience.

These children may be successful for a short period in their potty-training results, lose interest for a short period, and get back to it again. They always achieve a successful outcome, just not always on the timeline mom or dad might like. I have never met a Type 3 adult who is still wearing diapers, so you can rest assured they will get it soon enough. Just be patient as they move through this stage erratically.

⌒ **Child Whisperer Tip:** Because Type 3 children are naturally so confident, some parents assume that they should let their child take charge of potty training, but this actually backfires with these children. You need to explain the result you want and then be direct about what you expect. Instead of asking if they need to use the potty, just say, "It's time to use the potty now. Let's go." Type 3 children communicate in this direct, to-the-point manner, and so they will respond when you do, too. They put off using the potty because they don't want to break away from the activity or project they are engaged in, and are telling themselves, "I will get to that later." I know Type 3 adults who put off using the bathroom for this same reason. They want to get their project done in spite of the discomfort!

⌒ **Child Whisperer Tip:** Let your Type 3 child experience potty training as a task that gets a result. For example, you could create a chart where they earn a sticker or a checkmark every time they go potty. Continue to remind them that the result they're aiming for is wearing underwear, not just how many checkmarks they can rack up—otherwise, they may find a way to rig the system. "You did it!" is a good way to phrase your praise for your Type 3 child.

Sleeping: *Play hard, sleep hard*

Type 3 children would keep go, go, going all night if they could. They have a hard time letting down in the evening to go to sleep unless they've had enough physical activity during the day. Type 3 children who have had enough opportunities for physical outlets will often crash at the end of the day and sleep hard. You might think these children don't need naps, but up until age two, I recommend regular naps to keep their moods even. From about two and a half to four years, they may do well with a nap two to three days out of the week.

Type 3 adults have a tendency to "burn themselves out" more quickly than any of the other Types, due to their swift, determined approach to everyday tasks, not just special endeavors. Teach your Type 3 children at a young age that they will be able to accomplish even more if they pay attention to their bodies' need for rest. This habit will help them maintain balance throughout the rest of their life.

• • • •

JOSEPH'S STORY
Bedtime Adventure

When my grandson Joseph started climbing out of his crib, his mom knew it was time to graduate him to a toddler bed. Climbing out of his crib was too big of an adventure each night for the little mind of this Type 3 boy to ignore.

The toddler bed was a success, but a few other challenges engaged Joseph and kept him from going to sleep at night. One in particular was unzipping and taking off his footed pajamas and his diaper. My very creative Type 1 daughter solved that problem by putting his jammies on backwards where he could not reach the zipper. Out of sight, out of mind for this Type 3. When the challenges were removed, Joseph easily went to bed at night, as long as they made sure to run out his energy earlier in the day!

• • • •

Going to Pre-school and School: *Confident*

These children love to play, they love new experiences, and they are confident—a perfect combination for a new school experience! Sometimes, parents of Type 3s are disappointed that their children aren't a little sadder to see them go.

If your Type 3 child doesn't feel immediately comfortable going and playing in a new situation like pre-school, they may sense that the environment is more structured than they prefer. Help them see the ways they will experience freedom to be themselves and they will warm up quickly.

Being Left with a Babysitter: *Need a physical goodbye*

Type 3 children engage readily with new people, even if they are older. They get excited about playing with someone new. If they have a babysitter who lets them play actively, they probably won't want to leave when their parents show up to take them home. Before you leave, share some sort of physical expression of your love like a hug, a kiss, or a pat.

Dating: *Active, practical approach*

If your Type 3 child is raised true to their nature, they will have a lot of self-confidence by the time they are teens, which can lead them to create healthy and fun dating experiences. Group dating will be more natural for them, as they enjoy the higher, more active energy a group experience would offer. It is also natural for them to lead out with friends to get a group date organized.

In the areas where my children grew up during their teens, it was a popular practice at the high schools to have as many girls'-choice dances as boys'-choice dances. For Type 3 girls, this arrangement is very supportive, as they would not understand or appreciate why the boys would be the only ones who could choose to ask someone out on a date! It is becoming more acceptable for girls to initiate dates in Western culture, which is a positive cultural shift for Type 3 girls in particular.

Type 3s bring their very practical nature into their dating experience. When my son-in-law, Tanner, decided that he wanted to date with the intent to meet his future wife, he knew by the first date whether a girl was a match for him and someone he wanted to pursue or not. People gave him a hard time, saying that he wasn't giving the girls a chance. They would ask how he could possibly know in one date what he wanted. He just did, swiftly and confidently. For my daughter Anne's sake, I am glad he trusted his instincts.

High School Experience: *A lot going on*

Your child may sign up for all sorts of teams or clubs or extra activities that keep them going all day long and into the night. Encourage and support them to do the activities that they love most and that honor their determined nature. Do not feel obligated to keep track of it all for them. They will make happen what they feel most determined to do.

Because Type 3 children are so results-oriented, they can become addicted to action. They can burn out by getting too much going, making too many commitments, or taking action too soon. Since this is the time of life when they are becoming more independent, don't stifle them. Help them make choices about what would best serve their development and their nature without taking on more than is necessary. Also let them learn by experience, by burning the candle on both ends, only to find out they have too much going on and they are stressed out. This is a good time to help them see their tendency for this and support them in making more balanced choices. Learning by doing is a great way to burn the lesson into the memory of a Type 3!

Driving: *Possible over-confidence*

Type 3 children love speed, and they often take to driving quickly. Many Type 3 children generally love anything with an engine. I know of several Type 3 children who want to learn how to drive a snowmobile, or a 4-wheeler, or a motorcycle before they're even big enough to reach the pedals. Whenever I hear on the news the occasional story of a younger child (about age 9 or 10) taking the family car out for a spin, I think to myself, *It had to be a Type 3!*

⌒ **Child Whisperer Tip:** Type 3 children can be over-confident in their driving skills. When I first learned to drive, I got in an accident the first week I had my license. I am sure my over-confidence was the problem. I felt awful. Rather than punish me, my parents could see my own self-punishment was harsh enough. Before your Type 3 teen gets out on the road, tell them in a reassuring way that you think they will be a great driver and that they need to make sure they don't get over-confident at first. Support them in learning and gaining experience. I think it's a good idea to enforce a no-cell-phone policy with your Type 3 teen who is new at driving, regardless of whether or not cell phone laws exist where you drive.

. . . .

ANNIE'S STORY
Going Up in Type 3 Flames!

Nine-year-old Annie really wanted an electric scooter for Christmas so she could go faster than on her regular foot-powered scooter. It cost a little more, so her parents told her that she needed to wait. For her birthday, she told everyone in her extended family that she wanted gift cards to Target, where the electric scooter was sold. She received enough money to cover the cost—and more. Leave it to a Type 3 to make things happen.

When Annie went to the store, she found something even better: a new scooter that shot sparks out the back when used. You better believe that Type 3 Annie fell in love with the idea of zooming down the street with fire shooting out behind her!

. . . .

Physical Characteristics

Every Type of child moves around. How do you determine if your child is really an active, determined, Type 3 child? Facial features provide one of the most telling ways to identify your child's dominant Type. Take a look at the list of Type 3 features and then look at your child's own physical characteristics. Do any of them show up in your child's face?

Something to remember: Learning facial profiling for babies and children in a book without pictures or illustrations can be difficult! That is why I have created a library of free videos on my website called, "How to Profile Babies, Children and Teens!" To access this library visit www.thechildwhisperer.com.

Face Shape: *Angular facial planes with irregular, asymmetrical hairline. Square or angular jaw, pointed chin, prominent forehead. May have a cleft in the middle of their chin.*

Skin/Skin Texture: *One of the most telling features in Type 3 adult skin is deeper, textured lines, especially around the smile and eyes.*

At a very young age, though, Type 3 skin does not exhibit this trait as clearly. Baby fat and youth may make their skin look smoother than it will appear later in their life when it naturally becomes more textured.

What you will notice most in a Type 3 baby's or child's skin is irregularity. Type 3 energy is a higher, more textured movement, which will express itself in your child's skin as irregularities in pigment or in texture. Some Type 3 children exhibit dry patches on their skin, or you may notice several irregularly placed birthmarks, moles, or spots on their body. As they grow, these children can be prone to acne. Type 3 teenagers might try to eliminate the texture from their skin with products that ultimately won't work. Help your child recognize that their naturally textured skin is just a feature of their body, not a flaw.

Cheeks: *Various forms of triangles on the cheeks and in or around the mouth.*

It may be tricky to tell at first, as babies are generally known for chubby cheeks.

Nose: *Angular, beak, lump of clay, triangular nostrils that flare when reacting strongly to something*

Eyes: *Come to a point in the inside of the eye or outside corners*

Might be described as cat-shaped, with the outer corner located slightly higher than the inner corner. Angles in the lid area can create an exotic look.

Eyebrows: *Type 3 eyebrows come to a peak somewhere after the middle of the eye.*

If you drew a line connecting both eyebrows, it would look like a wide V-shape.

Hands: *Rectangular shaped fingers, rough and knobby texture, with wide knuckles*

Early Childhood Features: *One of the most telling features for Type 3 babies and toddlers is what I call the "Type 3 scowl."*

This is the furrowing or wrinkling of their forehead between the eyebrows. Both of my Type 3 grandchildren, Joseph and Katie, exhibited this characteristic from the first day of their lives. Add the classic Type 3 growl to the scowl and you can be sure your baby is a determined little one.

Body Language

Since Energy Profiling is an assessment of our natural expression of movement, body language is an excellent clue to your child's Energy Type. Pay attention to the way your child moves. Do any of these movements describe your child?

Crawling: Type 3 infants start moving early! Before they crawl, they may drag themselves across the floor, army style, to get to whatever toy or goal they have in mind.

They start crawling and often continue to do so for a long time. They get so good at crawling that they would rather just keep crawling to get what they want quickly, rather than take the time to learn to walk. They often wait until their bodies grow and mature to a stage where they can learn to walk quickly before they ever take those first steps.

Walking: A Type 3 walk has a swift, deliberate movement to it. These children probably spend less time walking and more time running everywhere they go. They will slow down to a more deliberate walk as adults, but while your Type 3 is a child, expect them to take off at a sprint when they decide they want to go somewhere.

With their strong movement, these children are also known for clomping around the house. Type 3 children are heavy-footed and you can hear them coming. My Type 3 grandson, Joseph, stomps around the house making growling noises, just as a natural movement throughout the day.

Sitting/Standing: These children sit and stand at angles. They put their hands on their hips or in their pockets, bending at the elbow, making angles and a strong stance. They may even sleep at angles, with one leg bent in an asymmetrical position.

You won't often catch these children sitting still of their own choice. And when they do sit still, they are usually tapping something or moving somehow. I know of one Type 3 child who gets out of his seat during meal times to make a circuit of the room on imaginary adventures. Another one insists on eating all of her meals standing. Your Type 3 child will usually only land for a while if they get completely absorbed in a project they're working on and trying to finish.

Voice/Language: Loud voice, medium pitch. When upset, a Type 3's voice can become explosive. They speak directly and their voice carries. Due to their louder voices and more abrupt manner of communicating, Type 3 children get shushed by their parents more than any other Type. Type 3 children do not know they are louder. It's just the way they are built and naturally express themselves.

Child Whisperer Tip: Your Type 3 child needs to learn that certain times are appropriate to use a quieter voice. However, in most of the situations in which parents tell their children to be quiet, the shush is for the parents' own comfort. The next time you want to tell your Type 3 child to shush, reconsider if it's really necessary. Just let them talk at their normally loud level and see if their volume really matters that much.

To be constantly reminded and told to be quieter than they are makes Type 3 children begin to doubt their assertive, expressive nature. If you feel your Type 3 child really is talking too loudly for a certain situation, rather than shush them, ask them to use their quieter voice in a manner that is honorable rather than embarrassing to them.

Personal Space: Type 3 children move swiftly, which means that their personal space may be a bit of a mess.

They **are not** trying to be messy, they're just moving so quickly that they may not have the time or attention to clean up after themselves naturally. They do want to help, so if you bring the mess to their attention and make cleanup a challenge, they will pick up in a hurry.

♡ **Child Whisperer Tip:** Don't try to prevent your child's big energy. Parents often sense their Type 3 child's powerhouse energy under the surface and they worry about just letting it go. They can just tell their child is going to DO something. They wonder, *what if it gets out of control?* Pray for inspiration to know how to direct that energy, rather than contain it. I'll say it again: Redirect, don't contain! Their energy won't get out of control if they feel safe to express it. Check your living space to see if it's supportive to a Type 3's exploratory, active nature. Make necessary adjustments. You'll end up telling your Type 3 child no a lot less often, and your child will be so much happier.

· · · ·

JOSEPH'S STORY
Another Bedtime Adventure

My grandson Joseph loves a challenge. I mentioned earlier how he climbed out of his crib and took off his pajamas and diaper at night, keeping him from comfortably falling asleep. Another bedtime challenge he loved was getting out of bed after Mom and Dad had turned out the light, and taking all of his toys out of his toy chest and closet.

Rather than go through the push-pull struggle of trying to teach a two-year-old to stay in his bed and leave the toys alone at night, Jenny just pulled the toy chest out of his room and into the hall and put a child prevention lock on the closet doors so Joseph had nothing in his personal space to challenge him at bedtime. As he has grown and matured in his sense of reasoning and understanding, she has successfully taught him that it's bedtime and not time to pull all the toys out. She no longer needs to remove the items from his space.

. . . .

Challenges as a Parent: Feeling Pushed and Keeping Up

Parents of Type 3 children experience the challenge of feeling pushed. These children tend to push their parents persistently until they get their way, using phrases like, "You should," or "You have to." If you don't understand and honor the movement behind these statements, you might think your child is trying to strong-arm or manipulate you. They're not. They're just determined to get what they want and they'll go for it directly. You may have noticed that even if you've told your Type 3 child no, they'll do it anyway. Their excuse might be, "You're not the boss of me."

♡ **Child Whisperer Tip:** You can be equally direct in your response to your Type 3 child. They will appreciate how open and to-the-point you are. You don't need to give a lot of excuses or explanations about why they can or can't do something—it will only make the issue muddy and open up other places where they can push you. It's important to realize that Type 3 energy is substantial and your child may need to grow into themselves! They are not aware of how pushy they can be, or how determined they are when they have their mind on something. Your job as their parent is to help them grow into the dynamic energy they naturally express, rather than squash it or shame it.

Parents of Type 3 children also mention that their child is so *loud*. They may have an immediate temper tantrum that seems like it came from nowhere. The intensity of a Type 3's emotion sometimes feels a little overwhelming, especially for a parent of a lower movement on the energy scale.

⌒ **Child Whisperer Tip**: Help your child feel like they can *do* something about their frustrations. Give them choices, redirect to another meaningful activity, or just give them space to experience their big emotions without trying to shut it down or contain it. Most importantly, do not match their level of intensity or their tone of voice. Their active nature might spark an explosive reaction in you, but you don't have to give into it. You have control over the way you react.

Here's a challenge that can actually be a lot of fun: keeping up with your child! Type 3 children are on the move all day long, which can sometimes exhaust their parents.

⌒ **Child Whisperer Tip**: You do not need to be (nor should you be) your Type 3 child's sole physical outlet. You will both get tired if you try. When your children are young, find a play group, a child's gym, a grandparent, a mother's helper, or someone who is willing to *do* something with your child. Your child will appreciate the variety, and you will appreciate the break.

. . . .

JOSEPH'S STORY
Stomping on the Downstairs Neighbors
My grandson Joseph is very heavy-footed and likes to stomp around the house. He also climbs a lot and

jumps off the ottoman and kitchen chairs. He got his older Type 4 brother going, as well, which made for two rambunctious little boys stomping and jumping around the house.

Unfortunately, this was not conducive to the second floor townhome their family lived in. After repeated complaints from the downstairs neighbor, who did not understand the nature of these two little boys, my daughter and son-in-law first attempted to quiet little Joseph. It only turned into a daily practice of shushing him and telling him to stop stomping around and quit jumping. Jenny became stressed and sad that she was teaching him he couldn't be who he naturally was.

After much consideration, Joseph's parents decided to move to a new townhome that was both a bottom and second floor where Joseph could stomp and jump freely. Jenny knew it was not supportive of her Type 3 son to try and contain his natural movement in his own home when it was not harming anyone! He also needed a yard to run and play in to get outside each day, which their new townhome offered them as well. This was a big decision, but they put their son's needs first and it turned out to be the most supportive thing they could do for their young family.

. . . .

The challenges of parenting a Type 3 child are overshadowed by the great joy that these children are to their families. These children love to try new things and be active together. They are easy to take to new places. They keep the family moving forward, getting things done. They love as passionately as they do everything else. When these children feel supported in living true to their natures, their enthusiasm naturally motivates others to become their best selves.

Express your love for your Type 3 child by doing something for them today. Whatever you've been putting off, telling them that you'll do it later or that they need to wait, get going and make it happen soon—today, even. They will see that you moved into action for them and it will make a huge difference in your relationship with them.

What inspiration do you have about how to help your child feel they are a gift in your family? Make some notes here. Then take action on what you wrote.

_____

_____

_____

_____

The Type 3 Determined Daughter

Type 3 daughters are fiery and passionate. Type 3 energy is active, reactive, swift and determined—not a stereotypically feminine movement. As young children, Type 3 daughters are active and engaging and may be seen as such in a positive light. They may organize games with their friends or lead the neighborhood children in adventures. They can run into the challenge of being told they are too loud or too rambunctious, which might set them on a path of trying to soften or ignore their naturally swift, dynamic nature.

The more they grow, the more they may hear the label "tomboy." Although I know that nobody intends harm when using this reference, I do not find it the most flattering way to label these girls' fiery, passionate quality of feminine energy.

In a culture that tends to recognize the feminine expression as one that is soft and gentle, a Type 3 female who expresses herself as swift, determined, or competitive is seen as more boy-like and referenced in a way that says she is somehow less of a girl. How inaccurate! How damaging! These girls need to know that their determined movement is perfectly fine and perfectly feminine. Let's eliminate the term "tomboy" and honor these strong, determined females for who they are. They have a lot to offer with their Type of feminine!

If they are not supported in living true to themselves, these girls may try to send a message to the world that is actually in conflict with who they truly are. Even though their nature is dynamic and determined, they may try to soften themselves in order to not be seen as so intense.

This is not the message the world receives. Instead of being perceived as softer, these girls may actually look more masculine than ever, and be perceived by others as overly aggressive or abrasive. When they are living true to themselves, this couldn't be further from the truth. A Type 3 girl who lives true to her nature is engaging, interesting, and truly beautiful.

The opposite may also happen. A Type 3 teenage daughter may decide that she's tired of being treated like someone she's not and go overboard sassy. She may take her edginess to an extreme that's too big, even for her. She may rebel as loudly as she can and take more risks than she should, to her own detriment. She plays bigger than she actually is in an attempt to prove that her true nature is not so bad.

♡ **Child Whisperer Tip:** Whatever you do, honor your Type 3 daughter's fiery, active nature as the beautiful, feminine gift that it truly is. Support her in moving forward with her goals. If she wants to start a business, encourage her. If she wants to be a rock star, sign her up for guitar lessons. If she wants to learn, or build, or do, ask her what she needs to make her plans happen. Her plans might be bigger than anything you could dream up for her, and you might not know what to do. Just remember that your approval and confidence in her natural abilities will make all the difference.

. . . .

KATIE CLAIRE'S STORY
Entering the World With a Bang

At the time of writing the Type 3 section of this book, I had the great blessing and honor of welcoming my third grandchild to our family: Katie Claire Brown, a beautiful, dynamic Type 3 little girl, daughter of Anne and Tanner Brown, my daughter and son-in-law.

Katie entered the world with a bang, very true to her nature. Anne was admitted to the hospital a week after her due date to be induced to start the labor of their new baby girl. After fifteen hours of not much happening, they decided to increase Anne's labor-inducing medication. A sudden change in the baby's heart rate created a rapid change of plans and put a ten-person medical team into action immediately for an emergency Caesarean section. Both mom and dad were panicked and scared for the life of this little girl. The C-section was performed in minutes and a healthy baby girl was born. She was very content after her delivery and Anne and I commented that she came into her life true to her nature and she seemed pretty happy about that!

As I was not raised true to my nature, you can imagine how grateful I am that my daughter and son-in-law understand little Katie's nature and will raise her in a way that will support this little girl in becoming a confident,

self-assured young woman and adult who lives true to her
natural gifts and talents.

. . . .

The Type 3 Determined Son

Type 3 sons are adventurous and confident. They experience a bit more understanding about their natural expression as children. Our cultural sense of Type 3 energy can be summed up in this statement: "Boys will be boys." As children, Type 3 boys are loud, adventurous, and rambunctious, and it's expected. While their energy may exhaust their parents, it is not usually seen in a negative light.

However, when school age arrives and these boys are expected to sit for long periods of time behind a desk, they can sometimes get into trouble. Their energy needs somewhere to go, and it can often find a self-destructive route.

Child Whisperer Tip: Even if your child encounters some stifling experiences out in the world, you can always make home a space where your Type 3 son feels free to play as big and as loud as he wants. Help your Type 3 son direct his energy into creating useful things. Whether it be a skill, a project, a group, a business, anything will work as long as he enjoys it and feels the activity is purposeful. Help your Type 3 son understand that he is a powerhouse of forward momentum and that he can use that to accomplish many great things throughout his life. Empower him with an understanding of his natural gifts.

The Type 3 Child Through the Years

Type 3 children express their true nature from birth to adulthood in a variety of ways. The following will give you some of the most common general tendencies they may express in their first 18 years of life.

At each developmental stage, your child has a specific emotional need. This is true for all Types of children. I offer some specific phrases to share with your Type 3 child to help meet each need. Use these phrases in words, or consider how you could express these phrases in action to help your child feel loved and wanted in each stage of life. When your children are supported in living true to their nature, they can more easily enter their adult experience ready and able to create emotionally healthy relationships. You can meet your child's developmental emotional needs in many ways—just use my examples as a way to get you thinking.

Baby 0 to 18 months

Primary Emotional Need: *To be validated for their active, reactive nature and to be supported in starting to explore and sense the world around them.*

The Type 3 baby is ready to go from the minute they're born. In fact, some mothers of Type 3 babies report that their delivery was a quick, intense push at the end and then their child suddenly arrived, already moving swiftly in this world. All Type 3s start their life experience with a primary connection to the physical experience of this world. People around these babies can sense their desire to move and explore. Others might observe that a Type 3 infant is a busy-body.

Type 3s are also relatively louder babies than the other Types. They scream loudly when they need something—or they just try to do it themselves! One mother mentioned that her Type 3 baby had barely discovered her fists when she was already grunting away in her bassinet, trying to retrieve her pacifier all by herself.

When they are hungry, they can cry angrily. They nurse quickly and then are content quickly afterwards.

My daughter Anne made this observation about her Type 3 newborn: "I was playing some soft tunes on my iPod when an intense classical song, Verdi's *Trovatore Anvil Chorus*, started to play. It's louder with faster instruments, totally a Type 3 song—and I was about to change it when I noticed Katie close her eyes and fall right to sleep and get really relaxed, so I am playing the song again."

Messages your Type 3 child needs to hear in this stage of life:

- Welcome to the world; we've been eagerly waiting for your active energy.
- We planned and prepared a special place for you.
- All your needs are important to us. You can grow at your own pace and we are here for you.
- We love your swift, determined energy—you are a gift to our family.
- It's okay to play; we will make it safe and comfortable for you to explore.
- You can be you and we will always love you.
- It's okay for you to be different from Mom and Dad. We will work out our differences in a way that supports you in feeling loved.

Child Whisperer Tips to support this stage: Type 3 babies do not have the motor skills necessary to provide all the active movement they want in order to feel comfortable. You can provide this for them, just in the way you rock them. Rather than a slow, soft movement, you need to bounce them a little more or walk around while you're holding them. They will actually settle better when they experience a higher movement.

Baby blankets are typically plush and soft. Since Type 3 energy is higher, these children actually enjoy a little more texture on their blanket than you might think. As your baby becomes more interactive, choose toys with varied textures for them to explore. Introduce foods that have variety. Be sure to give them plenty of time to look around, facing away from you when you hold them. They already want to take a close look at this big world they long to explore.

Toddler 18 months to 3 years

Primary Emotional Need: *Support in sensing, exploring, and doing in the world.*

The Type 3 toddler can begin to explore their world as they become more mobile through crawling and eventually walking. They want to get their hands on things, which you can notice in the way they just move into action whenever they see something that interests them. Language skills develop in this stage. You will notice that your Type 3 child's language has purpose behind it, and they are less likely to express themselves verbally unless it fulfills a purpose directly.

Messages your Type 3 child needs to hear in this stage of life:

- It's okay to be curious, to move, to touch and explore.
- We will make it safe for you to explore.
- You can be you and we will always love you.
- You can try out new things and find your own way of doing things.
- It's okay for you to want to move forward and trust

that your parents will support you in doing what's best for you.

- You are so determined and strong.
- You are so good at encouraging others; we are here to take care of you.
- You bring hope and encouragement to our family.
- I love you just the way you are.

⌒ **Child Whisperer Tips to support this stage:** I am pretty sure that Type 3 children in this stage of life created the phrase "The Terrible Twos"! Once a Type 3 child is mobile, they tend to want to get their hands on and into everything. This is the stage where they want to start exploring their physical world. When they are blocked from that, their tantrums can be terrible.

Type 3 children need to feel like they can move through the world without being contained. Make sure your home environment supports them in moving freely. Consider that your Type 3 child will feel more cooperative at home if they can play without always being told no. Spaces where they can move and jump and just get messy without you worrying about it will be supportive to them.

Pre-school 3 to 6 years

Primary Emotional Need: *Coming into their own identity and power.*

At this stage, you may find that your busy Type 3 begins to get a little feisty. They may even be intentionally destructive. You may wonder what you'll do with this child who seems so out of control! These children actually get out of control when they feel they haven't been given control over their lives. This is just the time when it shows up big time.

They often come to realize that their parents are worried about their big energy. They realize that not everyone else plays as big as they do, is as loud, or needs as much space. Their blow-ups are just efforts to establish their big personality as okay in their world. This is an important stage to recognize your child's voice and make sure that your child knows that they can speak as loud as they want. A Type 3 child hears the words "Shush" and "Be quiet" often enough. Responding to *what* they say, rather than to the volume at which they've said it, will help your child at this stage.

Messages your Type 3 child needs to hear in this stage of life:

- It's okay for you to move as fast as you want to.
- You are learning what is right for you—trust your instincts.
- We are glad you are starting to think for yourself.
- We love to spend time doing things together with you.
- Your persistent and determined energy is powerful. Trust it!
- You do great things; thank you for letting us share them with you.
- Thank you for the active energy you so willingly share with our family.
- You are an important member of the family. Your natural gifts and talents are a blessing to all of us.

◯ **Child Whisperer Tip to support this stage:**
Type 3s experience the world physically. So make sure you get out and do things with them. Ask what they

would like to do, and even if it's not your favorite activity, spend the time to do it with them. Type 3 children who see their parents invest in their connection in the world know that their parents are connected with them. They will feel more loved and honored than if you just said how much you loved them.

School Age 6 to 12 Years

Primary Emotional Need: *Fitting in, working with structure, knowing and learning*

At this stage, Type 3 children encounter limits and structures that put more bounds on their forward-pushing energy. Look out for signs that they feel stifled, stalled, or boxed in. Are they picking fights? Are they taunting their siblings more than usual? Are they blowing up emotionally with you? These are all signs that a Type 3 child is not experiencing enough forward momentum in their life. You can work on this by talking about what they want to do. They usually know right away and the quicker you can move into action to support them in doing it, the sooner these problems will be resolved.

During this stage, a Type 3 child might take on the belief that in order to fit in and have value, they need to do more. Help them clear this lie from their lives so they do not carry it into adulthood. I have met too many Type 3 adults who are trying to accomplish their way to value—but it doesn't work. Help your child recognize that they don't have to do a single thing in order to be valuable and lovable. When they truly believe that, their activities become so much more effective and enjoyable.

Messages your Type 3 child needs to hear in this stage of life:

• You are smart and brilliant, and you learn so quickly.

- You are able to move at whatever pace feels best to you.
- You can succeed at anything that feels right and honoring of you.
- Trust your intuition.
- You deserve to succeed.
- Follow what is right for you. You don't have to do things that do not honor you—and you can change what you're doing immediately.
- It is not your job to take charge of pushing the family to do the best things. We are in charge of our own happiness.
- Thanks for being so active and easy to get along with.
- You never have to go along with something if it is not right for you.
- You have a right to have boundaries and know what is important to you.

Child Whisperer Tips to support this stage: In this phase, Type 3 children enter school. Your Type 3 child may push back against the structures presented to them there. They may be scolded in school for being too loud or for not sitting still. Although Type 3 children are often pegged as rowdy or rambunctious, that doesn't mean that they won't do well in school. If they are shown the purpose of those structures, they will often work with them rather than against them.

Their movement is active, not explosive. It is determined, not out of control, provided that they are not reined in too heavily. Any conflict your Type 3 child experiences within the structure of school is an indication that they need more to do—either in the form of physical activity or of academic challenges. Give your Type 3 child free time during the day to explore and do. Consider having items on hand that allow them to experiment and play.

If you have not been parenting your determined child true to their nature by this stage of life, you will likely see signs of stress in their behavior and feelings, including anger and the early stages of rebellion. You can easily heal this pattern together with your child by being honest and accountable as a parent. Here's an idea of something you might say that would make a big difference for your Type 3 child: "I know that you always have things you want to do. What would be the most important thing I could help you do today?"

High School 12 to 18 Years

Primary Emotional Need: *Separating and creating independence from the family.*

When parented true to their nature, Type 3 teenagers are easy to support. It feels like that in this state, they are finally growing into their dynamic energy. They have a lot of confidence in their own life pursuits as they begin to create more independence. Continue to support them and they will experience successful outcomes in all areas of their lives.

Friends become very important in this stage of a Type 3 child's life. Their peers enjoy their engaging energy and will readily follow them on any teenage adventure they might cook up.

Messages your Type 3 child needs to hear in this stage of life:

- You can engage your friends however feels best for you.

- You do not need to please others to be loved.
- You can take all the time you need to grow up.
- We are happy with your choices.
- It is okay to make mistakes.
- You can take action and move forward with the things that are important to you; we're always here to help when you need it.
- You can go after all the goals that you feel are important to you.
- You don't have to do anything to be loved but be you.
- Good for you to think for a moment before you commit to a project.
- You can develop your own relationships, interests, and causes.
- You can learn about sex and be responsible for your needs, feelings, and behaviors.

♡ **Child Whisperer Tip to support this stage:** If your Type 3 teen was not parented true to their nature, this can be a difficult phase. They don't want you to get in their way and you may find they have a tendency to just do what they want and not include you in their pursuits. This can all be remedied and you can gain the trust of your teen by what you have learned in this book.

It's Never Too Late!

Even if your Type 3 child has grown past any of these stages, you can still validate and meet their emotional needs.

We are all every age we have ever been and we still carry our earlier unmet emotional needs with us. If your Type 3 daughter is 16 years old, you can still validate and affirm all the previous stages of her development. Even if your son is in his 30s or 40s, he would benefit from the messages in this book that he has not yet received from you as his parent. Your Type 3 child is receptive to your love and support as their parent at any age and will respond to your efforts to honor their determined nature. If you are a Type 3 adult, you can tell yourself the messages you did not receive during your childhood to help heal some of your own inner child's unmet needs.

Most of my work in the field of Energy Psychology helps adults heal their inner child's unmet needs. What a gift when a parent shows up and meets their needs at any age. It's never to late to become a better parent!

The Child Whisperer's Top 10 Things a Type 3 Child Needs From You!

To summarize, I've put together a brief list of what I feel are some of the most important points to remember when parenting a Type 3 determined child. This general list will be supportive to all Type 3 children. After reading through this list, please take a moment to add your own inspirations to it.

My goal with this list (and this book) is to bring out your own Child Whisperer gifts. As a Child Whisperer, you will receive your *own* inspirations and aha's, specific to your child and their Type. Make sure you write down those aha's!

1. *Physical activity*

   Remember the need for physical outlets that Type 3 children are supported by. Are they getting outside enough? Are they engaged in physical activities that match their determined nature and help them express their physical connection to the world? Are you making the physical contact with them that they need from you as their parent?

2. Challenges

Type 3s like challenges. Telling them no is almost an invitation for them to think to themselves, "Oh yeah? Watch me!" Help them channel their determined energy into healthy, productive challenges that help them feel they can accomplish great things for their age.

3. Projects

Having something to do will keep your Type 3 child from saying frequently, "I'm bored. There is nothing to do." Projects without a lot of detail or lengthy learning curve to get them going are best. They can be worked on in short lengths of time. They can be projects that are not finished in one sitting, but can be returned to frequently to keep your Type 3 actively involved with something to do that they find interesting and challenging.

4. Results

One of the primary reasons a Type 3 child likes projects is to create a result that they can admire and feel satisfied about. Make a big deal of their results and praise them for their hard work and efforts, like "Wow, look what you did. That is awesome!"

5. Encouragement to live true to who they are

Refer to the phrases in each of the developmental stages in earlier sections to continue to validate and encourage your Type 3 child to live true to their nature throughout all the phases of their childhood.

6. Time to do things with you

Type 3 children love to spend time with mom and dad in

physical activities and challenges. Go to the park. Learn a sport together as they get older. Let them help you make dinner. Take them camping. Let them get the food and gear ready, and show them how to cook on an open fire. Do a craft project together or take them to the hobby store and pick out some new projects to learn together. Ask your Type 3 child what things they would like to do with you and then make sure you follow through with them.

7. *Praise*

Praise your Type 3 child's accomplishments and results. Tell them you are impressed and think they do a great job at their activities. Appreciate their get-it-done nature even if they could have taken more time in planning details or may have missed a few steps. Lead with praise and correct and teach them later.

8. *Attention*

Attention is different than praise. You know your Type 3 is not getting enough attention when they start to do aggravating things that cause a negative reaction in others—that's a red flag that they just want to be noticed and interacted with more. When they behave in this manner, they unfortunately get the opposite response than they are subconsciously looking for, so make sure you remind yourself to give them positive attention rather than the negative reprimands this kind of behavior provokes. The negative attention is still a reaction, which is better than nothing to a Type 3 who needs an active, reactive experience from others. It is your job as the parent to give enough positive attention that supports your Type 3 in acting positively which then creates a positive reaction from others.

9. *Don't sweat the small stuff*

You'll experience plenty of opportunities to get frustrated over the more intense, determined energy your Type 3 child seems to have plenty of. Decide today to let go of some of that frustration and focus on the dynamic action and confidence that your child expresses along with their passion for life when they are honored and validated for who they are.

10. *Avoid these phrases and judgments:*

- Shush, you're too loud.
- You shouldn't think so big.
- Just calm down, you're too much.
- Stop being so pushy.
- I don't think you should try that.
- When are you going to relax?
- Settle down.

After reading this section, add to this list by writing the inspirations and ideas you received about what your own Type 3 child needs from you. Make your notes here:

_____

_____

_____

_____

The Type 3 Child Word Portrait

Refer to this word portrait list often as a quick reminder of the nature of your Type 3 child. Compare your child's mood and disposition to this list. Is your Type 3 child expressing these movements and qualities on a consistent basis? If not, what do you need to change in your parenting approach to support them in living true to their nature?

Type 3 children are often described as:

Adventurous	Mind of their own
Assertive	Mischievous
Busy	No nonsense
Busy body	Outgoing
Competitive	Passionate
Determined	Persistent
Down to Earth	Practical
Energetic	Quick
Enterprising	Rambunctious
Entrepreneurial	Resourceful
Feisty	Restless
Independent	Risk taker
Industrious	Rowdy
Into everything	Strong-willed
Little tiger	Swift
Loud	Take charge

Negative labels that are not honoring of Type 3 children:

Aggressive	Over-reactive
Demanding	Pushy
Hot-tempered	Wild

Type 4: The More Serious Child

Primary Connection to the World: *Intellectual*
Primary Movement: *Straightforward and exact*
Primary Need: *To be respected by their parents and family members and respect them in return*

The Type 4 expression comes from the element of carbon/earth, and its natural primary movement is constant, still, and reflective. A child with a dominant Type 4 movement will be independent, focused, and bold. With their introverted expression, they reflect perfection to create in this world. They express a low level to almost no movement. While this does mean they can hold still for longer periods of time than other Types of children, it does not mean that they sit still all the time. More about that in a moment.

These words also describe the natural movement of a dominant Type 4 child: mature, reserved, authoritative, logical, and respectful. Adults often describe a child with a dominant Type 4 energy as serious or older than their age. When I meet Type 4 children, I always notice that they hold themselves with a sense of dignity and inner confidence. Due to their more reflective nature, Type 4 children seem to sense that I understand them and respond favorably to me, when they are typically more reserved when meeting new people. I believe they sense my insight into who they are and feel my respect and love, which naturally endears me to them.

Perfecting their world and being their own authority are huge motivations for a Type 4 child. Some adults may see their tendency to perfect the world around them as a tendency to be critical. As Type 4 children grow, they may often hear that they need to lighten up, loosen up, and stop being so judgmental. If you acknowledge your Type 4 child's bold, reflective movement as a natural strength, you will actually notice their tendency to criticize diminish and your relationship with them flourish. Dominant Type 4 children who receive early support to just live true to their structured, authoritative natures grow into adults who respect and honor their gifts, rather than tending to criticize others and themselves.

. . . .

MAX'S STORY
Always Aiming for Perfection

Five-year-old Max opened a custard style yogurt and showed his brother how smooth and shiny the top of the yogurt was. His brother barely touched the top of the yogurt with his finger, ruining the perfect surface on the yogurt top. Max got irritated, spooned off the top portion of the yogurt, then got a new spoon before eating it.

If your child is a Type 4, you may start to notice instances like these in which they want things to be just right. Encourage and validate their eye for perfection, and they will use it to improve the world around them as they grow.

. . . .

Natural Gifts and Talents: Respect and Efficiency

Type 4 children naturally offer a unique gift to this world without even trying: *A keen eye for the big picture, which leads them to perfect their world and inspire respect in it.*

Type 4 energy brings us full circle in the cycle of wholeness. Type 1s start the cycle by providing ideas and optimism. Type 2s gather the details and make a plan. Type 3s move it into action. And Type 4s look at what has been created and naturally recognize inefficiencies that can be perfected to improve the end result. A Type 4 catchphrase sounds like this: *"Here is how we can make it better, and here is how we can duplicate it."*

Of all the Types, I believe Type 4 children are the most misunderstood. Our cultural perception of children strongly influences us to believe that all children are light and playful, like Type 1 energy. While it is true that all children exhibit their own degree of playfulness, a Type 4 child's playfulness expresses itself as more exact, linear, and straightforward. They come across as more serious or more mature than their chronological age.

These children have a firm presence, one that is not easily swayed and is often misjudged as being inflexible. Type 4 children see themselves as the primary authority in their own lives. In things they care about, they are organized, precise, and focused. They like to be in control and consider their way of doing things to be the best. They have a natural ability to step back and take in the big picture all at once, which allows them to figure out how things work and see in an instant how to perfect processes.

They naturally create more efficiency in their own lives and, if they are allowed, the lives of those around them. These children have a gift for seeing how all the pieces fit together to create a whole. They can perfect and systematize any process in order to create a desirable, repeatable outcome. For example, you might show your Type 4 child how to complete a certain household task and they will naturally find ways to complete that task more efficiently. Whatever you show them how to do, they are usually always thinking of a better way it could be done.

. . . .

JAKE'S STORY
The Gift of Perfecting

Type 4 Jake was eight years old when his mother asked him if anything bugged him. Without even pausing, he proceeded to give her a numbered list! "Okay," he said. "These are the things that bother me: #1. There's a girl in my class who spits when she talks. #2. This other kid. . ." He went on to name five things that got under his skin.

A mother who didn't understand her child's true nature might tell her son to stop being so critical and that what he'd said wasn't very nice. Jake's mother recognized these as natural gifts in her Type 4 son—his keen eye and innate desire to perfect the world.

Instead of asking their Type 4 children to stop seeing the world the way they do, parents who understand their child's true nature can help their children focus their discerning eye in positive ways.

. . . .

At times, your Type 4 child's desire for perfection may seem like criticism to you. You may find yourself just wishing that your child could be content and happy with the way things are—for just once! However, telling them to stop seeing the world the way they do is just another way of asking them to stop being who they are. If you do this, you will only encourage your child to turn that keen, perfecting eye inward. They will focus their gift on themselves and may begin to judge their own nature as flawed. You don't want to set them up for the inner criticism that many Type 4 adults experience later in life as a result of being told they were too critical when they were young.

◯ **Child Whisperer Tip:** Instead of dreading criticism, express your willingness to hear suggestions for improvement. Do this before your Type 4 child even offers an opinion next time and you may be amazed with the results. Consider using phrases or questions like these: "If you see something that would make this work better, please tell me." Or, "I'm sure you've thought of a better way to finish that chore and I'm excited to see it." "What do you think would be the best way to do this?" Then really listen to their reply. Your child will feel honored that you respect their opinion, especially since they value their own opinion so highly.

Let go of any anxiety you have about opening a flood gate of criticism. No Type 4 will share *all* their insights. It may seem like they are always correcting you, but an overload of judgment from your child is often a signal that they are feeling shut down or dismissed. If they know that you will accept and honor their input, they can maintain their bold stance without feeling the need to voice it at all times. The more open you are to feedback, the less "critical" your Type 4 child will actually seem to be.

Type 4 energy is an introvert expression that leads these children to be more reserved, private, and independent. Their nature is reflective and bold, characteristics that make them seem more solemn and mature, even at an early age. Their movement expresses itself as solid and structured, which is often a surprise to parents who expect their children to be carefree and random.

I know of a mother who felt concerned when her toddler son started arranging items in rows: his toy cars, her makeup pencils, or any other small item that he could line up. She worried that perhaps she had done something wrong to make him too uptight before he even turned two. She just needed to know that her Type 4 little boy was already honoring his own exact movement and attempting to structure and perfect his world in the small ways available to him.

A Type 4 child's nature is a great gift to them and to your family. They step back from a situation rather than jumping into it, and they can take in everything at a glance. As they grow, your Type 4 child will be more likely to think things through and be aware of their options before making big decisions. It's not something you'll have to teach them—they will do it naturally as long as they are supported in being their own authority in the decisions that they make.

While these children primarily connect with the world intellectually, they experience their emotions deeply. When parents mistake Type 4 children's emotional depth and assume that these children have everything under control, parents may emotionally neglect them. The neglect would be inadvertent, of course, but damaging nonetheless. Allow your child to feel safe in sharing their more private emotional experience with you on their terms.

Personality Traits: More Serious Than the Other Types

From the very beginning of writing this book, I spent quite some time considering the right word to describe the Type 4 child. Others often describe these children as focused, serious, or mature. I would like to take a moment to explain why I decided on the description of the more serious child as the Type 4 child's title.

Type 4 children take themselves seriously—not necessarily in a somber, straight-faced way, but in the way that they view themselves. They see themselves as someone worth taking seriously. These children are also reflective, contemplative, and more structured, which we tend to think of as a more serious, adult-like energy.

The word *mature* also made it into the running for the Type 4 child's title. Adults regularly use this word to comment on a Type 4 child's more intellectual, systematic approach and their lower level of movement. However, a Type 4 child's insistence on being their own authority can lead to behavior that may also seem immature at times. As Tori, one helpful Type 4 mother put it, "Type 4s, with our own agendas and insistence upon ourselves as authority figures, don't always prioritize traits that adults see as mature. For example, a Type 4 child who is 'into' a certain kind of toy or childish game may stay focused on it long after he or she has outgrown it. A Type 4 child may not understand the benefit of learning to get along and be agreeable with others in social situations, and may appear immature socially."

Whatever Type 4 children want to do—even if it is something that seems immature, such as wearing summer sandals out in the snow—they take what they are doing seriously. They look seriously at themselves and the world around them, which may or may not look mature to others. In this book, the Type 4 child is described as the more serious child. This title is meant to honor their natural gifts and approach to life.

• • • •

A 5-YEAR-OLD DANCER'S STORY
Keeping it Serious

The mother of a Type 4 little girl recently shared this story with me. Her five-year-old Type 4 daughter had prepared for a dance recital over several months. On the night of the recital this girl executed her prepared dance nearly perfectly. After the prepared dance, the teacher asked all the students to make up a dance in the moment to the music that was playing. This little girl chose not to participate in the random dance. Rather than make her daughter participate, the mom followed her Child Whisperer instincts and honored her daughter's choice not to participate.

After the recital, the mom asked her daughter, "Why did you not want to dance the silly dance with the other students?" Very seriously, her Type 4 daughter replied, "I don't dance like that. I only dance the dances I have practiced for." This mom shared with me that in the past, before she understood her daughter's more serious nature, she might have thought that her daughter was not child-like enough and would have worried about her. Knowing her daughter was a Type 4 reassured her that her daughter was living true to her nature and that she had nothing to worry about.

. . . .

From a very early age (as early as two to three years old, perhaps earlier), Type 4 children have an intrinsic need to be their own authority. This is just one more example of the ways they take themselves seriously. They want to make their own decisions about the structure and the direction of their life. It is common to hear "I want to do it myself" from the earliest stages of a Type 4 child's life.

You may be wondering what to do about children who see themselves this way. How do you parent a child who wants to be completely in charge of their life?

First of all, it does not mean you hand over the reins to their lives and say, "You're in charge of yourself. Best of luck—see you when you're 30." It means that you learn to parent your Type 4 child in a manner that honors their natural expression.

Second, Type 4 children want their parents to be a *partner* of authority in their life. Your child will not be able to do all of the grown-up things they believe they should be able to do (although they are capable of more than you think). They want you to be there, both to set a boundary when needed, and to validate their other age-appropriate decisions that you allow them to make on their own. Type 4 children express a naturally structured movement, and as a parent, you should provide some of the structure they need in order to thrive. Your solid, parental presence will help your Type 4 child establish a sense of security in this world, which will support them in growing up true to their nature. When your Type 4 child feels honored and respected, they will very deeply honor and respect you in return as their parent and a close lifelong bond will begin to form.

◯ **Child Whisperer Tip:** While Type 4 children never give away their personal authority, they do share their authority with people they trust and take seriously. They will take you more seriously as their parent if they respect you. You will naturally be seen as worthy of more respect in your child's eyes when you live true to your own unique nature. Do you know which of the 4 Types *you* express?

The serious, precise nature of a Type 4 child might be judged as a weakness by certain people, sometimes even you. These children might receive labels like: overly serious, too literal, loner, picky, or know-it-all. Type 4 children are indeed serious, literal, and discerning, but these qualities are strengths, not weaknesses! It is your job as a parent to help them recognize those strengths in themselves. When your child sees their natural qualities as tendencies to be honored rather than flaws to be fixed, they will naturally feel more confident and manage their tendencies with great success. Because these children value perfection, this comment is a good place to start: "You are perfect, and I love you just the way you are."

Thought and Feeling Processes: Black and White, All or Nothing

A Type 4 child's thought process expresses a linear, black and white movement. These children are deep thinkers and naturally look at the world around them with the intent to see how everything fits together. They try to see and understand the process that was used to create things. They can often see the whole picture from start to finish.

• • • •

JAKE'S STORY
Frosting on the Cake

Eight-year-old Jake stared for a long time at the piece of cake in front of him. Finally, he felt the scallop of frosting on the edge of the cake and said, "I know how they did this." He then explained to his mother the concept of the frosting tip and the process probably used to decorate the cake. He wasn't especially familiar with cake decorating techniques, but Jake could deduce the process just from looking at the shape of the scallop.

• • • •

A Type 4 child's primary connection to this world is intellectual. These children are always thinking. They go deep with their thoughts, and think through an idea thoroughly before committing to take action. They may wait until after their thoughts become entirely clear to share their opinion with others. This can make them sound argumentative at times because their thoughts seem inflexible to others. To a Type 4, they are simply committed to an idea they've already spent time looking at from every angle.

Type 4s of all ages may be labeled as stiff or robotic. This is an unfair and inaccurate judgment, as Type 4 children can pull back and see the big picture in a way no robot ever could. While these children may choose to take their time thinking an idea through, their thoroughness is quick. They can take in a situation in its entirety and see the imbalances immediately and easily.

Since these children relate best on an intellectual level, others may sometimes believe that they relate only with their heads and not their hearts. Don't make that mistake. These children feel their emotions deeply. They are just very selective about who they allow to see their emotional side.

Their walls are not something you need to break down; in fact, you shouldn't try because your child will just build their walls higher and stronger. Your Type 4 child needs to invite you in, which will only happen through respect and honor for who they are. Recognize that your child has a loyal heart and be okay that you do not have to be invited into it all the time. Allow them their space, respect their emotional boundaries, and you may find that you become more emotionally connected to them than you ever have been before.

• • • •

KIMBERLY'S STORY
Type 4 Boundaries

When Kimberly was a toddler, her grandmother came over to her house and wanted to hold her immediately. Kimberly continually reached for her mother until her grandmother handed her back. Kimberly's grandma tried to take her back a few times, but Kimberly refused to sit with her.

Then, a few minutes later, Kimberly decided she wanted to sit with her grandma. She crawled over to her all by herself and sat with her, as happy and content with her grandmother as she had been with her mother.

A Type 4 child needs to be the one to cross their emotional and physical boundaries first. They will engage with others as long as the decision to engage is theirs.

. . . .

Child Whisperer Tip: Relate to your child mentally before you relate emotionally. Don't try to connect emotionally first. Go through their intellect to get to their feelings. Do not start an emotional conversation. Instead, be direct about issues on a mental level, respect them, and they may choose to let their emotions open up. For example, if you and your Type 4 child are experiencing conflict about their chores, talk about the logistics and the efficiency of the tasks your child has been asked to do before trying to discuss how they feel about them.

We assume that all children are easily in touch with their feelings. But because Type 4s feel so deeply and first relate to the world intellectually, they may not be in touch with their feelings as readily as other Types, and may need support in connecting with them. I believe Type 4s need to be taught at an early age what feelings are and be supported in how to feel their feelings and how to express them.

. . . .

SETH'S STORY
Learning to Feel Sad

Whenever we visited our Type 4 grandson, who lives in a different state, I noticed that he started to act up and misbehave when it came time for us to go home. His acting up was unusual for him. I realized that he felt sad that Grandma and Grandpa were about to leave and he would miss them. I took him aside privately and told him that it was natural that he would feel sad that we were leaving and that he would miss us. So I pointed out the emotion and then told him that it made sense for him to feel that way.

I shared my observation with his mother and suggested that she pay attention to this for the next couple of days. She could privately talk with him about his deeper feelings and help him express them appropriately.

. . . .

As Type 4 children are supported at a younger age in learning how to connect with their feelings, they will naturally be able to connect with them as they grow. If your Type 4 child is older now and they don't readily share their feelings, there is still hope. If they are feeling sad, embarrassed or insecure, they will most likely lead by presenting an emotion of anger.

◠ **Child Whisperer Tip:** Rather than discipline your child's anger, consider it a red flag for you to help them make an emotional connection. Set the intention to help them connect with their deeper feelings of sadness or any other deeply held emotion. Some supportive phrases are: "I can see you are angry. What are you upset about?" "You are really mad. What is troubling you?"

Having parented a Type 4 son, I started to employ this approach when he was in his mid-teens. As he gained respect for me and trusted that I really cared about him and his best interests, he started to open up to me. He is now a young adult and readily shares his deepest feelings with me and allows me in to the most sensitive part of his nature. As you have the intention to deeply connect with your Type 4 child, many opportunities will present themselves. Use your newfound Child Whisperer skills with them, and it will change your relationship for life.

Like their thoughts, the feelings of a Type 4 child also reflect a black and white process. They feel their emotions in extremes—either very happy or very sad, without middle ground. These children either like things or they hate them and they're very expressive about both.

Child Whisperer Tip: Because Type 4 children express themselves boldly, parents may try to soften their child's reactions to certain day-to-day situations, especially with certain emotions that are judged as negative. Just allow your child to feel as strongly as they do. At some point, you may be inspired to point out logically the effect that your child's emotional expression has on others. You should only share this with your child with the intent to help them be more aware of their world, not to shame them into hiding their feelings for the sake of others. It is also wise to have emotional conversations privately with your Type 4 child. Emotions are a very private matter to a Type 4, and they will respect you more if you discuss them privately.

Child Whisperer Tip: Your Type 4 child may apply their tendency to view things as all good or all bad to themselves. They want to do things perfectly and when they can't, they may feel more frustrated than you might think they should. They are not just frustrated with the issue at hand—they are also seeing themselves as flawed. If your child has a particularly bold emotional outburst or seems especially withdrawn (always in black and whites), do not focus on the obvious issue. Focus on the fact that they feel weak or flawed. Reassure them that they are learning perfectly what they need in order to become the person that they want to be.

One of the most important things to know about a Type 4 child's emotions is that they cannot fake them. While some of the other Types more readily adapt to expectations placed on them, these children do not. Their structured nature makes it nearly impossible for them to put on a face and pretend they feel a certain way when they don't. This might make you nervous on birthdays when you want your child to respond enthusiastically to every gift they receive. Let those expectations go and recognize this as a gift in your child. You will always know where you stand with your Type 4 child and you can trust that the emotions they express are authentic.

If you don't feel emotionally connected to your Type 4 child, there's a reason. Consider the possibility that your child has one of these experiences with you:

- They think you don't respect their opinions.
- They think you talk down to them or treat them like a baby.
- They think that you don't trust them to make their own decisions.
- They feel like you put them on the spot or embarrass them.
- They do not think that you keep their personal information and concerns confidential when talking to others.

- They feel confused because they sense that their parent has judged their naturally structured nature as flawed.

Type 4 children don't just appreciate respect from you—they need it. It's just part of their nature. When you respect your Type 4 child's true nature, your child will feel safe with you and your relationship will flourish.

What other thoughts do you have on the experiences your Type 4 child has with you? How will you improve your relationship with what you know now? List your ideas here:

_____

_____

_____

_____

Communication: Logical and Concise

Type 4 children value respect, loyalty, and straightforwardness in their communication with others. They have a gift for sharing their thoughts clearly and in a few words. They hold back until they have something in mind that they are eager to share.

Their minds work in a logical, accurate way, so they express themselves literally. They may come across as matter-of-fact and sometimes blunt. These children may also take others literally when perhaps they are not meant to. Since their primary connection to the world is intellectual, they really think you mean what you say. They do not handle sarcastic remarks and teasing well, as they do not understand what's meant to be funny when it sounds and feels mean to them.

One funny story of how literal they can be (and a good reminder for me) happened with my Type 4 son, Mark. With his very precise and thorough nature, he is my go-to guy for getting my car detailed. We were texting back and forth about how much I would pay him to do this job for me when I texted him, "I'll pay you $100 for in and out." He responded, "$100 for in and out? Where did you get that?" It took me a moment to understand his questions until I realized he thought I was going to pay him $100 in a gift certificate for the popular hamburger fast food restaurant, "In-N-Out Burger." What I was referring to was I would pay him $100 for detailing both the inside and outside of my car!

When you speak to a Type 4 child, speak clearly, consider the literal, and take them seriously when they respond.

· · · ·

TAUSHA'S STORY
Lost in Communication

Tausha is a Type 2 mother whose 11-year-old daughter is a Type 4. They had done a lot of gardening together and her daughter got excited about buying some flowers to plant in her own little garden space. One Saturday, Tausha promised they would go and buy some flowers together soon.

To Tausha, soon meant sometime in the near future. To her daughter, soon meant as soon as possible. Over the next few days, Tausha's daughter asked when they would go buy flowers. But it wasn't ever a good time and Tausha continued to put it off.

On Tuesday evening, Tausha noticed that her daughter seemed upset. When Tausha asked what was wrong, her daughter said, "Mom, I don't want to hurt your feelings, but it is hard to believe you when you tell me you will do something for me, because you always put it off and do other things. I don't feel like I am on the top of your list." Her daughter told her this in a respectful tone, but with tears in her eyes.

Tausha says that before knowing her and her family's Types, she might have felt offended that her daughter corrected her, especially when Tausha was obviously so busy taking care of the family and house and everything. But she realized in that moment that she had not communicated clearly with her daughter and needed to honor her right then. She apologized, validated what her daughter said, and promised to work on putting her daughter's needs at the top of her list. Tausha told her daughter that she was more important than any to-do list.

She grabbed the keys, loaded the family in the car, and they went to buy some flowers that very minute.

. . . .

⌒ **Child Whisperer Tip:** If you need to communicate something important to your Type 4 child, talk in logical terms and trust that they'll understand quickly. Type 4s are so observant that you do not need to say much for them to get the idea you're trying to convey. If you can explain the logic of something on the level they can relate to at their age, these children can easily align with your reasoning and shift from being argumentative to very cooperative. I have used this numerous times with my young Type 4 grandson, and every time he understands the logic behind a request, he easily cooperates.

This expectation of understanding works both ways. Your Type 4 child expects you to understand what they mean logically, as they feel they have been clear. If they are not able to communicate their own thoughts and feelings clearly, they may become frustrated with themselves. Type 4 children communicate most clearly and effectively if they feel respected and trusted. Use these phrases to help them communicate better: "How do you see this situation?" and "What's your opinion about this?"

. . . .

JAKE'S STORY
Trying to Speak

Little Jake wanted to play a computer game that he saw once on the family's computer. He didn't know the name of the game, though, so he tried describing it. But nobody in the family knew which game he was talking about. When he couldn't get his point across, he lost it. Shouting and pushing things around, he said how stupid he was and that he couldn't do anything right, all because he couldn't clearly explain which game he was talking about.

This sort of frustration is difficult for a young Type 4 child. They know so clearly what they want, but when they can't articulate it, they just feel stupid. You can reassure your child that you hear them and that you'll work with them until their meaning becomes clear to you.

. . . .

One word pops up again and again in a Type 4 child's vocabulary: *stupid*.

Parents may try to discourage their Type 4 child's use of this word, especially when their child seems particularly critical of something or someone. Many parents see this kind of communication as something that needs to be disciplined or parented away, but this word is actually a gift. Constant use of this word is a huge indicator that your child is, indeed, a Type 4. Plus, it's a fabulous opportunity for you as a parent.

There are several reasons why Type 4 children refer to things as "stupid." They are embarrassed by something or someone. They feel insecure or inadequate. They are not feeling heard or respected, or they are bored. When they use that word in reference to something or someone, they don't feel they have any authority to work out a situation that makes them feel uncomfortable or inadequate. They don't know any other way to handle it than to deem it flawed and call it stupid.

For example, a Type 4 child might say that about their teacher, "That teacher is just stupid." This does not mean your child is trying to be rude about their teacher. It means they're having problems in their interaction with them. Your child is giving you information and you have the opportunity to recognize it and do something about it.

⌒ **Child Whisperer Tip:** Forget approaching whatever situation your child calls *stupid* by telling your child they are being too critical. Just validate that they feel it's stupid and they have a right to feel that way. Validate their authority to judge something in that way by asking, "Can you tell me why you think it's stupid?"

Then follow the conversation wherever they take it. Just remember that there's an underlying issue you need to discover. By saying something is stupid, your child is building an idea that if something doesn't work in their life, they have the right to judge an external force as stupid or wrong. As you listen to your child, ask yourself what is really causing the discomfort, sense of inadequacy, sense of powerlessness, or the feeling that your child can't be their true self. Turn on your Child Whisperer skills and tune in to the real message your child is sending you. That message might sound like this: "This is not right for me, I don't feel honored in this situation. I need your help changing this so I feel good about myself and feel supported."

Doing this makes any stupid situation easier. It leads you to the true issue and gives you the insight you need to approach your child to help them make changes so they can feel appreciation for themselves and their experiences.

I suggest some of the following phrases to use with your Type 4 child when they are referring to something or someone as *stupid*:

"You think that is stupid. What don't you like about it?"

"You don't like that. Tell me more about why you don't like that."

Once they have shared their feelings, you can follow up with phrases like these:

"I can see you don't feel respected. How can I help you change that?"

"What do you think a solution to this problem is?"

"What are you responsible for? How can you show up differently in this situation?"

Of course, the language of these approaches will need modifications to be age appropriate for your child. Because you are a Child Whisperer, you can take this idea and run with it, using inspiration to find the perfect words for your particular child.

Type 4 children communicate openly with select people whom they trust to honor and listen to them. They say what they mean and they expect others to do the same. If they say they will do something, they see that statement as a commitment and they follow through on it. This means that they also take others at their word, even if someone just offered a suggestion or an idea.

. . . .

LIZZIE'S STORY
On Follow Through

Lizzie's grandmother said that they should go out and get ice cream sometime. It was a nice idea, one that Lizzie liked the sound of, but it didn't happen that day. Or the next. Lizzie started asking her mother on a regular basis when Grandma was going to take her to get ice cream. She couldn't understand why Grandma hadn't called her yet to follow through on the idea that Lizzie interpreted as a solid commitment.

Praise and appreciate your Type 4 child's ability to make commitments and keep them. You may need to help them differentiate between others' commitments and suggestions.

. . . .

Type 4 children have a hard time opening up to people they do not yet know. They need time to situate themselves and allow the interaction to happen. And they will keep their heart and mind especially closed to anyone they feel is critical of them. Type 4 children want to feel safe to open up with their parents. You can do a few specific things to create a situation in which your Type 4 child feels secure in sharing with you.

♡ **Child Whisperer Tip:** Type 4s also do not like to have to repeat themselves, so if you ask your Type 4 child a question, pay attention and listen to their answer. They will lose respect for you if you distract yourself while they respond and will not be very willing to repeat themselves, which unfortunately makes them appear stubborn.

 Child Whisperer Tip: On a regular basis, give them one-on-one time with you where you give them your full attention and make eye contact. Every Type 4 child I have seen, including my own son when he was little, will grab their mom's face and say to them, "Listen to me, Mom!" Before you even sit down with them, make sure you can commit to listening. Just say, "I want you to talk about whatever you want. I just want you to know you have this time with me where you don't have any interruptions." These children give their full attention to those they are listening to, and they will appreciate that you take the time to do the same for them.

Once they start opening up and sharing, let them keep going. Don't interrupt them or start giving advice. Just listen. When they are done, ask them, "Are you done? Do you want any feedback from me?" If it is a younger child, it can be phrased as, "Do you want Mommy (or Daddy) to help you? Or do you want to figure it out on your own?" Communicate clearly, honestly, respectfully and logically with these children and they will respond in kind.

Communication with a Type 4 child can be very easy. Unfortunately, many parents of Type 4 children have the opposite experience. Most parents make one primary mistake: when their Type 4 child turns to them for support, they naturally start to advise and tell their child what to do. I learned from many experiences with my Type 4 son, Mark, an entirely different approach that helped him connect, both with me and with the insight he was seeking.

One afternoon, Mark came to me feeling troubled and stressed out and asked if we could talk. I was in the middle of something and told him I needed 10 more minutes. He asked,

"Mom, will it really be 10 minutes? Because you know me and I will be back in 10 minutes." Since I know Mark takes things literally, I thanked him for the reminder and told him it would be fifteen minutes. Mark returned in fifteen minutes and sat down in my bedroom. I asked him if he just wanted me to listen or to give him feedback. He replied and told me he just wanted me to listen.

I put down everything I was doing and engaged with Mark 100 percent with full eye contact. I let him share his thoughts and feelings and then something happened that I had never noticed before. Mark came to his own insights and the aha's he needed to resolve his current issue. All he needed was someone to talk it out with. We both recognized that he had come to his own awareness and that my role at that time as his mother was to give him the support he needed by being present for him. At other times, Mark invites my feedback and takes it very seriously and appreciatively. All I have to do is ask him how best to support him when he comes to me.

Behavioral Tendencies

Family Relationships: *Ever loyal, often misunderstood*

Type 4 children open up with people they know best. They remain incredibly loyal to those they love. They feel a deep love and loyalty for their family members.

However, these children are the most likely of all the Types to be misunderstood by their parents, siblings, and extended family. They can experience pain or conflict in family relationships that lead them to believe they need to take control, criticize, or withdraw. When this happens, Type 4 children can feel very alone. As a Child Whisperer, you can facilitate understanding between family members and help your Type 4 child feel respected and included.

⌒ **Child Whisperer Tip:** One of the most important ways to achieve harmony is to give your Type 4 child a voice in family rules and activities. These children need to feel like they have some say in what happens to them and the authority that is exercised over them. Don't worry that your child will make up ridiculous rules that allow them to do whatever they want. Because Type 4s are attuned to authority, they respect rules—particularly those rules that they've created themselves and committed to follow. Give them an age-appropriate voice in what is expected of them, and consequences if they disobey. You may find that they have a higher standard than you do!

Type 4 children will give you a signal if they do not feel they have enough of a voice in family situations: They will start to play in extremes. For example, they may rebel against *all* the family rules, even if some of the rules make sense to them. This sort of all-or-nothing rebellion is a statement that their voice is not being heard. Pay attention to it.

Type 4 children need to feel safe in their privacy at home. This means they need some of their own private space. They also need to feel safe that their parents will not talk about confidential conversations or personal matters with other family members without their permission. Their need for privacy also means not calling them out or chastising them in front of the rest of the family. They get especially upset when a sibling calls them out. They may react angrily when someone who doesn't have the right authority tries to play the parent, although they may try parenting their own siblings themselves from time to time. They like to take control, so you may need to remind them that you are the parent and they do not need to worry about anyone else's actions but their own.

. . . .

JAKE'S STORY
The Meltdown

Jake's brother came in the room to report to their mother that Jake had said a bad word. Jake immediately said, "I did not." And then he lost it, completely melting down. He shouted repeatedly that he didn't say a bad word and got surprisingly upset with his brother.

Whether he said the word or not doesn't matter. Either way, this is a classic Type 4 child's reaction to this kind of family situation. To be put on the spot like that by a sibling is a horrible experience for a Type 4 child. They have a level of expectation within themselves to do things right. Being tattled on like that and exposed is very embarrassing to them. They react to the embarrassment and the shame, not to the mistake itself that they made.

Jake's mom decided that in the future, she would tell Jake's siblings, "If you have an issue with your brother, come and tell me privately. Then I'll see if we even need to deal with it. Then I will talk to him privately." This allows her to correct Jake when needed without embarrassing him in front of the rest of the family.

. . . .

If your Type 4 child seems to overreact in certain family situations, don't try to resolve the issue in front of everyone. Invite your child into another room to talk with you. Don't even discuss what just happened, but try to discover the root of their bold reaction. Most likely, your child feels embarrassed, shamed, or stupid. This may not seem like a big deal to you, but for a Type 4 child, embarrassment is the worst punishment. To them, it's a sign that they have not lived up to their personal standard—and now everyone knows it. This feeling gives them the sense that they are no longer in control. It can be a frightening experience for a young Type 4 who doesn't yet know how to manage a sense of failure.

I have also noticed this kind of reaction in younger Type 4 children who get hurt accidentally. My grandson Seth was running and playing when he fell very hard and scratched his leg. He cried because it hurt and immediately ran to his mom for comfort. When the extended family that was around him all tuned into his accident and tried to soothe him, he pulled back, turned away and stopped crying suddenly. I recognized his embarrassment and quietly suggested to his aunts and uncles to change their focus and let his mom take care of it privately. He was only three years old then, and his nature was already so clear!

♡ **Child Whisperer Tip:** Do not tell your child to lighten up, get over it, or stop feeling that way. Their strong reaction to embarrassment is so automatic; it's just built into Type 4 programming. If you tell them that their authentic, automatic response is flawed somehow, you essentially tell them there's something wrong with being themselves.

You can better help them manage their reaction by validating their feelings instead. Consider saying something as simple as, "It seems like you feel embarrassed. Is that right?" If the answer is yes, you can team up with your child by telling them how you want to help. Ask them to help you see the best way to support them. Here's an example: "That seems really uncomfortable for you. I'm going to support you so you don't have to be put in this situation anymore. Let's come up with a different approach. I want to help you feel safe and comfortable in our family."

Type 4 children need solitude at home, away from family members. As they get older, some might take care of this themselves by spending a long time going to the bathroom. It is not unusual for a Type 4 to spend thirty or forty minutes in there. It doesn't take them that long to actually use the bathroom, but that's where they get their solitude. If you make accommodations for that in your house, rather than banging on the door and telling them to stop taking so long, your child will naturally get the solitude they need at home and be more pleasant to be around.

If at all possible, allow your Type 4 child to have their own room. It would benefit them greatly and allow them more privacy. If that is not possible, I have suggested to parents that they invest in some portable screens that could create more privacy in a shared room for a Type 4.

Privacy is not the only factor that Type 4s benefit from when they have their own room. They are also supported in having a space they can call their own and be the authority of. A good friend of mine who is a Type 4 shared with me that when she was growing up, she shared a room with her Type 1 sister. In their early teens, my friend drew an imaginary line down the middle of the room and told her sister, "This is my half of the room. Please keep your things on your half." My friend was very neat and organized with her space, making her bed every day and keeping her side of the room very clean. It was important to her to have a designated space that she could manage and where she could be her own authority. On the other hand, her sister's side of the room was usually very messy with a lot out and about. These two sisters now laugh at how true they were living to their natures— neither way being better, just different!

Friends and Social Settings: *Need their alone time*

Type 4 children express a unique movement, in that the

quality of their energy is very bold—when they show up, people notice them. But the movement of their energy moves inward. They are energized by their inner mental experience. Depending on their secondary Energy Type, some Type 4 children can handle expressing their bold energy easily in social activities. Other Type 4 children are much more inwardly focused and require less social contact than their parents might think they need.

Regardless of how comfortable they feel in social settings, all Type 4 children will need some time afterward to decompress and ground themselves again. After social situations, allow your child the space and time they need to regain their inner balance. Doing so will help them feel solid in their own energy when they encounter social settings in the future.

Before joining in any social setting, Type 4 children tend to observe. They need to see the big picture without feeling pressured to be part of it at first. Then, they will remain selective about how they choose to interact. They tend to have fewer close friends to whom they are very loyal, rather than a wide variety of friends who come and go.

Child Whisperer Tip: These children have a strong orientation to the rules and follow them with exactness. They may become very stressed out when other children disobey the rules and may report it to the authority in their life. Yes, these kids can be tattlers. You can help your child interact easier in social settings by removing the pressure to monitor everyone else. Explain who is in authority over whom (whether it be a teacher or the other child's parent) and explain what your child's job will be during the interaction. If they understand the hierarchy, they will let go of control over things that are not under their authority.

. . . .

SETH'S STORY
Who's in Charge at School

When my grandson Seth attended pre-school, it was his nature to want to make sure the other children there would follow the rules. His mom knew his tendency for this, so in preparation for his first day of pre-school, she told Seth, "You are your own authority and you should obey the rules the teacher tells you to obey. The teacher is in charge of making sure the other children obey the rules. She is their authority. Your job is to play with the other children and have fun with them." This helped create the guidelines Seth needed to relax and have fun and let the teacher manage the behavior of the other children.

. . . .

Parents may misunderstand their child's smaller group of friends and more selective social interactions. Many Type 4 children are told they need to smile more, to be more extroverted, silly, and playful. This usually just pushes a Type 4 child into social situations before they think they are ready and makes them feel unsure of themselves and their ability to engage others. These children can feel lost in the child world and wonder if there is something wrong with them. I find it interesting that Type 4s, with their reflective nature, mirror the opposite experience of Type 1 children, who grow up and often feel lost in the adult world because their animated, playful nature is judged as immature. Every child just expresses movement. We are the ones who attach the labels and the negative judgments.

Above all, remember that all Type 4 children will step into social situations that *they* choose, but they do not want someone else to put them there. Pushing your Type 4 child into social settings they do not want to join actually accomplishes the opposite of what you want. They will retreat into the comfort of their own solitude, rather than become more outgoing. If your Type 4 child wants to reach out socially but doesn't know how, you can help them find and join activities they enjoy that will naturally lead to more comfortable social interaction.

Timeliness: *Love consistency and routine*

Even from their earliest days, Type 4 children love routine. It's in their nature to duplicate and perfect things, so the more consistent schedule you allow them to keep, the more inner balance they will experience. For example, from the first few weeks of my grandson Seth's life, his need for structure and predictability started to present itself. So for the first year of his life, his mom and dad made it a predictable routine to give Seth a bath right before he was put to bed. This routine honored his nature, which made going to bed a much easier process. The few times they were not able to follow this routine, bedtime was more stressful.

As Type 4 children grow older, they do best if they are allowed some degree of input on what their schedule looks like. Since they experience a high degree of mental organization, they will remember their own schedule and keep themselves on track. This makes many aspects of parenting much easier for you. For example, if homework is just a scheduled part of your Type 4 child's day, they will often sit down and do it without reminders from you. If they commit to completing a certain chore at a scheduled time each week, you can bet it will get done.

Of all the Types, Type 4 children are usually earliest to grasp the concept of time and to value timeliness. They demand punctuality of themselves and may stress over being late to events that are important to them. However, they may not deem other family members' appointments quite as important as their own and may dawdle a little bit when they are required to support others' schedules.

If a Type 4 child understands time and does not prioritize punctuality for a certain activity, they usually have two reasons: Either they were focused on something else and could not be distracted until they finished, or they judged that particular activity as not as important as others that they value. For example, many Type 4 children get up on their own and get ready for school on time every day, even in elementary school. But a Type 4 child who does not view school as a worthwhile experience or their teacher as a valued authority in their life will give priority of their time to sleep or other activities. They may drag their feet getting ready, not because they can't get ready on time, but because they decide not to.

Jobs and Household Chores: *Thorough and reliable*

A Type 4 child's high degree of mental organization and their tendency toward routine can work in their favor when assigned household chores. When they commit to a task, they complete it thoroughly. They may prefer being assigned the same job at the same time each week rather than something different all the time. When they know their ongoing responsibility, they often complete it without being asked again.

As in all things, they resent being told what to do without the opportunity to add their input. If you assign your child a job without discussing it with them first, don't expect them to jump right in and do it perfectly. In these situations, Type 4 children are more likely to let everyone in the family know what a *stupid* chore they've been assigned to do. Ask them which chores they would like to be assigned, rather than telling them. Be sure to discuss structure, clear instructions, and a clear time frame when tasks need to be finished. Then trust that it will be completed. If you remind your Type 4 child, they may get irritated with you, as their nature is to easily remember these things and they interpret your reminder as an insult to their nature.

I learned this when I reminded my Type 4 son to do his chores. He would look at me and say, "I know, Mom. I am not stupid!" After the Child Whisperer light bulb went on and I realized that he did not need my reminders, I had a conversation with him to straighten it all out. I explained to him that my reminders were my way of supporting him. Yet, he was not feeling supported, so I said something like this from then on: "Mark, I trust you will get your chores done. Is there anything I can do to support you?" I also suggested to him that he not be so blunt, that he came across rude and disrespectful. We decided to reenact the entire conversation, each practicing our new approach that created mutual understanding and harmony.

♡ **Child Whisperer Tip:** Give your Type 4 child advance notice of chores with a list they help create. Do not add any additional chores to their list after you have both agreed on their assignment. If your Type 4 child knows beforehand what is expected of them, they can mentally organize those tasks into their day. Throwing something in there at the last minute is frustrating to a Type 4 child, especially since they have already decided on the perfect way to get everything done most efficiently.

· · · ·

JAKE'S STORY
Why Do Chores?

Type 4 Jake often voiced his opinion that chores were stupid. They seemed inefficient to him and so he asked why they had to do chores if everything was just going to get messy again anyway. Jake's Type 4 dad answered the question clearly and concisely with his own question: Why do you wipe your bum every day? That one question wrapped up the conversation pretty quickly.

. . . .

♡ **Child Whisperer Tip:** Once you and your child have agreed upon expectations for their chores, trust your child to follow through. Let them take charge of their responsibilities. Otherwise, your child may feel micromanaged. Type 4s who feel micromanaged turn around and micromanage others, particularly their siblings.

Type 4s may prefer organizational tasks like putting away silverware and dishes and organizing. Many of them also like doing things that require an air of authority. One mother I know gave her Type 4 child the job of calming down the baby when she was busy, which seemed like a very important job. However you choose to manage your child's household responsibilities, always communicate openly and allow your child to communicate in return.

Money Management: *Thoughtful about spending*

When taught how to manage money, these children can be given the authority to oversee their financial experience at a very young age. They are smart and very thought-out with how they spend their money and prefer to spend more on what they really want, rather than compromise. Not surprisingly, they are also keenly aware of how much they have.

Whatever they choose to spend their money on, they are specific about it and may buy it regularly. One Type 4 10-year-old often chooses to buy Gatorade with his money. Another Type 4 five-year-old saves up quarters for gumballs on a regular basis. They know what they want and use the system of money to repeat the experience often.

Recreational Activities: *One track at a time*

Type 4 children tend to enjoy activities that allow them to focus on a single mental track at a time. In your child's experience, this might look like hours spent with Legos, or repetitive activities like sledding or going down a slide over and over again. They enjoy activities—both indoor and outdoor—that they can become absorbed in. Whatever they are doing becomes the big picture that they see in that moment. For example, rather than just a sandcastle, your Type 4 child might build an entire sand city with an intricate system of roads they've envisioned in their mind. These children have laser-like mental focus, so if they're immersed in an activity, don't be surprised or hurt if they completely tune you out.

♡ **Child Whisperer Tip:** Fifteen minutes before you need your Type 4 child to stop a certain activity, give them a warning and a brief reason why they'll need to stop. Otherwise, the interruption can feel jarring and unfair to them and you will end up with a tantrum or a power struggle on your hands. If they negotiate for more minutes than you give them in your warning, agree to it sometimes. They will be more likely to stop what they are doing if they feel they have a say in when the activity ends. If there really is a pressing reason why they need to stop at a certain time, explain this logically to your child.

These children express the lowest level of movement of all the four Types. This does not mean they do not like to move and run and jump around. It simply means they maintain an inner stillness that needs to be respected in the activities they pursue. They love to play with friends like any Type, but also need time to play by themselves and have some quiet, reflective time. My grandson Seth does well in group play, but then needs quiet time alone, reading books or playing.

They do well with recreational activities that call for repetitive practice and precision. In activities that require performance in front of others, like competitive sports or dance, they need time to feel well prepared and grounded in demonstrating their abilities. As a parent, you do not have to wonder if a certain sport, hobby, or activity caters to your Type 4 child's natural gifts. They will probably let you know.

. . . .

MARK'S STORY
Type 4 Fun

My son Mark loved Legos from an early age. He played with them for hours on end. He especially loved the sets that included a picture book of the finished Lego project. He studied the picture to figure out how to put it all together. When he mastered the Lego world pretty well, we purchased a more advanced system that included more mechanical pieces and parts that required a lot more focus and precision to build the desired structures. To this day, Mark enjoys recreational activities that involve his single focus and perfecting nature. Snowboarding and competitive mountain bike racing have allowed him those outlets.

. . . .

It is especially important to find channels for your Type 4 child to express their inborn, critiquing nature. Otherwise, they just become very critical about things that don't really matter. For example, Mark and I were watching TV one night and he criticized nearly every commercial that came on. I turned to him and said, "I appreciate your natural gift to see the flaw in things, but right now I just want to watch TV! I am also excited for you to get involved in more pursuits that will allow you to use your gifts and talents in productive ways." Mark took my feedback to heart, and since we have a very close and trusting relationship, my directness was not offensive to him. We continued to watch TV—without the Type 4 commentary.

Activities to Help a Type 4 Child Develop Natural Gifts

Type 4 children will be drawn to activities they think they can do most perfectly in the least amount of time. They set high standards for themselves and hesitate to do a new activity if they feel they might not meet their standard. Allow your child to pursue activities they feel naturally good at, as well as try new activities in low-pressure situations where they will not feel embarrassed if they fail in front of others.

Type 4s can excel in all sports as long as they are allowed to approach it in their own, more serious way. Whether they are interested in soccer, basketball, swimming, gymnastics, tennis, golf, or baseball, help them see examples of the best players so that they can break down the movement and duplicate it themselves. Individual sports that require precision and repetition are also a good fit.

Golf is a particularly Type 4 sport. The players dress up a little more formally than for other sports, and their swing is a bold movement in order to create a very precise result. The majority of top professional tennis players are Type 4s. Martial arts also provide a very Type 4 experience. They require a lot of repetition and accuracy with levels of advancement that are rewarding to a Type 4. Whichever activities your Type 4 child enjoys, they will want to perfect their technique.

> ⌒ **Child Whisperer Tip:** If you attend your child's sporting events, do not shout loudly at them or call their name, even to cheer them on. It draws attention to them that they would rather not have, and it distracts their mental focus. Whenever I yelled my own Type 4 son's name really loudly at a sporting event, he turned to me and said, "Don't do that." Give your child your focus by attending the event, but don't single them out in front of others. If your child is not drawn to sports where you could be a spectator, this may be the reason they hesitate. In their tendency to look at the bigger picture, they have probably considered your presence at their event. In order to avoid an uncomfortable experience, they may choose not to pursue sports. Reassuring them that you will not cheer them on and call out their name may be just what they need to get active in sports.

Performing and entertaining may be another area for your child to pursue, as long as they are supported in having enough private practice before they have to go up on stage, and they have personally decided that they do want to perform. Ballet requires structured, precise, and rehearsed movement that they may enjoy. Other options might be drill team or ballroom dancing. Type 4 children tend to have a clear sound to their voice, so if they enjoy singing, consider voice lessons. Most instruments, like the piano or violin, require repetitive practice that these children take to naturally. Let them choose which instrument they prefer most, support them in their practice, and watch them excel.

Parents sometimes push their Type 4 children to branch out and try new things before their children are ready. Everyone should obviously try new activities that will challenge them, but Type 4s have a particular need to be allowed to approach the new activity in their own way. When a Type 4 child does not like the activity they are involved in, they often refer to it as stupid, which I mentioned earlier. Again, rather than label your child as harsh and judgmental, see that word as a red flag that the activity is not honoring of their true nature in some way.

A Type 4 child needs outlets in their life where they can express their natural gift of critiquing and perfecting things. Help them identify and participate in activities they feel they're the best at.

Of all 4 Types, these children have the greatest tendency to want to immerse themselves in video games. This is not true of every Type 4—always black and white, they are either completely into the video game world or they are out of it. If your Type 4 child is into video games, you may notice their tendency to want to play all the way to the end of a new game without stopping, to unlock everything in it. Video games can be an excellent outlet for a Type 4, but taken to an extreme can become more of a road to isolation than to the solitude that Type 4s need.

⌒ **Child Whisperer Tip:** If your Type 4 child enjoys video games, set an amount of time together that they decide to play, and do not let them go beyond that time limit. Make sure this is a matter of discussion between the two of you, not just a rule that you lay down. Otherwise, it won't work. Consider a leeway day where they get to play for a longer amount of time or don't have a limit on the first day they have a new game.

This tendency for overload is most obvious in video gaming, but it is a tendency that can show up anywhere in a Type 4's life, in any activity that they choose to pursue. Because they have a one-track mind, they can focus so well on one thing that they tend to overwork and overdo things and then not want to do them anymore. They go from too much of something to nothing.

As a parent, you can help your Type 4 child learn to achieve balance. Your child will relate to you describing their thought process as a track. By logically explaining that they can consciously shift tracks, you can support your Type 4 child in creating the balance they need.

Which activities would you like to involve your Type 4, more serious child in that would honor their movement? List a few here:

_____

_____

_____

_____

Learning Tendencies

Learning Style: *Duplication with improvements*

Observation is key for a Type 4 child. These children have a gift for taking in a process or concept by seeing how it works. They also have the additional gift of being able to duplicate something they've seen and improve upon it. They are hands-off learners at first, watching and taking everything in. As soon as they feel they have grasped an idea, then they want to jump in and do it themselves without anyone looking over their shoulder.

More important than the method in which they learn is the attitude of the person trying to teach them. A Type 4 will immediately dismiss someone who talks down to them. When someone speaks to them condescendingly, they may feel angry that they are not being treated as an equal or an adult. They may also feel threatened or weak if they think that the person teaching them thinks they know less than they do. Even when your Type 4 child is a toddler, speak to them in a more adult-like manner. When you do this, they feel honored and they respond enthusiastically.

Type 4s set a high standard for themselves. When they are interested in a concept or skill, they want to master it to perfection. They want to know that they can finish a project right (or do it better than their example) before they begin. Although mistakes are a process of learning, small stumbles can seem huge to a Type 4. They are all or nothing, and if they don't master it all, they may see their learning so far as a failure.

• • • •

MARK'S STORY
Mastering a Foreign Language

My Type 4 son Mark went to Slovenia and wanted to master the language, but he encountered some challenges because he didn't want to speak it until he could do so perfectly. It's difficult to master a language perfectly unless you speak it, mistakes and all. He saw the Slovene people as the authority of their language and he wanted to show them respect through his respect for their language. (Plus, he didn't want to look stupid.)

The key to a situation like this is to shift the focus from the end result to the process. Mark could not perfect the act of speaking correctly at first, but he could perfect his process of practicing the language. He could be 100% perfect in the amount of time he spent studying and the goals for new words to learn and grammatical concepts to master. He just needed to switch the focus to a kind of perfection he could actually attain.

. . . .

Classroom Behavior: *Adapt to structure if respected*

Their tendency to be very thorough and keenly aware of their responsibilities leads most Type 4 children to perform at high levels in traditional school systems. The routine of a school day supports their more structured movement, and they feel safe knowing that rules are in place that peers must follow. In a school setting, Type 4 children value fairness, structure, routine, time to focus, and time to adjust as they move from track to track. Fairness includes a teacher who treats students equally, without favorites or scapegoats.

. . . .

COLE'S STORY
Teachers Love Him

Cole's 3rd grade teacher said that if all of her students were like Cole, she would have a perfect class. In his music class once a week, the music teacher gives out small prizes to the best behaved children. Every week, Cole gets a prize. True to his Type 4 nature, he performs well within the structure presented to him.

. . . .

♡ **Child Whisperer Tip:** These children face the challenge of setting their own standard too high, with unrealistic expectations for themselves. They want to complete their projects perfectly. They aim for perfect scores on every assignment. They don't want to make a single mistake. Lofty goals are fine, but they can be damaging if a Type 4 child bases their sense of worth on them. Reassure your child that they do not need to do anything in order to be loved and worthwhile. They can pursue their goals, but the minute they feel less valuable for a mistake they've made, it's time to reevaluate the purpose of their goals.

The same qualities that help Type 4 children perform well in the classroom—structure, focus, and stillness—can make socializing with potential new friends feel awkward and challenging. They may feel comfortable in the classroom, but inhibited on the playground. Every family's situation is different and as a Child Whisperer, you will receive inspiration for what works best to help your child make new friends.

Some mothers have mentioned that their Type 4 children flourished through home schooling. As they are naturally self-motivated and structured, these children are able to accomplish their academic tasks without a lot of extra follow-up or hand-holding. And one mother noted that home schooling actually improved her Type 4 son's social skills, rather than inhibiting them. She said, "We did more together as a family than ever, and having the support of his parents and his siblings with him in social situations greatly helped his confidence and helped him practice in a safe environment."

One last note about school: This description of Type 4 children might sound confusing if your Type 4 child is resistant to attending school or working on homework. Remember that Type 4 movement reflects a black-and-white, all-or-nothing expression. While most Type 4 children look like the responsible, on-task, fully committed student that teachers love, others express exactly the opposite. They may rebel and boldly resist anything related to school. Their resistance to school is usually related to respect and authority. For whatever reason, they do not feel respected at school, or they have found a reason to reject the authority of the people who teach them. Rather than try to convince them why they should go to school, go deep and find the root of the issue. Ask their opinion about school and listen for the word *stupid*. Honor your Type 4 child's nature, be their champion and defend them if their teachers and their classmates don't understand them. They will respect you for it and appreciate that they feel like they are not alone.

Study Habits: *Repetition is useful*

Study routines work well for Type 4 children. Some of these children may just prefer to continue in their mental track of school and take care of their homework right when they get home. Others need some time to decompress after school and choose to work on their homework later. The key is a schedule that works for your child.

Repetition in their study is useful to them if the subject at hand is one that interests them. If a Type 4 child needs to work on homework they're not interested in, they don't understand, or they just plain don't like, they may complain about it loudly. In this case, they may add another red flag word to the mix when they call their homework stupid and *boring*. "That homework is boring." The task might be something they don't understand or know how to do, so they try to avoid it, or it might truly be boring for them. They may have already thought through a concept and felt like they mastered it before the rest of the class is ready to go on.

These children may not accept their parents as an authority on homework. Their teacher may have explained it a certain way and they feel there is only one way to complete a task. Do not be offended if they do not see you as an authority in their schoolwork.

. . . .

COLE'S STORY
Long Division

Cole was learning to do long division when he asked his mother a question. She asked him a question in return. Instead of answering her, he just huffed and took his homework into another room. His mother has said about his schoolwork experience, "If you have questions, he thinks you don't know and he's lost confidence in you."

Because this mother knows her son's Energy Type, she does not take offense or worry that their relationship is damaged. Her son might not look to her as an authority in long division, but will look to her for expertise in other areas of his life.

. . . .

Just like not wanting to be reminded to do their chores, Type 4 children don't like to be told to do their homework. Since they are so aware of their responsibilities, they know what needs to be done and have organized in their mind when and how they will do it. Many Type 4 children even make use of a planner or other system to organize their time. When checking up on the status of your child's homework, remember to use phrases that communicate your confidence in their natural ability to follow through: "I know you have a plan to finish your homework. Do you want my help with any of it?"

Physical Development

Learning to Walk: *Following the grown-ups*

Type 4 children want to do things for themselves, so they tend to walk fairly early. As these children grow, they take mental note of all the things that grown-ups do and try to duplicate them. Walking may just be one of the very first milestones where this tendency becomes apparent.

Learning to Talk: *Striving to speak perfectly*

Type 4s pay careful attention to language and then strive to duplicate it accurately. They do not express as much unintelligible babble as other children do. They wait until they can produce actual speech sound with language that is precise and clear for their age. This might mean that they wait a long time to speak, but when they do they will be very articulate. Even so, you still may struggle to understand them at times when they first learn to talk. You will notice that your child will become easily frustrated if you don't understand what they try to communicate.

. . . .

SETH'S STORY
Grown-Up Words

My grandson Seth learned to talk readily and enjoyed using his new found skill of speaking. As a toddler, he paid close attention to words he did not know and asked their meaning. I noticed his tendency to do this, so I asked him, "Seth, do you like to learn what words mean so you can use them when you talk?" He told me, "Yes, Grandma, I do." At an early age he often used very advanced words appropriately in sentences. For example, one day when his little brother who was only two at the time was whining and fussing to get something, Seth spoke up to his mom saying, "Mom, don't give in to Joseph's desperate pleas!"

. . . .

Potty Training: *Matter-of-fact*

These children are naturally tidier and more efficient. They dislike the mess and lack of control over their bladder. They need to hear about the process in matter-of-fact terms and will be more motivated to try it if you point out that all the adults use the toilet and no grown-ups are using diapers anymore. They want to be taken seriously and seen as more grown-up, so this is a big motivator for them. Let your child be their own authority and choose between the big toilet and a shorter potty seat.

⌒ **Child Whisperer Tip:** Keep their potty-training experience private. Do not share potty-training talk at the dinner table with the rest of the family, or tell potty training stories publicly to your friends. These children don't like it when their privacy is taken away in front of other people, especially in front of adults.

Sleeping: *Best served by a sleep schedule*

These children do best with a bedtime routine and a regular sleep schedule. They will stick with a particular sleeping pattern for a long time, repeating the same hours of wakefulness and lengths of naps day after day. Honor their need for predictability and repetition by keeping a regular bedtime for your Type 4 child. As a Type 3 parent, I was not as consistent with bedtime when our children were growing up. True to my son Mark's Type 4 nature, he took matters into his own hands. By the time he was in grade school, he had created his own bedtime and faithfully went to bed every school night at his self-appointed bedtime.

⌒ **Child Whisperer Tip:** Create a space where your child can experience stillness before they go to sleep. Make sure their bedroom feels calm and safe.

Going to Pre-school and School: *Need time to observe*

New situations always present an opportunity for you to help your Type 4 child feel safe. Early school experiences can be a tough adjustment for Type 4 children. When they arrive, they may hang back, just observing. They may not want to talk to anyone at first. All of this is normal behavior for a Type 4 child and should not be talked about as a flaw or a problem. It's a tendency, and they need to know they can still be respected for needing to take new interactions at their own pace.

Part of their underlying anxiety in situations like these comes from their worry of being unprepared or caught off guard. Being unprepared could potentially lead to situations in which they would feel stupid or embarrassed. The more sure they feel about what will happen, the more at ease they will feel at school and in other social situations.

⌒ **Child Whisperer Tip:** You can help make the transition easier by explaining the routine well in advance. Talk your child through the steps that will happen, one at a time. "First, you'll play with toys with the other kids. Next, you'll hear a story. . ." Describe the steps all the way up through the moment when you come to pick them up. If you don't know the preschool's basic routine, ask. Type 4s see and understand the bigger picture of what's happening in their world. When they know this, they are at ease. This is true for even very young Type 4s, even as young as three years old.

Being Left with a Babysitter: *Need advance notice*

Type 4 children may initially feel uncomfortable with being left somewhere unfamiliar or a new person coming into their familiar space. Regular babysitters eventually come to be trusted.

🌙 **Child Whisperer Tip:** Prep your Type 4 child in advance about what is coming up. Communicate the big picture—who's coming and for how long. Allow them to prep themselves mentally before the fact.

Dating: *All or nothing*

Due to their all-or-nothing nature, they will either love dating or feel no need for it. The more reserved your Type 4 child is, the longer they may wait until they feel comfortable dating. Group dating with friends they know really well helps them break into the dating world. Another caution is, due to their tendency for deeper connections with people, if your Type 4 teen does not feel deeply connected to you, they may create a relationship with a boyfriend or girlfriend to satisfy their need to share their deeper thoughts and feelings with someone. If this has happened to your Type 4 teen, rather than try and stop it and ban it, which may lead to them rebelling and doing what they want anyway, start to build trust and respect with them, so they value your wisdom and guidance.

High School Experience: *Fewer, closer friends*

Encourage your Type 4 teen to be themselves and find their place in high school. Smaller groups and fewer friends is their tendency, so remember not to push them to be more social and put themselves out there more. They may get really involved in high school activities and they may not—again, it's all or nothing for them.

• • • •

MARK'S STORY
A Positive Type 4 High School Experience
My Type 4 son Mark attended a very large high school where the culture subtly demanded that in order to be

popular, you needed to act a little more Type 1 in your behavior and personality. This is typical for most high schools and large social settings. Mark could have easily hated and judged high school as a very "fake" place to be. High school can be a very challenging time for Type 4 teens for this reason. They cannot fake their nature trying to be someone they are not.

Because Mark knew his true nature, he navigated the high school scene with confidence and without judgment. He had a few close friends who supported him in living true to himself. As his parents, we never pressured him to be more social than he was. We encouraged him to follow his interests, which naturally led him to get involved in activities where he met others with similar interests. We were always there to help him whenever he felt insecure about a particular situation. When he got bothered by how many kids tried to fit in and be popular, we just listened and told him what a good example he was as a role model to other students on how to be themselves.

· · · ·

If your Type 4 child is living true to themselves, there is a greater chance they will have a more positive high school experience and be capable of accepting others for themselves, too.

♡ **Child Whisperer Tip:** As I mentioned earlier, Type 4s can sometimes become so driven and focused that they go to extremes to follow something they are passionate about and committed to. Give them plenty of down time at home and help them be discerning in how many extracurricular activities they are involved in. Help them see that they do not need to pursue every extracurricular activity in their reach to perfection.

Driving: *Efficient drivers (and backseat drivers)*

Your little Type 4 child may turn into a backseat driver from a young age. Since their natural inner movement is stillness, they may express judgment for hitting too many bumps in the road or turning corners more quickly than they would like. My grandson Seth started to announce from his toddler seat in the backseat of the car what the speed limit was to his mom while she drove. He said, "Mom, the speed is 2, 5!" His mom would just thank him for letting her know and was thankful he couldn't read the speedometer from his seat.

They want to be mature, so they look forward to milestones like a driver's license that will prove that they are grown up. They have a high degree of mental organization and can take in many details at once. They will be able to find their way around well because they find the most efficient route in their mental map. Since they like rules and learn them quickly, you can count on them learning the rules of the road and carrying into their adult life the attitude that they are the best drivers on the street.

Physical Characteristics

One of the most telling ways to identify which movement your child dominantly expresses is to look at facial features and their body language. Your child's physical characteristics are often more accurate than personality, which can be altered by situation or expectation.

Type 4 children have a reflective quality to their appearance. They hold themselves with an erect posture and have a look that can make them seem older then they are.

Something to remember: Learning facial profiling for babies and children in a book without pictures or illustrations can be difficult! That is why I have created a library of free videos on my website called, "How to Profile Babies, Children and Teens!" To access this library visit www.thechildwhisperer.com.

Face Shape: *Symmetrical*
You could fold their face in half and each side would be a mirror image of the other. Shape is elongated oval or rectangle with parallel lines on sides of face and across hairline. Widow's peak is a classic Type 4 trait.

Skin/Skin Texture: *Smooth, clean, porcelain skin*

Cheeks: *High cheekbones with parallel lines*

Nose: *Straight, symmetrical nose bridge, sideways oval between nostrils, oval nostrils, two straight lines on sides of nose bridge*

Eyes: *Oval, bold*
If you drew a line from the outside corner of one eye all the way to outside corner of the other eye, it would make a straight horizontal line.

Eyebrows: *Straight lines or half of an elongated oval, bold*

Hands: *Long fingers are the same width all the way down the finger*
Fingernail beds are straight on both sides. Smooth, porcelain skin on top of the palm.

Early Childhood Features: *When you look at a young Type 4* *child head on, you will notice that the sides of their face run in two straight, parallel lines.*

Body Language

Since Energy Profiling is an assessment of our natural expression of movement, body language is an excellent clue to your child's Energy Type. Pay attention to the way your child moves. Do any of the following movements describe your child?

Crawling: Most Type 4 children's physical tendencies develop by the book! This means that they will develop their crawling and walking in the timeline that most child development books and experts suggest—in this case, crawling somewhere between 6 to 10 months. It is important to encourage them to crawl for a few months before they attempt to walk since research has shown that crawling enhances the development of the connections between the right and left hemispheres of the brain.

Walking: These children walk with a straight and rigid movement. Their arms stay closer to their body. They move in a straight line from point A to point B; even when they don't, they move in shapes that express Type 4 structure. One mother told her Type 4 daughter to stop running around in circles so they could get ready. "I'm not running in circles," said the daughter. "I'm running in squares!" One of our company employees, Kalista, who is a Type 4, used to balance books on her head as a teen to practice walking with poise and erect posture.

Sitting/Standing: Type 4 children sit straight up and down, with both feet on the floor. They have great posture, poised and erect. Of all the Types of children, Type 4 children are naturally capable of sitting and focusing for the longest period of time.

Voice/Language: As Type 4s mature, their voices have a lower pitch and a clean sound.

The language of a Type 4 is clear, concise, and bold. They say it like it is—or how they think it is.

♡ **Child Whisperer Tip:** Others may misunderstand your Type 4 child's bold nature and more blunt way of communicating. You may need to explain in a logical manner the way their language may be perceived by others. Help them manage their tendency to be blunt.

Personal Space: Type 4s function better in an organized space and they keep their personal possessions organized so they know where they are. They like to keep things clean and fairly spare, with a lot of open space and no movement. Cleanliness and organization in their personal space help them stay balanced in other areas of their life.

♡ **Child Whisperer Tip:** Do not touch their stuff! A Type 4 is particular about their personal belongings. They care for their preferred items carefully and do not trust others to care for them in the same particular way. If you disregard their personal space and personal items, you will compromise the trust in your relationship with your child.

. . . .

SETH'S STORY
Just His Toys

When I explained to my daughter Jenny that her Type 4 son Seth would benefit from keeping some of his favorite toys just for himself and not be expected to share them with others, she took this to heart. She talked to him about it when he was only four years old.

Seth loved being able to select his favorite items, knowing he would not have to share them with his little brother or friends unless he decided he wanted to. Jenny purchased a few plastic bins that fit easily under his bed where he could store them. Seth made a sign that said, "Seth's Specials, Don't Touch!" and taped it where it could be seen. When I visited Seth recently, I asked him about his toys and books under his bed and he explained, "Those are just for me. I only let my friends that treat them nicely play with them!"

. . . .

Challenges as a Parent: Power Struggles and Respect

Parenting a Type 4 child can be the easiest and simplest experience when you finally understand the few intrinsic needs Type 4 children have and you parent them with the intent to honor those needs. Parenting a Type 4 child can also be one of the most challenging and frustrating experiences of your parenting life if you do not understand these basic intrinsic needs and instead parent from the old belief that as the parent, you have all the authority and control. Take a moment to consider these common challenges of parents with Type 4 children and then try the straightforward tip that follows.

The number one challenge that parents tend to face with Type 4 children is a constant power struggle. Because one of the Type 4's basic intrinsic needs is to be their own authority, Type 4 children continually assert their authority in their own lives, which parents may interpret as rebellion or defiance. Parents who do not understand their Type 4 child respond by demanding more control in an attempt to be an authority figure in their child's life, which only leads their child to become more rigid and pull away in an attempt to be their own authority and experience more independence. Together, parents and Type 4 children create a cycle of power struggles.

Child Whisperer Tip: Become a partner of authority in your child's life. Your interaction does not have to be either/or—it can be both/and. Your child and you are both authorities and can work together in a partnership of mutual cooperation. In this partnership, your role as a parent is to raise them true to their authoritative nature, supporting them in learning how to use this natural gift to follow their own sense of what is right for them. As their parent, you are endowed automatically with a position of authority in their eyes. But that authority will only be respected if you recognize your Type 4 child as an authority in their own lives.

A child may lose respect for you as their parents as a byproduct of not being taught and supported in becoming their own authority. Don't assume that your child understands their nature to be their own authority. I have worked with hundreds of Type 4 adults who did not have a conscious understanding of this aspect of their nature. Once I pointed it out to them, it made perfect sense, since most of their life's struggles resulted from the limiting belief that they were not their own authority. They had this deep inner feeling that they wanted to be their own authority, but had not been given permission. When a Type 4 child does not respect their parents, they tend to ignore them and begin to do things their own way in an attempt to be true to themselves. They can put up emotional walls and refuse to let their parents in.

. . . .

JONATHAN AND MARK'S STORY
R-E-S-P-E-C-T

It took my husband Jonathan a few more years than it took me to understand our Type 4 son's nature. During Mark's high school years, he and his father had huge power struggles. Jonathan would not treat Mark with respect and support him in being his own authority. Jonathan also had a tendency to be sarcastic with Mark and he knew how to push his buttons, which only resulted in Mark becoming embittered towards his dad, pulling away and speaking very bluntly about how much he resented and did not respect him. He would say to Jonathan, "I am not going to respect you since you don't respect me."

I attempted to get involved and straighten things out for both of them. I saw how easy the solution was. I urged Jonathan to treat Mark in a respectful manner as his own authority. But Jonathan held on a while longer to an old parenting model that says, "I'm the parent. You should do what I say!" Once I let go of trying to mediate their power struggles, things started to shift.

Now, several years later, they have openly talked about their patterns and what each needs to feel supported. Jonathan learned to approach Mark in an adult-like manner with respect. When he trusted that Mark had deep insights to what would shift their relationship, it all started to change. They now have a wonderful father-son relationship and enjoy doing many activities together.

. . . .

Child Whisperer Tip: Never demand respect from your Type 4 child. Respect them first. Show that respect in the way you speak to them and you speak about them. Type 4 children express a reflective quality. If you give them genuine respect, they will mirror that same respect back to you, strengthening your relationship from both sides.

In my experience in parenting a Type 4 child, parenting became easy once I knew that two of a Type 4's primary intrinsic needs are a sense of their own authority and respect from others.

True to their nature of all or nothing, you can have it all: love, cooperation, enjoyment, closeness, easy communication. Or you can have none of it with a Type 4 child. It is up to you as their parent to be the one to initiate that opportunity. It is never too late, no matter how old they are!

Parents worldwide have found the information of Energy Profiling to be life-changing in the way they interact with their Type 4 children. Some of them have experienced the challenge of their child's resistance to being classified. Because they are their own authority, Type 4 children especially do not like the idea of someone telling them who they are.

♡ **Child Whisperer Tip:** Acknowledge your child always as a unique individual first. Honor their preferences if they do not wish to use the title Type 4 or do not want to use the language of Energy Profiling. You can always talk about this information in terms of your child's true nature, natural gifts, and tendencies.

Whatever challenges you face with your Type 4 child, the joys can easily outweigh them, especially when you reach a place of mutual respect and trust together. Your child is naturally reliable and responsible. They are deeply loyal. Their bold and blunt nature makes it easier for you to always know where you stand with them. Take a moment today to sit down one-on-one with your Type 4 child and tell them how much you respect them and admire the way they contribute to your family, just by their presence in it. Your earnest expression of respect will make a huge difference for them.

The Type 4 More Serious Daughter

Boldness and dignity are the keywords that come to mind when I think of a Type 4 daughter. Boldness in knowing who she is and the dignity of self to live it. Since some parents do not expect their sweet little girl to be so bold, they may be taken aback by her willingness to see the bigger picture of what she wants at a very early age and worry she is growing up too fast. Since Type 4 energy has not been classified by our culture as the standard feminine expression, you could easily repress your Type 4 daughter's nature at an early age.

Many moms of Type 4 girls have come to me very concerned that their little Type 4 girl is drawn to things that only older girls should be interested in. One mom shared the story of her six-year-old Type 4 daughter who came out of the bathroom and announced, "Mom, I just shaved my legs!" This Type 2 mom was shocked! She could not understand why her little six-year-old would even want to shave her legs. Little Type 4 girls watch their big sisters and their mommy and are drawn to things like makeup, clothing, hair—all the things that have to do with appearance and how to perfect it. I shared with this mom to not discipline her daughter for following her own instinct for wanting to shave her legs, but to redirect her focus to things that would be age appropriate, like playing with new hairstyles, giving her permission to put together her own outfits, and to let her master the skill of applying her own nail polish.

As your Type 4 daughter grows, she naturally takes time to reflect on who she is and what is important to her. She is not someone to follow the crowd. She may spend time alone, as this is necessary as part of her reflection time to discover herself. She is designed to grow into a beautiful, stunning woman who holds herself with dignity and expresses herself with clarity. She is a gift to others as one of her natural attributes is to hold a reflective light so others more clearly see who they are in her presence. Self-esteem comes naturally to her when she has been raised true to her nature. And in that gift of self-esteem, she esteems others to be of great value, thus leaving a beautiful footprint of her good character wherever she goes.

Child Whisperer Tip: Allow your Type 4 daughter to have a bold voice in your household. I have met many adult Type 4 women who have lost or never had a chance to develop their bold voice. This does not mean a loud voice, just a clear, bold expression of their own sense of self, their own values, and thoughts—a bold voice that also honors the voices of others. As your daughter grows, she takes on an air of dignity and regality. She knows who she is and respects herself, her body, and others. She is deeply caring and deeply sensitive.

The Type 4 More Serious Son

Honor and loyalty are the keywords that best describe a Type 4 son. These sons are very honorable and loyal from the very beginning of their lives. When you are on good terms with your Type 4 son, he is a joy and delight due to the respect and loyalty he shows to you. Since these sons do not share their feelings with just anyone, it is such an honor to know that you are someone in your Type 4 son's inner circle.

Type 4 little boys may not like to roughhouse and wrestle as much as some of their dads would like, but they will always enjoy learning new things. They have a love for learning about animals, machines, how the world works, and thanks to this time of internet access, they quickly learn how to get online and Google things to learn more. An iPad or similar tablet device can be a great investment for a Type 4 son.

Type 4 sons can be great at anything they put their mind to. Just don't expect them to be great at a lot of things. If they are into sports, that will be their primary focus. Or maybe they prefer academia and learning, or maybe they are into music. Whatever their focus they will naturally apply themselves to be the best they can be. Your job is to help them experience fulfillment by supporting them in creating reasonable expectations of their progress with whatever they are drawn to. Accept that they do not have a lot of diverse interests, but are drawn to fewer things that they want to master and perfect. Let your son lead the way in showing you what he finds the most interesting and fascinating in life.

Be respectful of their personal belongings: their clothes, bikes, phones, computers, or any other personal item that is very special to them. My son takes impeccable care of his car and his mountain bike. I know that those are two items I should not expect to borrow from him. He treats them with great respect and care and knows no one else will treat them the same.

These sons also love rules and following them. Give them a chance to make up some of their own rules to live by when they are small. It will be fun for you to see what they come up with.

♡ **Child Whisperer Tip:** If you are not close to your Type 4 son, I believe that can change over time. It may take some patience, as they need time to warm up to you and believe you can be trusted and that you have their best interests in mind. Follow the guidelines I have introduced to you in raising a Type 4 child. No matter their age, with proper care, they will come around to respect you and let you into their world.

The Type 4 Child Through the Years

The following are some examples of the many ways Type 4 children express their true nature from birth to age 18 as they mature and develop. They express many general tendencies in their first 18 years. The ones I note here are those I have seen most commonly.

At each developmental stage, your child has a specific emotional need. This is true for all Types of children. I offer some specific phrases to share with your Type 4 child to help meet each need. Use these phrases in words, or consider how you could express these phrases in action to help your child feel loved and wanted in each stage of their life. When your child is supported in living true to their nature, they can more easily enter their adult experience ready and able to create emotionally healthy relationships. You can meet your child's developmental emotional needs in many ways—just use my examples as a way to get thinking.

Baby 0 to 18 months

Primary Emotional Need: *To be validated for their inwardly still, structured nature and to be supported in starting to explore and sense the world around them.*

All Type 4s start their life experience with a primary connection to the intellectual experience of this world. They are observant from day one and take in their world through careful observation. People often note how reflective and still they are.

You may hear a lot of people comment that your Type 4 child seems very serious. They are the most serious of all children from the very beginning of their lives.

Messages your Type 4 child needs to hear in this stage of life:

- Welcome to the world; we've been eagerly waiting for your reflective energy.
- We have a special place prepared for you.
- All your needs are important to us. You can grow at your own pace, and we are here for you.
- We love your constant, still nature—you are a gift to our family.
- It's okay to watch and observe; it is safe for you to watch as long as you want before exploring in other ways.
- You can be you and we will always love you.
- It's okay for you to be different from Mom and Dad. We will work out our differences.

♡ **Child Whisperer Tips to support this stage:** Type 4 babies need structure and predictable routines in order to feel secure. Support them in finding a regular sleep schedule and do not interrupt or change it unless absolutely necessary.

These babies also respond well to structured movement on their bodies. Dress them in clothes that fit more closely, rather than loose-fitting garments. Swaddle them tightly and make sure they feel like you are holding them with a solid embrace.

Toddler 18 Months to 3 Years

Primary Emotional Need: *Support in sensing, exploring and doing in the world. Learning to do things by themselves!*

The Type 4 toddler is ever observant. They want to understand exactly how the world around them works and they pay particular attention to what adults value and do. They try to duplicate adult speech and behavior, which leads many to observe them as mature for their age. At this age, your child will often say, "I want to do it myself." The Type 4 child is learning to master this world, to think things through and know how things work. They need to do things themselves with your guidance and support.

Messages your Type 4 child needs to hear in this stage of life:

- It's okay to be curious, to watch, to think about, to touch and explore this world.
- We want you to explore. We will make it safe for you.
- We want you to learn to do things yourself. Mommy and Daddy are here to support you.
- You can be you and we will always love you.
- You can try out new things and find your own way of doing things.
- It's okay for you to make your own choices about what you want.
- You are so aware and observant.
- You are so loyal and caring. We are here to take care of you.
- I love you just the way you are.

Child Whisperer Tips to support this stage: Make sure your home environment supports your child's desire to explore how the world works. As they learn to talk, focus all your attention on them when they are trying to communicate something to you. Make sure you stop what you are doing and give them your full attention and eye contact. This is a practice that will serve and honor you and your child's relationship for the rest of your life. If you don't have time when they are demanding it, let them know and that you will give them your full attention in the time you decide. Put on a timer so they can relate to what that time looks like. They will gain confidence in their speech and in their relationship with you if they know that you will listen when they speak.

Pre-school 3 to 6 years

Primary Emotional Need: *Coming into their own identity and power and feeling a sense of their own authority.*

In this stage, you may notice your Type 4 child really start to assert their sense of authority in their life. They may refuse your requests to do certain things. They may also demand to do things you don't want them to. Your experience in parenting them will be a continual readjustment to find the right balance of partnered authority. Practice it now while the stakes are lower and simpler. You will receive inspiration to know when to give your child responsibility and when to take more parental control.

At this age, they also need to develop an understanding of the bigger picture of their lives so they can put things into a logical order in their minds. They may ask incessantly throughout the day, "What are we doing today? When is this going to happen? When is so-and-so coming over?" They need to know what to expect and what direction things are going.

When we planned a visit to our daughter's home, Jenny expressed some concern and hesitation about telling her Type 4 son Seth we were going to visit. She knew from the day she told him that he would ask every day, "When are Grandma and

Grandpa coming?" I suggested she make a paper chain with him with one link representing each day until we arrived. She has used this strategy successfully in many situations when she needed to relate a timeline to her young son. She helps him make the chain, they hang it in a place where he can neatly cut off a link for each day that goes by.

She has also learned to share with him the plan for the day so she doesn't hear all through the day, "What is happening next, Mom?" Recently, she shared a story of telling Seth their plans on a Saturday, which included getting haircuts, going to the grocery store and a few other errands. Seth got his own piece of paper and, as best he could, noted the plan. Jenny is a Type 1 and can easily make a change in her plans, which she often does. This can cause great distress in her Type 4 son's life if it becomes the norm.

In this case, they were driving in the car, going about their plan, when she saw a garage sale sign. Jenny loves garage sales, as they are full of possibilities and surprises and great deals. Rather than just divert from the plan, she asked Seth, "Do you mind if we stop at this garage sale?" From his toddler seat in the back he said, "No!" She clarified and asked, "So you don't mind?" He quickly replied, "No, I DO mind, I do mind!" very emphatically. Jenny chose to honor Seth and the day was very pleasant.

Jenny is not required as a mom to give up what is true and right for her, but she knows it's a matter of taking one day at a time and striking a balance that works for both her and her children.

Messages your Type 4 child needs to hear in this stage of life:

- It's okay for you to know what you want and make your own decisions.
- You are learning what is right for you—trust your instincts.

- We are glad you are thinking for yourself.
- We love to hear about the things you think.
- Your strong and serious nature is powerful. Trust it!
- You understand things clearly; thank you for sharing your thoughts with us.
- Thank you for the lessons you so easily teach our family.
- You are an important member of the family. Your natural gifts and talents are a blessing to all of us.

🌙 **Child Whisperer Tips to support this stage:** Since Type 4s experience the world intellectually, give them opportunities to learn about what interests them. They like to look at processes and systems to learn how they work, so involve them in activities with several sequential steps, showing them how things work. Take stock of how much down time you give them at home to make sure they stay centered and balanced.

School Age 6 to 12 Years

Primary Emotional Need: *Fitting in, working within structure, knowing and learning*

Type 4 children naturally move through life with a structured expression, so they usually move into school-age years with ease. They may express initial worry about certain new experiences that come with this stage of life, but as long as they have enough advance information to mentally prepare and they know the routine of their new environment, they will be able to make the transition.

Messages your Type 4 child needs to hear in this stage of life:

- You are smart and brilliant, and you learn so thoroughly.
- You can have as much structure and routine in your life as you want.
- You can succeed at anything that feels right and honoring of you.
- Trust your thoughts; they are brilliant.
- You deserve to succeed.
- Follow what is right for you. You don't have to do things that are not honoring of you.
- It is not your job to make sure that others are following the rules. We will take care of your siblings and your teachers will take care of your classmates.
- Thanks for being so loyal.
- You never have to talk to other people when you don't want to.
- You have a right to have boundaries and know what is important to you.

♡ **Child Whisperer Tips to support this stage:** Type 4 children in this stage are interacting with the structure of school and learning how they want to create their own personal structure in their lives. You can help them remain centered and happy by supporting them in making a schedule they feel good about.

Due to their tendency to be very literal, experiences like Santa and the Easter Bunny can be a sensitive issue in the life of a Type 4 child. I know Type 4 adults who were so let down and felt they had been lied to when they learned that Santa was not real that they refuse to create a pretend Santa in their children's lives. My grandson announced at age four that Santa was not real and followed by sharing all the logical reasons why he was not. Rather than try and convince her son that Santa was real, his mother said he was not real, but he represented the spirit of Christmas by giving gifts and that it was fun to pretend. Seth made the decision in his own mind that Santa gave each family member one gift and the rest came from Mom and Dad and shared that conclusion several months after he had figured out Santa was not real.

Jenny is just letting Seth lead the way on the Santa experience rather than trying to make it something that may not be worth the issues of trust that can come up for a Type 4 if they feel they are being lied to.

High School 12 to 18 Years

Primary Emotional Need: *Separating and creating independence from the family*

In this stage of a Type 4 child's life, friends take on a high level of importance. Social interactions and creating a social network of friends is a big focus at this age. This may be challenging for your Type 4 child, especially if they are expected to be naturally social and outgoing. This is not their nature. Remember, their natural energetic expression is more reserved. Honor and support them in having a smaller group of close friends they feel they can trust.

Messages your Type 4 child needs to hear in this stage of life:

- You can have a small group of close friends.
- You can interact socially in a way that feels safe to you.
- You do not need to do things perfectly in order to be loved.
- You can take all the time you need to grow up.
- We are happy with your choices.
- It is okay to make mistakes.

- It is okay to take your time to think about things.
- You are allowed to focus on the things that are most important to you.
- We respect you for being who you are.
- Good for you to move forward after you've thought things through.
- You can develop your own relationships, interests, and causes.
- You can learn about sex and nurturing and be responsible for your needs, feelings, and behaviors.

Child Whisperer Tips to support this stage: Being with their friends takes on a priority in this stage of life. When it comes to making and having friends, your Type 4 child is very capable of creating a social network that honors them. Remember to not push them to have a lot of friends and be more outgoing. Support them by helping them have a friend over and doing things in small groups. They are not comfortable going to birthday parties where they don't really know anyone, so don't force them to attend events and parties that will make them uncomfortable. Instead, work with them in developing confident social skills that honor their more reserved nature. When they are familiar with people, and understand the scope of their relationship with them, they have no problem engaging.

It's Never Too Late!

Please note that even if your Type 4 child has grown past any of these stages, it is never too late to validate them and meet their emotional needs. We are all every age we have ever been and if we have unmet emotional needs, we carry them with us into the next stage of our lives.

No matter if your child is 4, 14, or 44, you can express your respect for them and affirm all the previous stages of their development. If you are a Type 4 adult, use this information to heal your childhood wounds of being misunderstood and start a new chapter of respect and inner balance.

Most of my work in the field of Energy Psychology helps adults heal their inner child's unmet needs. What a gift it is when a parent shows up and meets their needs once and for all! It's never too late to become a better parent!

The Child Whisperer's Top 10 Things a Type 4 Child Needs From You!

To summarize, I've put together a brief list of what I feel are some of the most important points to remember when parenting a Type 4, more serious child. This general list will be supportive to all Type 4 children. After reading through this list, please take a moment to add your own inspirations to it.

My goal with this list (and this book) is to bring out your own Child Whisperer gifts. As a Child Whisperer, you will receive your *own* inspirations and aha's, specific to your child and their Type. Make sure you write down those aha's!

1. *Support in being their own authority*
Recognizing your Type 4 child's need to learn to be their own authority from the earliest stages of their lives will make all the difference in your parenting experience. Instead of power struggles and frustration, you can experience mutual cooperation that creates a life-long bond.

2. *Respect*
Express respect for your child's sense of authority, their

logical nature, and their bold stance in their opinions. These children naturally inspire respect wherever they go and they will respond dramatically to you when they experience respect coming from you. Type 4 children easily respect those that in turn respect them. If you fall out of respect in the world of a Type 4 you can expect it to take a little time to gain that respect back. Believe me, it's worth it to go through that process when it is your child.

3. *Privacy*

Respect their need to have space and time that is solely theirs. Giving them privacy includes reprimanding them privately and teaching them new skills in private, rather than in front of siblings, neighbors, or even another parent at times. Allow them to make the decision about what they will share with the world and what they will not. Never embarrass them in public. They need to feel that their mistakes are safe and not exposed to the world. Respect their nature by treating their belongings as their private possessions, especially those they care the most deeply about and are hesitant to share with others.

4. *Encouragement to live true to who they are*

Refer to the phrases in each of the developmental stages in the previous section to continue to validate and encourage your Type 4 child to live true to their nature throughout all the phases of their childhood.

5. *Time for reflection*

Don't demand instant answers to the questions you ask them. Your Type 4 child may need some time to think deeply and thoroughly before sharing their opinions about something new. In new situations, let them observe first without pushing them to engage or move forward. Allow them to take the time they need to size up a situation and decide what they think about it. Encourage them to take time to be alone and reflect on things, even on a daily basis. Type 4s need solitude and quiet to let everything get sorted out that is going on in their minds. Support them by teaching them this at a very young age. Even my grandson at 3 years old had quiet time for 30 minutes a day in his room by himself to quietly play with toys or read or just listen to music. He has been taught from an early age that his quiet time was important time to connect with himself.

6. *Undivided attention when communicating*

When you are communicating with your Type 4 child, look them in the eye, listen to them without distractions or interruptions, and if you ask them a question, listen to their answer and don't make them repeat themselves. These are great communication skills with anyone, but are especially honoring of a Type 4 child. They will respond with respect for you, listening with the same undivided attention you have given them, truly taking in what you share. You will not be able to give your Type 4 child undivided attention at all times. If you are too distracted at the moment to listen to your child without interruptions, set a time in the near future when you can give them undivided attention. (And keep your appointment!)

7. *Help to see the bigger picture by giving them advance notice*

Keep your Type 4 child in the loop when it comes to daily plans, weekly plans, and family vacations. When they are aware of the bigger picture of what's going on, they are able to mentally organize and move forward with ease. Let them know as soon as you can about expected changes in their lives and their routines. They need time to process and to mentally reorganize. Fifteen-minute warnings are a good rule of thumb to use on a regular basis. Before you call them to dinner or ask them to move on to the next activity, give them a 15-minute warning that they need to wrap up what they are doing.

8. *Social help*
Enable them to find one best friend who has similar interests and abilities. Encourage this relationship, even if the friend moves. Do not push them to make lots of friends or be engaged in large social activities with a lot of people.

9. *Don't sweat the small stuff*
You'll experience plenty of opportunities to feel challenged by your Type 4 child's perfecting eye and seemingly endless criticisms. Decide today to let go of your frustration and focus on showing respect to your child in order to create mutual respect between you.

10. *Avoid these phrases and judgments:*
- You are such a loner.
- Stop being so picky.
- What a know-it-all.
- Smile more!
- Lighten up.
- You're uptight.
- Quit being so critical.

After reading this section, add to this list by writing the

inspirations and ideas you received regarding what your Type 4 child needs from you. Make your notes here:

_____

_____

_____

_____

The Type 4 Child Word Portrait

Refer to this word portrait list often as a quick reminder of the nature of your Type 4 child. Compare your child's mood and disposition to this list. Is your Type 4 child expressing these movements and qualities on a consistent basis? If not, what do you need to change in your parenting approach to support them in living true to their nature?

Type 4 children are often described as:

Articulate	Precise
Bold	Poised
Clear	Polite
Concise	Proper
Deeply loyal	Reflective
Dignified	Reserved
Efficient	Responsible
Exact	Serious
Focused	Still
Honorable	Structured
Literal	Thorough
Logical	Well mannered
Mature	Well behaved

Negative labels that are not honoring of Type 4 children:

Bossy	Judgmental
Brash	Know-it-all
Condescending	Loner
Critical	Opinionated
Harsh	Rebellious

How to Profile Babies and Toddlers

You may wonder how early in life a parent could assess a child's Energy Type. I speak from experience when I say that you can identify it as early as the day they are born. Depending on the nature of pregnancy and labor, you may even have a sense of your child's Type even earlier! Since Energy Profiling offers the unique opportunity to profile your child even at birth, I felt like a full section should be dedicated to giving guidance in that opportunity. I am not aware of any other profiling system that offers you assessment tools to learn your child's true nature even the day they are born.

While I was writing this book, my daughter Anne gave birth to a little girl. Three weeks later, my oldest daughter Jenny gave birth to a little boy. In both cases, we could recognize each baby's Energy Type on the day they were born. I am asked frequently how we could possibly tell what their Types were so early in their lives. I think people ask this question because they are thinking of Energy Profiling as a personality typing system. Since babies have not developed personalities yet, it would be impossible to know their Type.

This is the beauty of Energy Profiling: As a profiling system, it looks at human nature as an innate quality of movement that creates our inner nature. Because of the ability to assess movement and physical features, it is possible to successfully Type a baby, even before their personality has developed.

In the case of my oldest daughter, Jenny, she knew even before her son was born that he was probably a Type 2. She based this on her intuitive knowledge of Energy Profiling and how her baby moved in her womb. She felt a peace and calming with this baby, even in utero. The day he was born, you could see his Type 2 nature written all over his face! He had a very obvious downward movement to all of his features, with blended cheeks and even a double chin! He made a lot of soft purring sounds and subtle winces. The most common feedback the nurses shared about this little baby boy was that he was so mellow.

My other daughter, Anne, who is also highly skilled at profiling, felt that her little girl was either a Type 1 or a Type 3, due to her baby's higher movement while in the womb. She noticed swift kicks and jabs as the baby grew. Just like her cousin, this little girl had her Type written all over her face the day she was born—a Type 3! You could easily see the angles in her hairline, and she had exotic eyes, which were also set at an angle. She had a more substantial nose for a baby and she made a lot of grunting and growling sounds. Both moms were able to greet their new little ones with full acceptance and understanding of their true nature from the moment they were born.

The Essential Key to Typing Babies and Toddlers

When assessing your toddler or baby's Type, remember this one essential key: movement.

Your child's nature is completely intact as a quality of movement from the first day of their life, but their personality is still forming. Energy Profiling assesses nature, which is first identified as movement (for more information about the movement of all 4 Types as they express in the nature kingdom and in adults, see the appendix in the back of this book).

All babies have the ability to play, learn, and have fun, especially in an environment where they feel comfortable and safe to be themselves. The movement with which they do so is distinct. Let's look at all four of those movements expressed in toddlers and babies.

Type 1 Babies and Toddlers

Movement: The Type 1 child's movement is upward and light. They enjoy free movement where they can kick their legs. They look outside themselves to see what they can connect with and they enjoy interacting with a variety of locations, sights, and people. Their random, higher movement makes them less likely to adhere to a structured sleep schedule or accept doing the same thing at regular times. They love to be bounced and sung to playfully.

Features: Their face has a cherub or pixie look to it, with a round structure and animated shapes in the features—like circles or star points. They make sounds that rise and fall and when they shout, they can easily reach a high-pitched shriek.

What to Notice: If your baby or toddler is a Type 1, you will notice their higher movement. While all babies are "cute," a Type 1 baby or toddler exudes the energy of cuteness with their social, outgoing nature. They seem friendly, more animated, and bright-eyed. If your young child does express a higher movement, but you are not sure if they are a Type 1 or a Type 3, consider the quality of their energy. A Type 1's high energy feels like a bouncing ball (random and playful), while a Type 3's higher energy feels more like a push forward momentum. Type 1 babies make cute, gurgling noises to entertain themselves.

Challenges: Type 1 children thrive in environments that have a lot going on and a lot to stimulate their love for newness. If your baby is required to sit still for extended periods of time or is in too quiet of a house during the day, they may be bored and get fussy. If your toddler does not have the regular opportunity to interact with a variety of people, they may become grumpy or sad.

⌒ **Child Whisperer Tip:** Sit your Type 1 child up in a swing or walker so they can engage with their world in an upright way. Mix up the locations where you put them so they always have something new to see. Turn on some upbeat music. Consider lovely scents you can add to their environment. Do they have toys that stimulate their curiosity and excitement for life? Make sure that as they grow into toddlers, they have plenty of opportunities to play and interact with other children.

Type 2 Babies and Toddlers

Movement: While all babies offer an energy of love, Type 2s in particular have an energy that expresses a steady, heartfelt connection to those around them. They seem quieter, more tender and more sensitive than other babies from the earliest moments of their life.

Features: Like their natural movement, the features in a Type 2 baby's face will move downward with a blended quality. Cheeks blend into the jawline. The eyebrows, corners of their eyes, lips, everything will have a softened, downward quality to it. They may also have a quieter cry than most babies and will try to get your attention in subtle ways when they are hungry or tired.

What to Notice: Other people will give you clues that your baby is a Type 2. The most common perception you'll encounter (as long as baby's comfy!) is that your child is so easy or so calm and mellow. These children have a quieter cry and all-around quieter affect to them. Their baby sounds are subtle and soft, which could be compared to a purring.

Challenges: With their sensitive, relaxed nature, these children can experience challenges if things do not feel comfortable for them. You will have a fussy baby or a whiny toddler if clothes or sleeping arrangements are not comfortable, or they do not have a space to feel cozy in. They may also feel stressed if there is too much loud noise, like TV shows that have intense background music, or even quarreling parents or siblings. As they grow, these children do not have a natural tendency to speak up for what they need. So as they develop, they can whine, fuss, and get moody if they feel their needs are not heard.

♡ **Child Whisperer Tip:** Lucky for you, most items in the baby world are comfy and soft, which will support your Type 2 baby in feeling safe and cared for in this world. To prevent excessive whining, you need to consciously support them in learning to speak up. Make sure you do this in a way that's supportive and comfortable to them, and does not communicate that their tendency toward subtlety is a flaw. If you are arguing or talking loudly, do it out of range of your Type 2 baby or toddler.

Type 3 Babies and Toddlers

Movement: The Type 3 child's movement is active, reactive, spirited, and fiery. Their energy has a forward push to it and they are focused on results. As babies, they get really hungry, nurse quickly, and then they're done. They crash, sleep hard, and then they're up again. Baby or toddler, Type 3s are always ready to go, go, go.

Features: Their faces have more textured, angular features that aren't necessarily soft and cute. They have more substance in their nose, angular hairlines, texture in their hands, and cat eyes. For Type 3 girls, cute pink bows in contrast with more angular features will look a little silly. The Type 3 baby's most distinguishing trait is the Type 3 scowl. They furrow their brow intensely, more than any other Type.

What to Notice: Type 3 children express a higher movement like Type 1 children do. But Type 3 energy shows up as more pushy and adventurous, rather than bouncy and bright like a Type 1. Your Type 3 child will meet challenges head on. They make more guttural, growling sounds. As they learn to walk, they have a weighty, heavy-footed energy.

Challenges: Because we expect babies to be soft and snuggly, parents don't often expect a Type 3 child's active movement or know what to do with it. From the beginning of a Type 3 child's life, their parents may try to get them to stop moving. Because they want to get their hands on everything and they react to being told no, they can be labeled as rebellious, destructive, or pushy. They don't have trouble, though, when sufficiently engaged.

⌒ **Child Whisperer Tip:** Keep your Type 3 baby engaged with sounds and move them around to different spots in the house. This sort of variety will match their movement better than staying in the same place or too quiet of a home. To avoid the pushing they may do when they become toddlers, keep your Type 3 child physically engaged and provide safe places for them to roam and explore.

Don't always tell them no. And when they do something big and unexpected, be impressed by it before anything else ("Wow, you're so adventurous." "That's really cool you did something hard."). Then you can say something like this: "What would help Mommy is for you to come and tell me so that I can support you in doing what you want."

Type 4 Babies and Toddlers

Movement: The Type 4 child's energy moves inward, so they are naturally more reserved, particularly in new environments. They are supported by structure and repetition and will often start to create structure for themselves by falling asleep at the same time or wanting to eat on a schedule. Stillness does not mean sitting still (although they are more capable of it than the other three Types). It means an inner stillness, a quality of being grounded and centered, which you may sense from them, even when they are a baby.

Features: Their most obvious facial feature is the shape of their face. It has a boxier look, with the sides of the face creating two parallel lines, and the forehead being more rectangular. They typically have eyebrows that go straight across, even if the eyebrows are faint. The sides of their fingers form parallel lines all the way to the ends of the fingers.

What to Notice: Even at a very young age, these children focus intently on what holds their interest. Type 3 and Type 4 children tend to be independent, but with a different quality to their movement. Type 3 children will want to do something on their own because it's a challenge. But Type 4s will want to do something by themselves because they want to figure it out. As they grow from babyhood to becoming a toddler, learn to recognize if your child is engaging with activities on an intellectual level, rather than a physical one.

Challenges: Type 4 babies will have a more serious expression than what you may expect in a baby. This still, authoritative quality is not a challenge, unless the baby is judged for not wanting to be passed to strangers or the toddler is told they need to smile more. Even at a very young age, these children want to be their own authority. As soon as they start attempting to communicate with you, they will express that they want to do things themselves. You can see this as an opportunity, rather than a challenge.

♡ **Child Whisperer Tip:** Offer your Type 4 baby structure with eating and sleeping schedules. Too much noise all the time can be very stressful for them, as their inner stillness requires periods of each day to be in a quiet environment. You may even find these babies enjoy lying in their cribs for a short period of time after they wake up from a nap, just to enjoy some solitude.

Above All, Remember Movement!

- Type 1 energy moves upward and outward.
- Type 2 energy moves downward in a steady flow.
- Type 3 energy moves forward with a push.
- Type 4 energy remains constant, still, and reflective.

Knowing your baby or toddler's true nature even before they can speak is a great gift to you as a parent, and it is a gift that you also give your child. It offers you a huge window of insight into your unique parent-child relationship. Your Child Whisperer skills give you an intuitive advantage to make decisions on behalf of your child in order to support them in feeling safe, loved, and cared for properly in a world that they are just getting to know!

You may have some thoughts or feelings about which Type your child is. What do you notice or remember about your child's experience as a toddler? Take a moment to jot down your insights, or a few experiences you remember about how they moved, what they did, or what they said that might indicate your child's Energy Type. In the next section, I'll share some added tips to help you identify your child's Type.

Which Type is My Child?

Now that you have learned about all 4 Types of children, it's time to identify which Type matches up with your child's natural expression. When you know that, you will take another major step toward becoming a Child Whisperer. Like I said before, your child may express all 4 Types, but they will lead with one dominant Energy Type.

If you feel unsure of your child's Type, I offer you the following supportive questions and tips to help you identify what your child is trying to tell you about their true nature.

How Do They Move Through Life?

You can better understand your children by observing the way they move through everyday activities. The little, unedited moments of daily life will help you see their Type more clearly. How does your child get ready for school? How does he clean his room? How does she play with friends?

- *Type 1*: Unstructured and more carefree, finding delight in simple pleasures. The key words to remember here are *random* and *fun-loving*.

- *Type 2*: Steadily and calmly enjoying whatever creates comfort. The key words to remember here are *sensitive* and *gentle*.
- *Type 3*: Focused on the end results with swift determination. The key words to remember here are *determined* and *adventurous*.
- *Type 4*: Straightforwardly, concisely and precisely knowing where they stand with themselves and others. The key words to remember here are *exact* and *particular*.

When you clearly see your child's natural movement, Child Whispering becomes so much easier. Everyday events like bedtime, homework, or chores work out effortlessly because you know how to support your child in moving through the experience in their way.

For example, you will know your Type 4 child will choose to execute their chores in a structured, systematic way. Or you will know your Type 1 child needs to incorporate randomness and fun into studying. No more fights—just an expression of movement that's supported and honored.

What Are They Telling You About Themselves?

Your children tell you exactly who they are and what they need—even in the language they use. Observe the way your child speaks and the words they choose. Do you observe any of these common phrases and words used by your children?

- *Type 1*: They might light-mindedly make fun of someone, then quickly say, "Just kidding!" When they like something, they say, "That is so fun!" They giggle often.

- *Type 2*: They may apologize more than necessary. Before asking a question, they announce it: "I have a question." Adults often ask them to speak up.
- *Type 3*: They speak directly and abruptly. When they feel someone is taking too long to explain, they lose interest and interrupt. They talk loudly and are told to shush.
- *Type 4*: Their favorite phrase when agreeing is "Exactly!" To describe something they like, they often say, "Perfect." Things they dislike are usually "stupid."

An understanding of your child's natural speech patterns is such a handy Child Whisperer tool! When you know your child's Type, you won't waste time trying to change your child's speech to be louder or quieter or somehow different than it naturally is. Instead, you can see your verbal interaction with your children as an opportunity to understand their expression and the intent behind their words. Your children will feel heard and validated when they talk with you—which leads to greater cooperation, trust, and better relationships.

What Do Other People Tell You About Your Child?

We tell each other every day what we think of others' natures—both positive and negative. The commands and judgments we give children are often the most telling peek into their true selves. What are your children told at home, at school, or at play that shuts them down or builds them up?

- *Type 1*: Stop moving. You're such a busy little kid. You never sit still. You are too hyper, too bouncy. You live in a dream world. Settle down. *On the positive side:* You are so fun to be around! You make friends so easily. You are such a bright light!

- *Type 2*: You're shy. You are too sensitive. Hurry up, you take too long. You ask too many questions. Speak up. You're always awkward around new people. *On the positive side:* You are so nice and kind. You are sweet. You are so easy to get along with. You are so sensitive to others.

- *Type 3*: You are too demanding. You're too pushy. You are such a tomboy. You need to be more ladylike. You are too rough. Calm down, relax. *On the positive side:* You get things done so quickly. You're a natural leader. What a great athlete! You always know just what you want and go for it!

- *Type 4*: You need to be more social. You are such a loner. You are such a quiet little kid. You need to make more friends. You are so picky. You are so critical. You're a know-it-all. You are too serious. You need to smile more. *On the positive side:* You act so grown up and mature. Everybody knows where you stand on an issue. You are so independent. You are so responsible. You are so polite. You are very trustworthy.

To become a true Child Whisperer, you need to give up negative labels. It's one of the most powerful things you can do to support your child. Every time a child hears one of these judgments, they trust their true nature a little less. You remember the judgments you heard about yourself as a child and the damage they caused. Do not subject any child to that sort of wounding and worry! When you truly stop seeing your children's tendencies through eyes of judgment, they will feel the change and respond in positive ways you cannot yet anticipate.

. . . .

ELIZABETH'S STORY
Rockclimbing With Two Types

Elizabeth took her two daughters rock climbing at an indoor gym. Neither her Type 1 nor her Type 2 daughter had ever gone rock climbing before. They wanted her to show them first, so she climbed up.

Then it was her Type 1 daughter's turn. Elizabeth called down that it was fun and exciting and her daughter climbed up immediately.

But her Type 2 10-year-old felt scared and didn't want to climb. Elizabeth stood there saying, "It's fun! You'll love it!" when it suddenly hit her—this wouldn't work for a Type 2 who felt nervous! She immediately changed her language and told her daughter to take her time, to make sure she was comfortable, and to ask her mom for whatever she needed to support her. She used the word "comfortable" several times. And guess what? Her daughter didn't need any more convincing. That beautiful Type 2 girl started to climb.

Both daughters felt empowered and confident because they went about the activity in the way they needed to, not in the way that their mother wanted them to. Parents the world over experience small victories like this in their families every day because they use what they know about their children's Types and act on the inspiration that comes because of it.

. . . .

What Does Your Child Think?

You might have a good idea of your child's dominant Energy Type. But what does your child think? If your child is old enough to have a conversation with you about the 4 Types, I recommend that you have a conversation with your child to hear what they think about their dominant and secondary Energy Type. Even if you're still wondering, they may already know for themselves.

Always frame this kind of conversation in terms of wanting to help your child to be happy and understood. Present the information in an age-appropriate way. Tell them you want to understand them better so you can help them be happy. Children respond positively to parents who genuinely want to help them live true to their nature.

How to Identify Your Child's Secondary Energy Type

While there are 4 Energy Types, your child is entirely unique. Your child will naturally lead with a dominant Energy Type, but your child's secondary Type will influence natural movement and behavior. Sometimes, understanding how secondary Types show up can help you identify your child's dominant Energy Type, which you should do first before spending a lot of time considering a secondary Type.

Here are some pointers to help you recognize your child's secondary Type, and some phrases you can use to support them in living true to their nature.

Secondary Type 1 Energy

What to look for: A child with a secondary Type 1 nature will express a cuteness, a sparkle, or playfulness about them at times. It's not their primary expression—just an added animation in their dominant Type. In family gatherings, they might try to lighten the mood or make you laugh. Support them in keeping things light.

Phrases to support them:
- Thank you for wanting to make sure I'm happy; I know how important that is to you.

- I appreciate your happy nature. It's safe to be who you are.

Secondary Type 2 Energy

What to look for: A child with a secondary Type 2 nature will express a gentle quality to them that softens and adds sensitivity to their dominant Type. Recognize their emotional awareness of others and their desire for others' feelings to not be hurt.

Phrases to support them:
- Thank you for your sensitivity, and how you care so much about others.
- Thank you for noticing when someone's feelings are hurt and caring for them.

Secondary Type 3 Energy

What to look for: A child with a secondary Type 3 nature will express more orientation to wanting results, with a bit of a push that backs up their dominant Type. They like to take on challenges—not in the same, head-on way as a dominant Type 3. You need to help them realize they don't need to get results in order to have value, especially if this is not their primary Energy Type. Don't let them depend on their secondary too much to get recognition.

Phrases to support them:
- I love how you can take action so quickly when you've made the right decision.
- Results are secondary to your being. You don't have to do anything to be loved.

Secondary Type 4 Energy

What to look for: A child with a secondary Type 4 nature will express an ability to step back and look at the big picture with a keen eye. You'll also notice their ability for perfecting the world around them—but to a lesser degree than a dominant Type 4. Support them in enjoying what is already created and experienced and fulfilled right now.

Phrases to support them:
- You have such a gift for seeing the bigger picture. Thank you for sharing that.
- I love how you want things to become better and more beautiful for people.

Which of these explanations speak to your experience with your child? Making a few notes here may help those insights become clear. What have you noticed that may help you identify your child's secondary Type?

_____

_____

_____

_____

As a parent, you have a responsibility to support your child in understanding and living true to their nature. While Energy Profiling is interesting, support for your child should be your number one priority as you identify your child's dominant and secondary Energy Type. As a parent, you should always strive to communicate to your child that he or she is perfect just the way they are.

We Need All 4 Types in This World!

We need the upbeat energy and optimism that come so easily to Type 1 children. We need the sensitivity and calming that Type 2 children share so willingly. We need the determination and adventurous spirit of Type 3 children. And we need the quiet loyalty and strength of purpose that Type 4 children live by. No one Type is better than the other. In fact, if we were missing one, this world would be incomplete.

As you determine your child's Energy Profile, consider the possibility that any of your child's perceived flaws or shortcomings that get on your nerves may actually be their greatest gifts! When you identify your child's natural movement by determining their Type, you will also learn how to encourage those traits in your children. Your change in perception will empower them to develop their natural tendencies into obvious strengths. One day, you'll notice that your relationship with your child is full of greater peace and mutual respect than you even dreamed it could be. And that's when you'll know: You really *are* a Child Whisperer.

The 4 Types of Parents:
Motivations, Challenges, and Tips

Let's take a moment to talk about *you*.

After all, you're becoming a Child Whisperer. A moment of self-reflection will be supportive to you in becoming the best Child Whisperer you can be.

Just as your child expresses a dominant Energy Type, so do you. Maybe you already knew your Energy Type before picking up this book. Or you discovered it during your reading. Or maybe you're still not sure about your Energy Type. Wherever you are in your own journey to self-discovery, these explanations of the 4 Types of parents can help you better understand your own unique interaction with your child.

You express all 4 Types to some degree. But certain motivations are more dominant for certain Types of parents. When our children aren't the same Type as we are, we can be counterproductive and wound our children because we're not separating our nature from our parenting approach, or because we're not living true to our own nature. In order to become a Child Whisperer, you need to live true to your own nature. If you are not, it can be challenging to see and support your child's true nature. Your own childhood wounds may be getting in the way of allowing your child to live their truth.

We need to understand ourselves clearly enough that we can step back and ask ourselves, "How do my children need me to show up in a way that's true to them?"

Important! One last thing before you read up on the 4 Types of parents. Parents tend to be their own worst critics. They see where they fall short, rather than where they succeed. Even parents who are not Type 4s see their flaws so keenly! While you read these descriptions, focus on remaining in an energy of love, both for yourself and for your child.

The Type 1 Parent

Parenting Priorities: For an upward, light Type 1 parent, making sure their children are happy and having fun is really important to them. They love having all their family together, enjoying each other's company, having fun and laughing together. They check in on their children with the intent to ensure they are happy. When their children are stressed or having problems, they want to make things lighter and easier for them.

Their Concern: These parents might worry that their random nature makes them inadequate in some way. They may experience anxiety or frustration over things they did not follow through on. They may judge their success as a parent by standards that are not true to their upward, light nature—like how much structure they can maintain, how much they get done as a parent, and how efficient a household they run. If this is the case, they will always feel like they are falling short and are ineffective parents. They may blame themselves if their child is unhappy.

♡ **Child Whisperer Tip for Inspiration:** Let go of anything that brings you down. Use this affirmation: "I am consistent in all the things that really matter. I am trusting that everything else takes care of itself." Change your standards of success to ones that match your nature, like, "How happy are my children?" "How much fun are we having together?" "How much hope and positive energy do I add to their lives?" Getting things done is always going to happen—after all, you are a parent. Just don't make it your standard of measurement for being a great parent!

Remember to keep your energy light, but do not insist that your children need to be light with you. For example, Type 2 and 4 children may be hurt or offended when their Type 1 parent makes light of their worries and concerns. Even though the Type 1 parent is just trying to lighten things up, the energy does not match their child's nature and the child may misunderstand. You don't have to be serious in order to show that you care, but you don't have to insist that your children look on the bright side as quickly as you naturally do.

Tip for taking care of yourself and your nature: If you are a Type 1 parent, do what you need and want to in order to keep things light for yourself. What do you have in your life to look forward to that's just for you? You can't channel your gift of light and hope to others if you're not taking care of yourself.

The Type 2 Parent

Parenting Priorities: More emotionally oriented, the Type 2 parent focuses on helping children feel comfortable. They are sensitive to the emotional atmosphere of their home and the emotional state of their children. They check in emotionally with their children to make sure that everyone is feeling comfortable. They want to create a safe place for their children.

Their Concern: These emotionally connected parents are the most natural worriers of the bunch, about any possible detail. They may try to prevent their child's potentially bad choices or any uncomfortable confrontations between family members.

⌒ **Child Whisperer Tip for Inspiration**: Get in connection with your inner peace using the visualization of a river. Let worries about your children float down that river, instead of trying to stop them. Whatever you do as a parent, allow it to come from a feeling place. Connect with your children from the heart, no matter your child's Type. Instead of worrying, trust your heart!

⌒ **Tip for taking care of yourself and your nature**: Do things that help you connect with what's comfortable in your life. Don't take emotional responsibility for everyone else's stuff. Because you are so emotionally tuned in to what is happening with your children, you may pick up the negative energies of everyone in the family. If you do this, your energy can feel like mud to your Type 1 or Type 3 children. Send your love to your children, but don't smother them with it.

The Type 3 Parent

Parenting Priorities: More physically active, Type 3 parents focus on engaging children in activity. They give the family a forward push to get things done and experience the physical aspect of life. They often look around to make sure that their children have enough to do. They move fast and want their family to move fast, too.

Their Concern These active, dynamic parents can potentially overreact. They may worry in hindsight that their fiery energy affects their children in negative ways. They may move too fast for their children or push too hard. The best way to work with this is to own it and give your children opportunities to voice their concerns and frustrations.

⌒ **Child Whisperer Tip for Inspiration:** Practice being still for a few moments each day in order to avoid using "doings" as your measurement of success—both for yourself and your child. Do whatever you need to in order to stay in touch with your physical body. Notice how much you may push your children in ways that may be overwhelming and stressful to their nature if they are different from yours. Be mindful when you are getting ready to leave the house, and also when you are out and about, not to hurry your children faster than is natural for them. You move at a quicker pace on your own, so when you are with your children make some adjustments to honor all of you.

⌒ **Tip for taking care of yourself and your nature:** Create space in your life to get a lot done without rushing your child. If you are a Type 3 parent, you will get frustrated if you are not able to move a lot of things forward. Consider hiring a parents' helper—a teenager in the neighborhood or someone similar—to come into your house and entertain your children to give you some time to get things done. You don't even need to leave the house, but you will appreciate the extra hands. As a Type 3, you will be a better parent when you feel you got some things done and then can relate to your child at their energy level.

The Type 4 Parent

Parenting Priorities: Structured and good at running very efficient households, Type 4 parents focus most readily on their children's progress. They create routines and systems in their home that keep everyone on track. They regularly check up on how their children are progressing.

Their Concern: These naturally organized parents can get lost in rules and sequences. They may worry about missing out on spontaneous moments with their children, simply because they are not built into the system.

⌒ **Child Whisperer Tip for Inspiration:** Allow more spontaneity into your life, rather than trying to always keep everything running on track and in the timelines that you want. Don't let your logical mind override your intuitive mind. Allow some room for synchronicity, even if this openness is something you need to consciously plan. Enjoy the journey. Your mind is so sharply focused on what to improve that you may pass by the moment of fulfillment that's being offered. Recognize your current successes!

⌒ **Tip for taking care of yourself and your nature:** Create standards of measurement that fit your child's nature. If you are a Type 4, you parent with deep commitment and strong values. You want to be the best parent. You may end up criticizing yourself as a parent too much if your standards for your children are not aligned with who they truly are. Energy Profiling will help you align your standards with your children's gifts so you can assess their progress more accurately.

Parenting True to Both Your Natures

Raising a child true to their nature and staying true to your own nature in your parenting style is a daily balancing act. You are not meant to abandon what is natural for you in who you are as a parent. As a Child Whisperer, you learn to take each day at a time and follow your intuition in knowing when you need to accommodate your child's nature over yours and when you need to be true to yourself and have your children support you. As you hold the intention that everyone will be honored in the process of your daily family life, that is what you will experience.

It is also important to let go of your negative judgments about yourself as a parent. Commit to becoming a better parent by living true to your nature and managing your natural tendencies. Look at the natural dynamic of your relationship with your child through the lens of both of your Types. How and when are you pushing each other's buttons? Now that you know this information, how will things change?

Write some of your thoughts and inspiration here:

_____

_____

_____

_____

Popular Parenting Approaches That Do Not Work for All Types of Children

The truth is, most classic parenting approaches don't work for a lot of children. In this book so far, you've already explored some of the reasons why each child is unique. So you understand now why a one-size-fits-all approach would just create frustration, both for children *and* for parents. Some popular parenting approaches lead to more focus on discipline and disciplinary tactics than we actually need in order to raise our children.

Together, let's reexamine some common disciplinary tactics and parenting beliefs that many parents incorporate into their parenting. You are becoming a Child Whisperer. So consider the possibility that some of the tactics you are using are not serving your child. Consider the even greater possibility that when you honor both yourself and your child, parenting will naturally become a more cooperative, enjoyable experience for you both, which means that you'll have less need overall to discipline your child.

Common Disciplinary Tactics

Before we look at specific discipline tactics, let's consider where the need for discipline even comes from.

Most parents are drawn to a parenting approach that's consistent with their own true nature, rather than their child's. They're just naturally drawn to something that appeals to them personally. This is understandable. However, children resist parenting styles that move contrary to their natural expression. Parents often interpret their resistance as disobedience, defiance, or rebellion; then, a parent responds with disciplinary measures to try and eliminate the negative reaction.

Discipline is Judgment

In a way, discipline is judgment. We discipline in order to change a movement, a tendency, a reaction. In other words, on some level, parents discipline their children in order to change who they are. Our children might submit in the short-term to discipline that tries to change them, but they will not respond positively in the long run. And discipline that works contrary to their nature will not ultimately help them live more true to their nature as adults.

When you mindfully honor your child's true nature, discipline actually takes on an entirely new look because it's supportive to your child, rather than punitive. How you choose to correct your child actually works in tandem with who they really are. In turn, your children become naturally more cooperative and responsive to your guidance. I really believe that if you consciously manage your own tendencies and work with your child's true nature in a way that honors them, you will actually eliminate a huge amount of need for discipline in your home.

Take a look with me at the practical application of how to shape (or discard) certain kinds of discipline for each Type of child:

Time Out
Time Out is a go-to tactic for many parents. And it gets the job done in many ways: It removes a child from a high-stress

situation, and it feels like a solution when a child's reaction seems inappropriate or out of control. Unfortunately, it can also lead to greater frustration and struggle. Consider the possibility that time-out may not be an effective measure for your child, or that in order to maintain a strong connection with your child, you may need to modify the way it is implemented

Type 1 in Time Out: A long, solitary time-out for the Type 1 child feels like a day of torture. Given their high energy, they're not likely to just sit still anyway. You may find yourself in a pattern of struggle that every time they get out of time out, you add minutes to the clock, but it just gets dragged out so long that you don't want to do it anymore. You get frustrated and your child feels weighed down and confined, which makes them even more frustrating to deal with.

Child Whisperer Tip: Time out is not a good option for a Type 1 child. Making the connection between what they did wrong and being confined in a chair doesn't make sense to them, and the imposed structure just makes them more boisterous than they were before. If your Type 1 child is out of control and you simply need them to bring down the energy level (for a good reason—not just for your own convenience), consider distracting them with something fun. If they are resisting a request you've made, try turning cooperation into a game. **Consider whether or not your child is out of control because they feel overly controlled.** If you take care of the root of the problem, the perceived need for time out may actually disappear. If they have hurt another child, solitary time out still may not be the best option, as it removes them from the social context where they can make amends.

Type 2 in Time Out: These children will often comply quickly if threatened with time out. If sent to time out, they will usually sit quietly. But if you send a Type 2 child to time out, you run the risk of making them feel emotionally disconnected from or rejected by their parents. This is a terrifying feeling for these children. On the outside, they may look very compliant; but on the inside, they may turn inward and try to disconnect from you because they feel rejected or emotionally unsafe. This is not the emotional place you want your Type 2 child to be.

> ♡ **Child Whisperer Tip:** If you need to remove a Type 2 child from a situation where they are whining or acting out of control in any way, go with them. Ask them to tell you how they are feeling and how you can help them to feel better. Their acting out is a signal to you that they need you to ask this question. They often calm down when they are invited to express how they feel.
>
> Yes, this may take more time than just sending them to time out alone, but it will be more effective in the long run. **You will teach your child that they can speak up to have their needs met,** and their whining or moodiness will naturally decrease because of it.

Type 3 in Time Out: Time out will make these children feel stopped or thwarted from their current goal, which is one of the worst experiences for these driven, determined children. When they are asked to sit still in one place with no obvious purpose, they just end up feeling frustrated. Without any place or action for that frustration to go, they may express their energy in explosive anger or become physically destructive to the place where they are sent to time out.

🌙 **Child Whisperer Tip:** Time out is just not a good option for these children. They won't see the purpose in it (even if you explain that the purpose is to think about what they've done). **They relate to the world physically and so any reason you give for sitting still will not resonate with them.** Rather than time-out, give them a motivating challenge, a project, or a job. It can be something they're asked to do as a consequence for some way that they've disobeyed. Whatever you do, allow your Type 3 to have a result from it, and respond to their result by expressing, "Wow, that is impressive. Look at what you did!"

Type 4 in Time Out: With their still, reflective nature, Type 4 children have a lower movement. If you send a Type 4 to time out, especially if it's in their room where they can do things that they choose, it may actually feel like a reward—unless, of course, you've made the announcement of time out public to their siblings or friends. In that case, they will spend every minute in time out focusing intently on how small you've made them feel.

🌙 **Child Whisperer Tip:** If your Type 4 child is acting up, consider the possibility that they feel too scattered and they need to center themselves. Get them into a single, linear activity and they will usually calm down a bit. For example, when my son Mark was too wired up and stressed out, I would have him do an activity that required a lot of his focus. It worked like a charm to help him get centered and balanced again.

If you need to remove your Type 4 child from a situation, do it without drawing attention to them. **When you show respect for your child's need for privacy, they will more likely respect the form of discipline you choose.**

Time out might actually be appropriate as a relief, but you should leave the situation with your child and then speak with them privately to get their input on whether or not they need some time alone. Communicate that time alone is meant to support and not shame them.

Revoking Privileges

Some parents tell their children that unless they behave in a certain way, they won't be able to attend a birthday party, or play video games, or drive the car. These sorts of consequences are useful, but may backfire if used in the wrong way with the wrong Type of child—especially if your child has not been informed that their privileges will be revoked for misbehavior and you choose to revoke them on a whim as a response to your frustration and anger. If you choose to revoke privileges, always communicate that information well before misbehavior happens.

Type 1 Privileges: A Type 1 child may not make the same connection between the two events (their mistake and the privilege taken away) and only see that you're shutting down their fun. If shutting down their fun is exactly what you want to do when your child has disobeyed, consider the possibility that you are choosing your method of discipline based on your own desire to get back at your child or show them who's boss. You can more effectively correct your Type 1 child if you keep things light for them. When your child is young, this might look like playing peek-a-boo in order to get their attention off something they shouldn't do. As they age, this might mean just using a tone of voice that seems happier, rather than taking discipline so seriously.

Type 2 Privileges: A Type 2 child may become extremely emotional about missing out on something they had planned. They have already thought through the details of upcoming events and will struggle with their future plan being taken away because of something they did in the past. If you truly feel you need to revoke a privilege for something your Type 2 child has done, take a bit of extra time to sit and talk it through with them. Allow them the time to process the details and create a new plan in their mind. Otherwise, your child may feel they cannot count on the plans they make because those plans may be taken away at short notice. This puts a Type 2 child in a stressful state.

Type 3 Privileges: If you revoke the privilege to do a certain thing, your Type 3 child may go ahead and do that thing anyway. This can lead to taking away more privileges. You will just create a cycle of getting in your child's way and stopping them, which will lead to reactive outbursts from them and frustration for you both. Instead of taking things away, give your Type 3 child activities to do. They could agree to do certain extra tasks around the house when they have been disobedient to rules in your home.

Type 4 Privileges: If you take away a privilege you have already promised to a Type 4, they will find it terribly unfair. And they may have a bold reaction to the news. You can take away privileges with a Type 4 child, but do not do so arbitrarily or from a position of absolute authority. Talk together with them to establish the rules and the consequences. They will accept the consequences of their behavior more readily if they are involved in the initial conversation to decide what those consequences are.

Handling Tantrums in Public

You've seen that child in the grocery story (perhaps your own at one point) who has obviously gone into meltdown mode. Screaming, flailing, tears, you name it. Parents try everything—

ignoring their child, shushing them, leaving the store. As you put your Child Whisperer skills to use, you will experience fewer episodes like these. Just in case you experience one again, consider the following:

Type 1 Tantrums: Put simply, the fun-loving child is not having fun. Perhaps you've been running errands all day. Or this trip to the store is just too structured and confining. If your child has already reached a place of being out of control, do not try to control them more or contain their energy. Stop what you are doing and focus on creating a fun experience in that very moment. This will look like different things in different places. Be your child's Child Whisperer and listen to your inspiration.

Type 2 Tantrums: The sensitive child will not usually throw loud tantrums, but they may become weepy or whiny. This is a cue for you that they are feeling overwhelmed, that their plan has been disrupted, or they are not feeling heard, or they are just plain tired and need the comfort of their home. The minute you get down on their level and tell them you want to hear how they feel, they will usually respond in a way that resolves the tantrum. Listen and respond in an inspired, child-whisperer way.

Type 3 Tantrums: The determined child is just plain determined to do something else. Their tantrum in a public place is just an outward attempt to move on to other things. Depending on your child's age, you might turn your current errand into a challenge. Alternatively, ask them what they really want to do and then promise to help them make it happen as soon as they help you finish the errand that you're on. They will jump in to help you achieve that result.

Type 4 Tantrums: The more serious child may need a moment of solitude to center themselves if you've been out all day. No matter how many errands you run, your child needs a say in the schedule of their day. Before you ever leave the house, have a conversation about what both of you expect from your day. Take their own hopes into account as you explain the bigger picture of what they can expect.

Spanking

Spanking is not the dominant disciplinary tactic used at the time of this writing. It is not necessary to talk about how each of the four Types respond to spanking as most do not respond well.

Of all the Types, Type 3 children may respond to a little spank, as it may be the most direct and swift message they need to get their attention before they dart off into the street or take on a challenge that is not safe and appropriate for their age. It is a physical message that distracts them from doing something physically unsafe. Be very direct in saying, "Mommy or Daddy spanked you because what you were about to do was very dangerous and not safe, and I love you enough to make sure you are always safe."

In other situations and for other Types of children, this message will not be as effective. You may try and go about spanking as a punishment in a logical way by explaining to your child why you are doing it, but it does not have the intended effect you may try to achieve. Regardless of what you say, the message your child may hear is that their parent struck them in an attempt to get them to comply or submit. That is damaging for a child and makes them feel flawed. It is simply not effective, nor is it appropriate, to systematically strike your child in order to get them to comply with your wishes.

Discipline in General

In some of these cases, you may be thinking, "So that tactic is seen as a punishment for my child—isn't punishment what I *want* to be doing?" Perhaps. But *consider what you want your end result to be*.

If you want to punish your child, to make them feel bad or belittled for something they did, then one of the tactics above can do that, depending on your child's Type. However, if your goal is cooperation, understanding, and mutual respect, then you need to forget about punishment and focus on Child Whispering.

You may think that discipline is supposed to be a painful punishment. But discipline at its best is educational, instructional, inspiring, and motivating. It's an opportunity to teach. Consider whether or not you approach discipline this way and why, as well as why you wouldn't.

Remember, you may have been punishing your child for behaviors and tendencies that are true to their nature, which only sends them the message, "It is not okay to be you. Who you are is upsetting to people!" This is critically important: Being parented contrary to our nature is the number one reason the self-help industry is booming. So many wounded adults in the world were sent the message as children that it wasn't okay to live true to their nature, so they created personality traits and beliefs about themselves consistent with that message.

Is your child's "bad" behavior an attempt to get your attention or send you a message? Is the "bad" behavior just a difference in your movement, or an attempt on their part to get more of the kind of movement they need? Is their "bad" behavior a negative reaction to feeling controlled or shut down? There are so many more possibilities open for you to explore when you know your child's nature. If you focus on the end result that I assume you want (cooperation, understanding, connection, and respect), you can consider other ways to guide and correct your child's behavior.

Type 1 Discipline: Type 1 children want to see a smile on others' faces, so keep whatever discipline you have for them light. Never keep things too serious with them or yell at them. They'll just disconnect and won't get the point you want to make with them anyway. Always approach them with a light manner.

Type 2 Discipline: Talk in terms of emotion. Speak gently to your Type 2 child. They do not want to upset you or let you down and may have a strong reaction if you give them a single look of disappointment. They are sensitive, so never be severe or aggressive with them or they will break down or withdraw. Use a few more words with them to reassure them of where they stand with you.

Type 3 Discipline: Be direct and to the point, and mete out any discipline as something they can do. These children can be very reactive and may draw a strong reaction from you—stay calm! Give your child a meaningful activity to redirect them and try to give them opportunities and appropriate ways to express themselves. If you push them, they will push back, so make sure your disciplinary approach is one that is clear and direct.

Type 4 Discipline: Connect at the head and use logic and reason. Explain why they should or should not do certain things. Allow them to decide on their own consequence together with you—with their high standard, they might choose something with a higher standard than you would. Do not discipline your Type 4 child in front of others. And never mock them, even if you are teasing in an attempt to lighten them up.

Parenting Myths and Milestones

Parents also run up against an army of opinion and cultural assumptions, telling them what children need to do and how they are supposed to be. Let's look at some commonly held parenting beliefs in our society. These beliefs lead to fights and struggles that parents have every day, and they just don't need to anymore. As a Child Whisperer, you can rethink them and try something better.

Sharing

We want our children to be gracious and generous. In an attempt to help children interact with others, parents often tell their children to share. Sharing is tricky territory because sharing toys in every instance is not always supportive to your child. Before you ask your child to share their toys again, consider why you are doing so. Do you want your child to be accepted as the nice child? Do you want to look like a good parent? Is your request truly supportive to your child's development?

Type 1 Sharing: Type 1 children are the most likely to adapt to others. They want others to be happy, so they are generally willing to share and they disconnect quickly if another child takes their toy. They share pretty easily if you reassure them that they can play with the toy again later.

Type 2 Sharing: Type 2 children do not naturally tend to speak up for what they want or need. If they don't want to share a toy, or a toy was taken from them, support your child in feeling heard in social experiences.

Type 3 Sharing: Type 3 children will just go for what they want, not realizing they are plowing over other children or taking toys from them. Consider helping your child see working together with other children as a goal. How can they work together with the toys and each other? Perhaps they could build a tower together or have a race. The focus will be diverted from sharing and move to an end result.

Type 4 Sharing: This discussion of sharing is probably most important for parents of Type 4 children. They are selective about the people they allow to share their things—not because they are greedy, but because they care for their possessions in certain ways and they worry that someone else might not take the same kind of care with them. These children are sometimes judged as stingy or territorial when they really are just worrying that others won't handle their possessions properly.

♡ **Child Whisperer Tip:** These children need to know there are certain things that nobody touches—not even Mom or Dad. Let your child mark them. For example, my Type 4 grandson, Seth, has a labeled box under his bed of certain toys that are just "Seth's Specials." Even Seth's siblings know they are not to get into them without his permission. Explain to your child that they probably shouldn't take those special toys to the park or a friend's house because other children will want to play with them and they don't want to have to waste their time guarding their very favorite items.

Eating Vegetables

How many bites until your child gets dessert? This fight around the dinner table can set children up for unhealthy eating patterns later in life. You obviously want them to eat healthy foods, but consider the possibility that there's another way to do it, true to their nature.

Type 1 Vegetables: Type 1 children may not like to eat their vegetables because those foods are not often portrayed as fun foods. The structure of your meal may also give dessert a celebratory feel, while the rest of dinner feels structured and planned. Does dessert get the fun-food title in your house?

♡ **Child Whisperer Tip:** Consider making vegetables into fun food, just like every other food on their plate. Don't demand a certain number of bites or a structured set of rules for earning treats. Type 1 children have a random nature, so you can give them a random mix of food. If they have dessert served right along with their meal, they will be able to take random bites of both and be more likely to see all foods as equal resources that they can manage wisely. Also, let them have some fun preparing the healthier foods. There are a lot of resources online showing examples of how to make vegetables fun by making them into pictures and shapes along with fun recipes to try out with your Type 1.

Type 2 Vegetables: Type 2 children want to eat food that makes them feel comforted or cozy. They tend to stick to foods they feel comfortable with and don't like to feel put on the spot to try something new that they are not prepared for. They also have sensitive palates and constitutions that are more likely to react to strong or spicy foods. Pushing them too hard to eat certain foods can influence them to become emotional eaters later in life.

♡ **Child Whisperer Tip:** Allow your Type 2 child to try new foods at their own pace, even if it is slower than you would like. Let them return often to foods that feel comforting. Tell them you would like to help them feel comfortable to try new foods and ask if they would like to help you plan or prepare some new dishes. Teach them why eating healthy foods is good for them. These extra details will encourage healthy eating.

Type 3 Vegetables: Type 3 children eat fast and they're done. They want the result of having eaten swiftly and being finished. They also like variety in their food, so eating the same thing over and over is not supportive to them.

♡ **Child Whisperer Tip:** Let them make food into a challenge. How many new foods can they eat? Ask them what new foods they'd like to try and then prepare them. Type 3 children can sit at the table and eat their food with the family, but do not demand that they stay at the table for a long period of time, waiting for everyone else. If you want them to be with the family, perhaps they could be in charge of starting to clear the table when they finish.

Type 4 Vegetables: Type 4 children do not need much variety in what they eat. Their tendency toward repetition starts to show up in their eating patterns around three to six years old. They tend to want to eat a few things over and over again. For this reason, parents tend to label them "picky eaters."

♡ **Child Whisperer Tip:** If your Type 4 child has the same pattern of only eating a small list of items, make sure there are some healthy choices on that list and don't worry about their limited menu plan!

Giving Up Blankets and Pacifiers
This is a big one. How old is too old for a child to use a

pacifier or carry around their security blanket? Given everything you've learned in this book, you may assume (correctly) that it depends on your child's Type.

Type 1 Security Items: These children disconnect and connect. So they will be unattached to security items and then attached again. They might feel like they're ready to give up a blanket and then they'll want it back. Give them the opportunity for some randomness by putting their pacifier or other item in a place where you can get it again when they need to feel a little connection. Then put it away when they disconnect again. They may just end up forgetting about it.

Type 2 Security Items: Of all the Types, these children have the hardest time letting that blankie go. They are highly connected to items that root them in the past and help them feel comfortable. When these items are taken away without preparation or their consent, they perceive the event as trauma. It will be particularly painful for Type 2 girls who are especially tender.

. . . .

ANNE'S STORY
Her Blanket

When my Type 2 daughter Anne was born, our women's church group gifted me with a blanket for her. She loved her blanket and as she grew through all the stages of her developing years, her blanket remained very precious and important to her. As a toddler she carried it around, and as she grew into her school-age years, she slept with it every night. If she spent the night at grandma's or a close friend's, it always went with her. As a Type 3 mom, I guess I was too busy to even think about taking it away from her, because I never even considered it. By the time she was a young adult, her blanket was very worn and thin, but she still loved it. When Anne went off to college, her blanket did too.

When Anne was 21 years old, she decided to spend 18 months doing volunteer work in Bulgaria—and her blanket went with her. Just a couple weeks after her departure, I received a package in the mail. Inside was her blanket with a note, which said, "Mom, please take care of my blanket. I don't want anything to happen to it, so I am sending it home for you to take care of until I return." You can imagine my tears. At this point in my daughter's life, I now had knowledge of her gentle nature and need for comfort and security. I was honored to be the caretaker of her blanket until she returned home.

We joked that when it came time for Anne to get married, she should wear her blanket as her veil! She is married now and has her blanket. Since her husband is her new security blanket that she sleeps with, she stores her blankie in a safe place to have the rest of her life.

· · · ·

♡ **Child Whisperer Tip:** Allow your Type 2 child to hold onto their security items. If allowed, your Type 2 child may keep and cherish their blanket or favorite stuffed animal until adulthood. When you decide that they need to let go of using certain items in public or they will not be allowed to take those items to school, prepare them in advance. Help them make a plan for what they will do in those situations to feel comfortable without their item.

Type 3 Security Items: These children are so busy that they probably won't care or notice. In fact, taking a special blanket from them probably won't even be an issue because they won't have one.

♡ **Child Whisperer Tip:** If your Type 3 child does happen to have a security item, turn the experience of giving it up into a practical and direct one. Consider the possibility that you are actually more attached to certain items than your child is.

Type 4 Security Items: Type 4 children may hold onto security items out of repetition and habit. These children look at adults for cues and then try to duplicate what they do. They will realize that nobody's carrying around blankets and they won't want to, either.

♡ **Child Whisperer Tip:** If your child does not naturally let go of their security item in order to be more grown up, do not take it from them without letting them in on the conversation. Point out, logically, that grown kids and adults don't use pacifiers or blankets and they will make the decision on their own. Once they're committed to letting the item go, they generally won't go back.

Testing Your Boundaries

This is a common myth about children—that they will test your boundaries to find where your limits are or "what they can get away with." This creates an adversarial sort of mindset that does not strengthen your parent-child relationship. If your child is testing anything, they are testing the world to see what it's like and how safe they are to be themselves!

Type 1 Boundaries: Type 1 children just have naturally big energy. They move randomly and with animation. Think of air: it fills any space it enters—so will your Type 1 child. When entering a room, they may bounce around randomly, seeing what fun they can find in it. They are not doing this to test you. They are doing this because it's their nature to do so.

   ♡ **Child Whisperer Tip:** Allow your child space and time to be free. If your child seems to be testing boundaries, take a moment to consider where in their lives they feel confined. Their energy never becomes too big if they have a good balance of spontaneity and fun in their lives.

Type 2 Boundaries: These children want to be appropriate and don't want to disappoint anyone, so they are less likely to look like they are testing boundaries. If anything, they may hang back and feel a bit hesitant to test the boundaries of their world.

   ♡ **Child Whisperer Tip:** Help your child to feel comfortable to try new things and test the boundaries of their world in a manner that's true to their nature. Let your child know that you're on their team and that you will support them as they explore their world and that they can always come back to you in order to feel more comfortable.

Type 3 Boundaries: These children aren't even thinking about your limits. When you do impose boundaries, they just see that you're getting in their way. Of all 4 Types, these are the children that will push against your boundaries the most. Remember that it's not about you; it's about their forward push toward exploration and big results.

◠ **Child Whisperer Tip:** Consider, "Why am I really telling my child no?" Is it because it's more convenient to say no? Less messy? Is it because their desired project is something you're not really interested in? Instead of closing off a boundary, offer your support and allow them to try things on their own. If their desired goal is not age appropriate, help them modify it or divert them to another goal they want just as much.

Type 4 Boundaries: A Type 4 child is not trying to test the parents' boundaries, but simply trying to establish their own. They need space for themselves and authority in their own lives.

◠ **Child Whisperer Tip:** Partner with your Type 4 child in being an authority in their own life. If you focus on giving your child this one thing in all aspects of their life, they will feel respected and will respect you in return.

Terrible Twos (and Terrible Teenagers)

The dreaded Terrible Twos frustrate parents and fill them with dread, but the twos don't need to be terrible at all. At two years old, children have entered the phase of life in which they are sensing, exploring, and doing in the world.

What that looks like for your child may look different than it did for you if you are different Energy Types (or may bring up some similar behaviors and issues if you are the same Type). Let's look at what the Terrible Twos look like for each Type and how you can prevent them.

Terrible Twos for the Type 1: A Type 1 who looks like they have the Terrible Twos will become increasingly cranky and demanding. They may throw frequent tantrums with a high-pitched squeal.

♡ **Child Whisperer Tip:** The Terrible Twos are a symptom of a Type 1 child feeling too restricted, structured, or boxed in. Free them up and you will see them relax.

Terrible Twos for the Type 2: Around this age, these children may become weepy, whiny, or moody.

♡ **Child Whisperer Tip:** An over-expression of emotion is a sign that a Type 2 child does not feel they are safe or invited to share their feelings on a regular basis. They may act out emotionally in an attempt to be heard and feel connected to you. Pick up earlier on their more subtle cues and you will find that their larger breakdowns diminish.

Terrible Twos for the Type 3: I bet the first time someone used the phrase "Terrible Twos," they were talking about a Type 3! I believe the label was created because Type 3 children who are physically oriented to this world are mobile enough when they hit two years old to get their hands on everything—and they have the most natural determination to never give up on going for what they want. These children are not terrible, but the experience of trying to shut down or contain their fiery energy certainly can be! They may become reactive, defiant, or especially loud if they feel they are not being honored or allowed to express their big energy. These children are most likely to receive the "Terrible Twos" label, and it's just not honoring of them.

♡ **Child Whisperer Tip:** Always give them enough physical outlets for their energy. If they are moving forward and being active, they are generally happy. Set up a home environment that allows them to get their hands into things and to explore rather than a home that has many opportunities for them to get into things you don't want them getting into!

Terrible Twos for the Type 4: These children want to be independent, often before children of other Types generally do. You may run into conflict with them if you are unwilling to give them authority in their own life or you make them feel like a baby.

◠ **Child Whisperer Tip:** The more grown up you treat them, the more grown up they will act. Acknowledge their tendency to look to the adults around them to duplicate proper behavior and point out behaviors they may not have noticed that they can duplicate. Never shame them in front of others unless you want to deal with a tantrum.

Teenagers also receive labels that are not supportive to their true nature and they often rebel. But your child's teenage experience can be one of immense success. This topic is big enough that it deserves its own section, which you'll find in the pages that follow.

But first, as you read this section, you probably had ideas of things you might want to try or change at home to help your child become happier and more cooperative. List your ideas and aha's here:

_____

_____

_____

_____

The Real Reason Children Rebel

I have already mentioned the idea that childhood and teenage rebellion are not inevitable experiences for your child. I would like to take that idea one step further and discuss the real reasons behind rebellion and what you can do about it as a Child Whisperer.

Teenage Rebellion

Rebellion happens most dramatically in the teenage years—the time of life when children are working to establish their own identity and individuate from their family. Add to that bodily maturation, hormone changes, self-image development, and the increasing awareness of their place in the larger world. It quickly becomes clear that teens have much to navigate at a pivotal time in their lives.

Rather than support these young people who are transitioning from childhood to adulthood, our society often talks about them like they are nuisances, delinquents, or rebels. The idea of teenage rebellion has just become a given in our current cultural environment. Most people accept it as if it were just something that teenagers do, but have we ever asked this question: What are they rebelling against?

Rebellion is a byproduct of not feeling understood. It's a teen's attempt to live true to themselves. No matter how many times a child is shushed, ignored, shut down, or put on the spot, their inner nature remains constant and longs to be free to express itself. The teenage years are often the time of life when children have enough autonomy to do something about it. If they don't trust themselves or don't feel supported, they may resort to the dysfunction of rebellion. However, if they understand their true nature and feel supported, they can live true to it without rebelling against anything.

Let's take a moment to look at what teenage rebellion might look like for each Type and what you can do if your experience with your child has already reached a rebellious place.

Type 1 Rebellion: Type 1 teenagers will rebel by not taking care of themselves. Patterns of overeating and apathy start to develop in their teen years, as a result of too much structure. Overeating and apathy is a Type 1's subconscious way of saying, "I'll do what I want by eating too much and not do what you want by being apathetic." They may also connect with other teens who are rebellious because they can be accepted for who they are, and be easily influenced by others, due to their adaptable nature.

⌒ **Child Whisperer Tip:** Lighten up on your Type 1 child! Let them feel more breathing room to be themselves. See them as successful, responsible individuals, rather than labeling them as irresponsible.

Type 2 Rebellion: A Type 2 child's nature is to be subtle, so rebellion can look very passive aggressive with the pattern of procrastination included. They will tell you they are going to do something, but then never do it. They will put things off and complain when they are finally forced to do them. They will act very victimized and mope around in a state of sadness.

⌒ **Child Whisperer Tip:** Type 2 teenagers rebel against not feeling emotionally heard. They want you to know about their feelings, but may not know how to communicate them in a healthy way, particularly if they were not supported in doing so as a child. Tell your teen you want to hear about their feelings, even those feelings that they worry are too negative. Explain that you will not support them in becoming a victim, but that you will support them in expressing their emotions and helping them feel comfortable in all the changes going on in their lives. Do not ever say that they are *too* emotional, even when they are not in your presence—your judgment will only add to the problem.

Type 3 Rebellion: The best phrase to describe what rebellion looks like for a Type 3 child is, "Oh yeah, I'll show you!" Type 3s naturally have a reactive nature, so when they are not feeling honored in their teen years, they tend to disregard their parents. When challenged by a parent they feel misunderstands and controls them, they will fight back and get very loud and be willing to argue it out. When they feel pushed, they push back. And they are the most likely to outwardly exhibit their anger.

⌒ **Child Whisperer Tip:** Consider the reason your Type 3 child is fighting you—they are willing to yell and scream, all in an effort to be heard and understood. These strong-willed children need you to believe in them and to give them the trust and support to do their own thing. Remember, these are the hands-on children and they need to see for themselves what results their actions create. Trust that their practical common sense nature will guide them in the right direction for their lives. And express this trust to them personally.

Type 4 Rebellion: Type 4 children are all or nothing. They either love and respect you and are very cooperative, or they feel completely misunderstood, have absolutely no respect and take no regard for you as a parent by the time they are teenagers. These children have very strong wills and will start to tune you out at a very early age if they do not think you recognize them for who they are.

Their rebellion can look very black and white as well. They may turn completely inward, just disconnecting from you and tuning you out, all while working within the system of your home life until the minute they can get out. Or, unfortunately, their tendency for rebellion can go to the boldest extreme of any of the 4 Types. They may run away, move out as soon as they can, or break all your rules in an effort to live by their own rules, even if their rules are destructive and get them into trouble.

After a recent news story reported an unfortunate and tragic incident of two teen boys taking guns to school and shooting other classmates, I was curious about which Type of child would go to such extremes in their behavior. I found a USA Today article that listed the dates of teen shootings that had occurred over the years and the names of the teen boys who carried them out. I did a Google search on each boy to see their facial features and determine their Types, only to discover what I suspected. They were all Type 4s. I believe they had lost control of their sense of reason and respect because they felt so disregarded and disrespected in their personal lives, which often involved personal trauma and stress.

These boys are obviously the most extreme cases, and I am not saying this is an inevitable end for a Type 4 child's teenage rebellion. But these boys' tragic choices do show how strongly a Type 4 may feel or choose to act when they are so deeply wounded. They may resort to dysfunctionally bold actions in order to be seen, heard, and respected.

♡ **Child Whisperer Tip:** At this point in the book, I may sound repetitive. But clear repetition is the nature of a Type 4, so saying this again fits: RESPECTING your Type 4 child's right to be their own authority and partnering with them in that authority is essential to avoiding a rebellious Type 4 teenager.

What a Rebellious Teen is Trying to Say

A rebellious child is a sign of a child fighting to be seen as who they are. They create an extreme behavior they don't really even want in order to live true to themselves. When you honor your child and see them for who they are, they no longer feel the need to rebel.

No matter the age of your child—very young, already-rebellious teen, or adult—you can always approach your child with the intent to honor them. Although a child may seem resistant to you, they are resisting your misunderstanding and lack of respect for their inner nature, not you as their parent. They want your love, your approval, and your respect. If you offer it without strings attached, just with the genuine intent to support them in living true to their nature, they will feel your love and naturally respond.

Force vs. Guidance

In your efforts to not force your child, you might make a

mistake. You may assume that allowing your child to express their true nature means allowing them to do whatever they want. It does not mean doing whatever they ask for fear of wounding their nature. Hearing your child does not mean just going along with them.

When your children are young, you can say, "I hear you, but the answer is still no." You can give your child a choice you are okay with. Then they feel like they have a voice and you can still set boundaries. As your child grows, the boundaries will need to widen and you will need to communicate why some boundaries for behavior still exist.

It is your responsibility to set age-appropriate boundaries with your child. You know the choices available to them better than they do. Your parental role should never involve force, but you should be your child's trusted and effective guide. As you hone your Child Whisperer skills, you will do this more and more effectively with your child. They will be grateful to know that they can look to you for guidance that honors them.

You may have had some thoughts as you read through this section of how you might be forcing or restricting your child in unproductive ways. Write down your thoughts and your inspirations to better guide your child to make choices true to their nature:

_____

_____

_____

_____

How Your Family Culture
May Be Wounding Your Child

Family is the space where children learn about their place in the world. They learn how to connect, whether or not they are safe, and how they belong to a group. Children who feel judged, punished, or belittled for who they are in their family group often grow up as wounded or repressed adults. My work for decades has focused on helping adults heal their lives, and I have seen family wounds affect adults many years down the road.

When a parent does not understand their child's nature, they increase the likelihood that they will accidentally wound their child. Each of the 4 Types receives certain wounding messages from their parents and family that often lead to a few dominant dysfunctions. Look honestly at your family situation and see if you are sending one of these negative messages to your child that may contribute to a future struggle in their adult life. You may also recognize messages that wounded you as a child, which can illuminate dysfunctions in your own life so you can clear them.

Type 1 Wounds

The wounding messages Type 1s receive from their family:
- You're too silly.

- You're too talkative.
- You're too much movement.
- You have too many ideas.
- There's too much of you—settle down.

Because their movement is naturally more random (especially in structured scenarios), parents may try to impose even more structure on them. When they are not recognized for their true nature, these children try to contain or shut down their energy. Parents can do much to help their child trust their nature and allow it to grow into something valuable.

What happens to the wounded Type 1: These children can start to doubt their natural gifts, which are spontaneity, ideas, and hope. They feel nervous, like they'll get in trouble whenever their nature bubbles up. There's a constant checking of their spontaneity so they won't irritate others, always checking it and trying to rein it in. They don't feel safe to just be themselves without being called silly or naughty.

Common adult dysfunction: More than any other Type, adult Type 1s struggle with their weight. Why? They're living in a world where they believe they have to live in structure, and that their natural light movement is not okay. Working out and dieting is just another world of structure, and it's one that they can control. Food becomes a way to spite the world—it's their inner child's way of saying, "Nobody will tell me when or what I can or cannot eat." So they eat randomly, spontaneously, and snack a lot. They also carry the belief that since it's not okay to be themselves anyway, why would it be okay to look good? Their upward, light movement naturally creates happiness. And if they don't get to be light, they don't feel happy, so they act it out in their bodies. They literally weigh themselves down with extra weight.

♡ **Child Whisperer Tip for the Type 1 child**: Enjoy their big, bright energy. Provide them with situations where they feel safe to talk, to sing, to shout, to dance, and to make friends. When you are at home, never allow your child's other siblings to make fun of them for their animated, childlike approach to life.

Type 2 Wounds

The negative messages Type 2s receive from their family:
- You're shy.
- You're too slow.
- You ask too many questions.
- You're so indecisive.
- You're too sensitive.
- You never talk loud enough.

Because a Type 2 child's movement is lower and they tend not to be as vocal as other children, their family members often refer to them as shy. They are not shy—their energy just naturally moves inward. They hesitate before they share because they want to be sure they have all the details and feel comfortable. They wait for an invitation to move forward. When they are singled out for this tendency, they actually tend to hesitate even more.

What happens to the wounded Type 2: When a Type 2 child is shamed for their nature or emotionally ignored in their family, their questioning tends to turn inward. They question themselves unnecessarily and incessantly. Their questioning nature is meant to be a functional ability that helps them gather details and flow through their lives in a calm, confident manner. But taken to its extreme, it creates a lot of worry. Their mind tries to resolve questions about the past and the future, creating assumptions about what others may have meant in the past or will do in the future. Their inner conversation can start to include other people, assuming motives for others that are not accurate. This can lead to extreme anxiety problems.

Common adult dysfunction: As they grow, wounded Type 2 children grow into adults who withhold their voice. They don't believe they can speak up, or that their naturally subdued tone has a right to be heard. If they think they need to act more aggressively in order to be heard, they can suffer physical side effects. They have more sensitive physiologies, and running all that aggressive energy can take a physical toll on them.

⌒ **Child Whisperer Tip for the Type 2 child:** When your Type 2 child worries about what someone else thought or meant, encourage them to ask questions before drawing conclusions. Reassure them that they can be recognized in their world and their voice can be heard. In fact, many Type 2s are very successful. Some examples include Bill Gates, Warren Buffet, Mark Zuckerberg, Mother Theresa, and Einstein. Help your child to love their sensitive nature and recognize it as a gift.

Type 3 Wounds

Negative messages Type 3s may receive from their family:
- You're exhausting.
- You're too determined.
- You move too much.

- You're really aggressive.
- You're way too loud.
- You're so demanding.

These children get the message sometimes that they are just plain too much. They hear all the time that they need to calm down and stop being so loud and active. Boys do not generally receive as much negative feedback, as their active nature is culturally expected. But Type 3 girls have a hard time. They are often called tomboys, which leaves them feeling unfeminine and conflicted between their true nature and their perceived idea of the feminine.

What happens to the wounded Type 3: If these children are wounded in their families, they tend to carry a lot of anger that can come out as overreaction in certain scenarios. They may come across as pushy or intense to others, mostly because there is not an outlet for their naturally dynamic energy to go.

Common adult dysfunction: They may get fired up and take their anger out on spouses or children in ways that the Type 3 adult later regrets. Without a healthy physical outlet, they may feel imprisoned and have an intense impression on others, or give the sense of an energetic intensity they're trying to mask. Adult women who have tried to shut down their Type 3 nature tend to look worn, stressed, and they age much earlier (it's hard work to repress that much dynamic energy). Men may become overly aggressive and not allow their emotional side to show up.

◠ **Child Whisperer Tip for the Type 3 child:** Help your child to get out into the world. Help them do something physical that challenges them and gets their body connected with this world. Allow them to learn a new skill that thrills and challenges them. Give them a place to be in their own movement and compete—even if it's just with themselves. If you were wounded as a Type 3 child, find a physical challenge you would really like to pursue and then go for it!

Type 4 Wounds

Negative messages Type 4s may receive from their family:
- You're too serious.
- You're so critical.
- You can be such a know-it-all.
- Stop being such a stickler for the rules.
- You're not social enough.
- You need to be more outgoing.

Type 4 children may receive negative messages from family members who perceive their naturally serious nature as critical, stifling, or bossy. Parents may worry about their more serious nature. And these children are often told that they are too critical and are told to change the way they naturally are.

What happens to the wounded Type 4: Whatever the Type 4 child does takes on a black-and-white, all-or-nothing quality. Depending on their secondary Type, they will become even more structured and rigid (all Type 4), or they will try to erase or soften their true nature (no Type 4). They may become so rigid, analytical, and controlling that their mind takes over everything and they can become blunt and rude. This is just a symptom of a wounded Type 4 who is no longer connected to their heart. Or they will give all their authority up because it only brought them trouble. Whichever coping mechanism they use to avoid being wounded by their family is an extreme of who they actually are. Their extremes are a symptom of being misunderstood and disrespected.

Common adult dysfunction: As adults, a wounded Type 4's critiquing mind may become a critical mind. They automatically criticize in a bold way and express a lot of willingness to share those opinions when they feel they are not being respected or heard.

Child Whisperer Tip for the Type 4 child: Consider your child's two best qualities: boldness and stillness. Boldness doesn't mean an outward expression—it's a stance, not necessarily a movement. It's a clarity of knowing what's going on. And stillness is an inner quality, not a behavior. In other words, it does not mean all-day meditation, but it means a sense of reflective stillness within their being that carries them. If you can give your child respect for their boldness and time to anchor their stillness, they will grow into centered and grounded adults.

If you have wounded your child

You may have parented your child in a way that has wounded them. Before you finish this book, we will talk about the reasons why it's never too late to be a better parent—even if your children are grown and are raising children of their own.

This is a good message for all children, no matter their Type or age: "It wasn't ever my intention to hurt you, but now I recognize that I hurt you when I… and I want to support you in loving yourself and trusting your greatest gifts."

No matter your child's age, they will appreciate your genuine, heartfelt intention to help them live true to their nature.

How the Public Education System
May be Wounding Your Child

You are not (nor should you be) the only adult in your child's life. Your child will interact with many adults who are placed in authority positions over them. Teachers and coaches especially have a powerful influence over how children create their perception of themselves in the larger world. You should pay attention to anyone who plays a big role in your child's life, who gives them structures or tries to affect them, especially if they are a different Energy Type from your child. As your child is honored in their classroom or on their team, they will be supported in creating greater success in their lives as they grow.

As a Type 3, I am practical and direct. I recommend that you give this book (or a copy of it) to your child's teacher or coach. It's easy to do, especially when you explain this book in terms of how much this knowledge has already changed your own relationship with your child.

Another way to train your child's teacher or coach in honoring your child's nature is through a parent-teacher conference or other meeting in person. You can meet with teachers when scheduled or request a conference at any given time. The most important thing: Don't wait until a problem gets out of hand. Be proactive in opportunities—particularly at the beginning of the school year—to express support for your child's teacher and get them on the same page with you.

5 Keys to the Perfect Parent-Teacher Conference

How you enter a situation with a teacher or coach makes a difference in how well they will hear you. Remember these five keys when you meet with your child's teacher:

1. *Clear anything that's coming up for you.*

If your child's teacher pushes your buttons in any way, they're stirring up emotional issues in you that will get in the way of you engaging with them. Did you have a teacher or adult in authority who shut you down? Are you angry because your child is being wounded in some of the ways you were? Acknowledge and clear your own childhood baggage before you try to engage with your child's teacher. For help in clearing emotional baggage, you can refer to Appendix B in the back of this book.

2. *Set an intention that it will be a positive experience.*

You can energetically influence the space where you will meet with your child's teacher before you ever arrive. Setting an intention helps to create a harmonious interaction. Imagine the nature of the space you want to experience. And remember that you are inviting your child's teacher to be on your side.

3. *Write out your intentions.*

When you write out your intentions, you more consciously create what you desire and set the right energy into motion.

Here are some ideas: "My child's teacher is understanding my child's nature more fully." "They are supporting my child in learning true to their nature." "They are hearing the truth about my child and honoring it." See the teacher as someone who has your child's best interest at heart. Establish in your mind that you're on the same team.

4. Decide who will attend.

Whether you bring your child with you to this meeting depends on age and the topic of conversation. A young child may not need to be there, or could be involved in a two-step meeting in which you talk with the teacher and then invite your child in. The older your child is, the more they need to be there so they feel honored and can express themselves. They may just need you to show up to support them in expressing their own voice. Allow your Child Whisperer intuition to lead you in making this decision.

5. Say the most effective words.

Your goal as a parent is to help your child's teacher understand your child's nature—their natural tendencies, needs, and motivations. Talk in terms of nature, character, and tendencies. Teach the teacher about who your child is, not about the 4 Types (at least, not at first). Here are some ideas of how you might begin a conversation:

"I would like to help you understand my child's nature. It's really helped me in being able to support them in their manner of being successful."

"I want you to see the best results from my child, and so I'd like to talk about how to approach them in a way that they understand and appreciate best."

(If your child has already experienced a problem with the teacher) "I want to resolve the behavioral issue in your classroom. I think we can do that best if we get to the actual root cause of the issue. I'd like to discuss how my child interacts with the world."

Then you can discuss your child personally, according to their age. Refer to yourself and your own personal story with your child, including your own successes and failures. Explain what you've learned about them, what you've tried, and where you've experienced the most success. Open the door to talk about your child's true nature.

Type 1 students

- *Emphasize*: Their brilliance and facility to learn quickly.
- *Explain*: If they are required to sit for long periods of time, they will create their own distractions, which will look like they're not doing their work.
- *What gets in their way*: Being required to focus on a single subject for an extended period of time.
- *Recommend*: Unstructured, social, hands-on learning. Consider explaining that you help your child to do their homework in short bursts with the opportunity to change activities or to move several times an hour.
- *Request*: If your child needs to be disciplined, ask that you consider together a different method than being kept inside from recess. Type 1 children need that social outlet, and without it, they'll just become problematic in the classroom.

I hope that this information will help both parents and

teachers understand the quick and brilliant learning style of Type 1s, who are the most commonly mistreated children in our current education system. If we accommodate their learning style, we will benefit from their brilliant minds that naturally bring us new ideas, as well as their steady optimism to make this world a more light and cheery place.

Type 2 students

- *Emphasize*: Their methodical process and sensitive nature.
- *Explain*: They learn better at the front of the room where there are fewer distractions and they feel they can speak up.
- *What gets in their way*: Getting put on the spot.
- *Recommend*: Advance notice if your child will be asked to participate in front of the class—either the day before or the morning of. They don't think well on their feet, which is stressful for them when they are so sensitive and want to do everything appropriately and in a way that wouldn't upset anyone. If they can feel prepared in thinking things through, they will excel.
- *Request*: Your child will be very concerned with how everyone in the classroom feels. Let the teacher know that your child would love to have an assignment to lend a hand to another child who may need some added help.

In many ways, Type 2 children fit into the traditional classroom structure quite well. As they are naturally more quiet and want to do things appropriately, they often comply with teachers and directions. Help your child's teacher see that they can do much to help your child feel empowered to speak up and participate in their own way.

Type 3 students

- *Emphasize*: Their hands-on ability to learn and desire for challenge
- *Explain*: Because they move swiftly toward a goal, they ignore details that sometimes they shouldn't. They want results and they want the job done, almost to the fault of not getting it done well enough, so they need some support in that.
- *What gets in their way:* Long periods of detailed instructions
- *Recommend*: A challenge! Your Type 3 child will enjoy being called up in front of the classroom to see if they can figure out something quickly.
- *Request*: If a big project takes weeks at a time to complete, your child will wait to do it so they can move through it quickly, which will look like procrastination. Perhaps deadlines of projects that take a long time could be modified. Also, missing recess as a punishment for these children can lead to defiance because it takes away their physical outlet.

Type 3 children may receive many negative labels in the classroom if the teacher is a Type with a lower level of movement. Help your child's teacher recognize their great facility in on-the-spot, hands-on learning, which is truly a gift to get everyone else in the classroom moving in a forward direction. Your child will be well served if you can find a teacher who recognizes your child's natural tendency toward leadership.

Type 4 students

- *Emphasize*: Their ability to see and understand the big picture.
- *Explain*: They have a need to be their own authority and respect their teacher as an authority. Once they feel respected, they automatically reciprocate that respect.
- *What gets in their way*: Being teased or told to lighten up.
- *Recommend*: Recognition as their own authority. Consider sharing that once you were able to parent from a place where you respected them, you didn't need to remind them to do things. They could see the bigger picture and if they felt respected to follow through on their responsibilities, they did.
- *Request*: Your child may come across as a know-it-all. The key to correcting that is simply thanking them and reminding them that the teacher is the authority in charge of helping everyone else to learn. Request that any discipline or conversations to correct your child should not take place in front of the entire class.

In many ways, Type 4 children look like the ideal student. They are consistent, punctual, and responsible, as long as they respect the authority of the teacher and their rules. If your child experiences difficulty in a classroom, always make sure that issues of respect—either from the teacher or other students—are addressed.

Notes for Your Child's Coach

All of the previous suggestions may also apply to conversations with your child's coach. Here are a few additional notes to help your child excel in sports and other activities:

Type 1: Express your child's need to have fun. If an activity no longer feels like a game, your Type 1 child's heart just won't be in it.

Type 2: Express that your child will perform at a high level if they don't feel pressure. It's not effective to yell at any Type of child, but Type 2 children especially will retreat.

Type 3: Explain that your child will go all out if they feel inspired and challenged. They need to feel pushed, which is the opposite of a Type 2 child.

Type 4: Express that your child performs best when they feel respected. Share how your child wants to do perfectly whatever they've committed to and that they need support to not be too hard on themselves.

These notes can be applied to your child's experience with a piano teacher, drama coach, choir director, or any other adult in a position of instruction and authority.

Your Role in the Parent-Teacher Relationship

Your job is to support your child in living true to their nature in successful ways, and to help them navigate their experience with the other adults in their life safely and with as much support as possible. If your child encounters a problem in school or on their team, listen to what your child is complaining about and then look beyond it to discover the actual issue. Your child is not yet equipped with the vocabulary, tools, and authority to speak to and resolve the issues that may arise with their teacher. They don't always have the capacity to know what is shutting them down and why. Ask them, "What didn't you like? What did you like?" Tell them why you're asking because it's really important to you to help them have an experience that they like and that helps them learn.

You can create a supportive environment before your child ever walks in the classroom door by getting to know your options of teachers well in advance. Ask parents in the neighborhood with children older than your child what they thought of their child's teachers. Just let them know that you'd like to get to know the nature of the available teachers and their teaching style.

Ultimately, it is your right as a parent to request a different teacher for your child. If you find that a teacher demeans, belittles, or disrespects your child, you are responsible to try and resolve the situation and then remove your child from it as quickly as possible if the teacher is resistant. Your supportive response will have a much greater impact on your child than the negative impact of the teacher, and will help your child in feeling empowered to speak up and live true to their nature in the future.

How Your Religious Culture
May Be Wounding Your Child

As a parent, you may want to pass on your religious experience or spiritual orientation to your children. You want them to be happy with a belief system you have found beneficial in your own life. If that's the case for you, it's time to consider how you can influence your child's religious experience to be supportive to their true nature. If you do not make accommodations for their particular needs and motivations, or your child feels judged for their true nature, they may decide to reject what you are sharing without understanding what it is they are rejecting.

Use your Child Whisperer skills to consider what your child needs at church or in the religious atmosphere in your home that they are not currently getting.

Type 1: These children need fun. They need their spiritual experience to feel light and free, and this includes their experience at church. This does not mean you need to let them run everywhere whenever they want. If you ask them to be quiet, turn it into a game or a time to imagine with you. Above all, make sure the experience feels light and inspiring to them.

Type 2: These children are highly intuitive and are often pretty connected to the spiritual aspect of life. If they are resistant to settings where they can have those experiences, they may be resistant for emotional reasons. How do their teachers or other adults at church treat them? Are they ever put in a position where they're on the spot? Do they feel emotionally safe with their peers to express their feelings? Check in with how they feel about spiritual matters.

Type 3: Type 3 children who like to go, go, go, often do not find an experience supportive to their needs in a church, as it usually often involves a lot of sitting and listening. You can give your child things to do with their hands during meetings. Don't worry that they are not listening because they switch focus erratically and can move forward several things at once. You can suggest to the teacher of your child's class to give them little projects to do during class to keep their hands busy.

Type 4: These children are capable of sitting still for the longest amount of time, which is often conducive to a church experience. If they respect the authority of the rules they find in the religion, they will want to follow them with unwavering devotion. As they grow, this can become frustrating, as they will never do everything perfectly. Help your child give themselves some leeway in following the rules, otherwise they may abandon their spiritual pursuits altogether. Type 4s are also the most reflective and deep-thinking about their personal belief and value system. Respect them for that and help them find the truths that support them in having a beautiful spiritual experience in life.

For all 4 Types: Getting your child to stay quiet in church is one thing. Supporting them in creating a unique spiritual experience and feeling a connection with a higher power is another. If your child's church or religious experience is supportive to their nature and they feel honored in living true to themselves, your child will be more likely to search out true principles for themselves and live true to their highest self.

What About Labels?

I would like to address any concerns you may have about labeling your child as a certain Type. We use labels to make sense of this world. We give names to things so that we can understand and talk about them. As people, we do this naturally and constantly, so the very act of labeling is not a problem. The labels only become a problem when they limit children, rather than support them.

Many labels cause problems for children—labels such as hyperactive, shy, rebellious, or bossy. Your children will fulfill those negative perceptions. If you feel negatively about your children, they will sense that energy from you, and together, you will end up creating a pattern in your relationship that you don't want.

As a Child Whisperer, you can use the Energy Profiling model as a tool to help you recognize your child's greatest strengths and talk about them in a way that your child understands. By understanding your child's Type, you also understand their primary motivations, greatest needs, and innate natural movement. We are already labeling our children's behavior anyway. Why not do so in a way that empowers and frees them?

Your Sneaky Negative Perceptions

Some of our negative perceptions of our children are not so obvious. Because parents love their children, and deep down they want the best for their children, they may not even realize the negative messages they sometimes send.

You can zero in on the negative perceptions you didn't even know you had about your child, just by paying attention to the words you use. The way you talk about your children creates your experience with them. So stop and consider what you say in these three particular situations that may be damaging your relationship with your child:

1. What you say about them when you're upset.
In the heat of the moment, our most negative judgments often rise to the surface. What you say during those moments of anger reveals a lot about what you actually believe about your child. And those words will stick with your child for years to come. If you find yourself making judgments about who your child is when you're upset, clear those negative beliefs away during times of peace. If you don't have those sorts of negative judgments anymore, they won't come out inadvertently.

2. What you say about them when they're not around.
Do you complain about your children when they're not around? This can be an indication that you have not taken care of yourself the way you need to—and you're taking it out on your children. This energy can damage a parent-child relationship and make your children feel like burdens, rather than the gifts that they are. Go take care of yourself and stop putting that strain on your child.

3. What you repeat from your own childhood.

If you were silenced, belittled, or shamed as a child for who you are, you may re-create that pattern in your child's experience in surprising ways. Do you ever hear yourself say hurtful or irritating things that your parents said to you (especially things you promised yourself you would never say)? You will usually repeat patterns that are familiar to you unless you consciously choose to change them. It is important that you choose to create a healthy pattern today and work to make it become familiar in your life.

♡ **Child Whisperer Tip:** When you recognize your negative patterns or energies with your children, go to them and acknowledge it. Have a private conversation with your child—or each of your children, if you have more than one. State your intention to change the pattern and make things right with them.

You can give your child the voice you felt you didn't have by empowering them with words that you both agree on. For example, I encouraged my children to use this phrase with me: "Mom, please change your tone." I told them that they could use it whenever they felt that my own active nature was pushing them too much or being too reactive. It was a cue for me that my children were not feeling honored and I needed to stop what I was doing and reevaluate.

Whatever words or phrases you choose, practice together in a moment of peace and ease. Help them feel like they have permission to speak up and use words that help you to honor them for who they are. When your children feel they have a voice in the relationship, you will find that any negative perceptions you might have of them are less likely to take hold for very long.

As soon as you change your perception of your child to a more positive one, you will find that the relationship naturally becomes more positive and mutually supportive.

The Top 5 Things I Did
That I Am Really Proud of
as a Parent

Now that you know what you do about Child Whispering, you may have a similar response to parents I have already heard from. Many of them wish they had known about Energy Profiling when their children were very young so they wouldn't have made the mistakes that they did.

I developed Energy Profiling after my children had already grown through most of the stages of development I have discussed in this book, so I understand that feeling. Are there things I would have done differently had I known? Yes. Are there things I know better now? Absolutely.

Yes, I would have done some things differently. But there are some things that I am really proud of as a parent. Before I share some of the most common mistakes, I want to reassure you that you are doing great. And I'd like you to consider your current successes.

These are five things I'm most proud of as a parent. As you read, pay attention to your own inspiration about the wonderful things you're already doing right.

The Top 5 Things I'm Happy That I Did as a Parent

1. *I was accountable.*

Above all, I was willing to see my own error and dysfunction. I was willing to own up to it all, and willing to heal it as I became aware. I never excused myself as a parent just because I was a parent.

In my opinion, many parents have given themselves a little too much room to excuse themselves with the statement, "Because I'm the parent." Our children are subordinate until they are old enough to get out on their own. But that's not a good enough reason to exert our authority over them. Being accountable as a parent and communicating your genuine desire to change for the better is the number one thing you can do to heal any past conflict with your child and create a healthy relationship moving forward.

. . . .

MY STORY
Becoming an Accountable Parent

In my late 20s, I started to recognize that I really needed to make some changes or I would pass on dysfunction to my young children. That realization was the catalyst for me getting into the field of personal development. Issues and emotions had become very distorted and misunderstood in my life. I started talk therapy, which helped me see my own actions more clearly. I participated in a 12-step program for just over two years, which made me accountable to other women who were also facing challenges. I then became a follower of John Bradshaw's work. I still use the concepts and methodology from Healing the Inner Child to help others heal their inner children.

In all, I put myself in programs and in places where I held myself accountable and I had to share with others how I was doing. As dysfunction became apparent, I cleared it, which helped me become a better person and a better parent at the same time.

. . . .

⌒ **Child Whisperer Tip:** Do not let guilt or embarrassment prevent you from becoming an accountable parent. You can acknowledge your own accountability to your children, but don't make it your children's job to keep you accountable. Show them that we all have the ability to change and get better, but don't make them hold you to it. That's just one more way of avoiding true accountability.

Don't ask your spouse to hold you accountable either. They have their own issues to be accountable for and you don't want to create any resentment. Choose a supportive third party. All you need is the intention to find support and support will show up.

2. *I didn't hold onto guilt.*

When I did make mistakes, I didn't hold onto guilt after it had done its job. Guilt has value. It can be used as a mechanism to help us recognize the need for change. That's what I used it for. And then I let it go and didn't hang it over myself.

Guilt can also be used as a false belief that limits you. When you get stuck in that kind of guilt you feel bad and worthless.

I couldn't function at a high level of confidence as a parent if I felt bad and guilty all the time. If I had, my children would have had to live with me in that energy. That energy binds children energetically and I didn't want them growing up in that energy. Learn from your choices. Let guilt be a mechanism to get your attention. And then let it go.

3. *I chose to be the creator of my life.*

I recognized in my early 20s that I depended on my doings to feel a sense of worth. That foundation began to crumble in my early parenting years. I remember sitting alone, feeling regretful, when the thought came to me, "You will always be you. You might as well learn to be your own best friend and love yourself." I knew that's what I had to accomplish and I worked with persistence to let go of all the conditioning that had led me to that place.

I knew that I wanted my children to experience true self-confidence, rather than a false sense of confidence through their life doings. Through my experience of clearing away my own limiting beliefs, I learned to speak in affirmations and my children did not hear me compromise myself in the way I talked about myself. I definitely experienced my own self-doubts and limiting beliefs, but I worked on them for myself. I did not put myself down in front of my children and did not hold them responsible to take care of me. I took responsibility to create my life myself.

4. *I taught all this to my children.*

I taught my own children accountability. I taught them not to get stuck in guilt. And I taught them how to be creators of their life. My own children are currently creating incredible lives, true to their natures. And I am so proud of them.

5. *I raised my children to be friends.*

I truly believe that my parents did the best they knew how and I am so grateful to them for it. But I was not raised to be my brothers' friend. Now that my brothers and I are adults, we are cooperative and we hold a respect for each other. But I yearned to be good friends with them as we grew up. I saw that as a possibility for my own children and from the early years of my parenthood, I set this intention: "I am raising my children to be best friends."

You can do this for your own children, but you can't force it. You must hold the intention and then allow it. Opportunities will then present themselves to form lasting relationships of friendship between your children.

To foster friendship between siblings, I taught my own children to never speak ill of each other. Using hostile humor and sarcasm toward each other was not allowed because it was not honoring. We also took road trips together when they were little, which allowed them to work out their issues, work on their friendships, and experience opportunities to have fun together.

At the time of this writing, three of my children work for us. Their spouses also work for us. And even when they're finished with work, where they've spent a lot of time together, they still get together. They have their own friends, but they are also each others' go-to friends for social experiences. As a parent, I am delighted that they enjoy one another's company and that they look to one another as true friends.

Bonus: *I took care of myself.*

As a mother, I took care of myself. I liked a clean home, so I hired someone to clean. As a determined Type 3, I needed to get lots of things done, so I hired younger girls to come in and play with my children while I was there. What do you need as a parent? You might need time to just let down to do something that's gratifying. Give yourself that time and recognize that your child's life experience doesn't have to all come from you. You can't meet everyone's needs because you don't have all the dominant energetic expressions. Don't strain your energy. Take care of yourself and you'll better take care of your children.

Your Successes as a Parent

These are just five of many things you may already be doing right as a parent. I personally believe that they are five of the most important. There are others, depending on your situation and your relationship with your child. It would be fabulous for all of us to know that we are really good parents. I want you to believe that about yourself because if you believe that, you'll create it. Recognize all the success you've already experienced!

What are you proud of as a parent? Write them here and appreciate them:

_____

_____

_____

_____

What I Would Have Done Differently If I Knew This Earlier

ow it's time to talk about the mistakes we sometimes make when we don't understand our child's true nature. I have 5 children: a Type 1 daughter and son, a Type 2 daughter and son, and Type 4 son. Had I known this about them when they were young, I would have done some things differently.

What I would have done differently:

1. *I would have spoken in affirmations and validations for my children.*
From the very beginning, I would have honored my children with messages that honored their true natures. From their earliest years, I would have affirmed and supported my children with specific messages they needed to hear at different stages of their development.

Type 1: "It's so fun to have you in our life. Thank you for bringing an uplifting, effervescent energy to our life. There is nothing you have to do to get your needs met. Thank you for being the bright, shiny, being that you are."

Type 2: "Thank you for your gentle, sensitive, kind nature. Take all the time you need to grow up and feel all your emotions. You're so heart-felt and understanding, I'm here to make you comfortable and safe in this world. I love you and I'm here for you."

Type 3: "I'm so grateful for your adventurous spirit, for your determined nature, and for your desire to make a difference in this world. Let yourself be who you are. Push forward, but there's no rush. I love you and I'm here to take care of you."

Type 4: "I love you. You are such a strong, stable being. Thank you for bringing structure and your strength to my experience. I know you need time to be still. I know that silence supports you at times. You do not need to take on any of my energy. Be your own person. Thank you for your strength, for your solid quality of being. I love you and I'm here to take care of you."

2. *I would have honored each child's Type even more.*
Type 1: I would have focused on keeping things light and playful in their lives. I would have made sure my Type 1 daughter and son didn't get too heavy with things, and that I checked in with them to see their world through that lens. If they were stressed or grumpy, I would have known to ask, "What is bearing down on you? What's weighing you down? How can I help lighten your experience and continue to validate you?" *Most importantly, I would have had more fun with my Type 1 children.*

Type 2: I would have asked myself frequently, "Are they

comfortable and are they comforted? Have I comforted them in the way that they need?" I would have supported them being more in their flow. If they ever got high-strung, I would have looked for where they felt too pushed or where situations were too aggressive in their life. *Most importantly, I would have sat with them more, held them more, listening to and comforting them.*

Type 3: I do not have any Type 3 children, but I know what would be supportive to them. I would encourage this child in exploring life. I would make sure I created an environment that was safe to explore and that sustained their hands-on nature so they didn't need to hear "Stop that," very often. I would let them take more risks on a more physical level. I would help them become entrepreneurial early on and take pleasure in their results. *Most importantly, I would take the time to appreciate their results with them.*

Type 4: I would have made sure I noticed if situations or spaces were getting too energetically overwhelming. If they were too much to handle, I would have taken my child out of those spaces and given the space needed to regroup and realign. I would have parented him in a way that was more of a partnership in teaching him about his own sense of authority. I would have said, "Good for you. Of course you want to do it yourself because you want to see what you can do. You don't have to do it yourself, but you can if you want to. I'm here to support you." I would have helped him understand the steps he needed to execute whatever he wanted to do. I would have asked, "Do you understand what you need to do?" I would have let him talk things out. *Most importantly, I would have sat without any distraction and let him tell me what he was feeling or thinking.*

Why It's Never Too Late to be a Better Parent

Every parent has great gifts to give their children. And every parent has plenty of room to improve. No matter how you feel you have done or will do as a parent, no matter your fears, anxieties, or regrets, and no matter the current age of your child, you can do something to become a better parent today. And this opportunity is bigger than you think.

There's a false perception that you can only influence your children when they are small. Stop believing that. You can do a great deal of good if your children are at home in your primary care. But you can have just as great an influence on your children even if they no longer live with you or are raising children of their own. Your kids are longing for you to show up and be the kind of parent you were meant to be.

Everyone's psyche contains an inner child and as we grow into adults, we try to meet whatever needs weren't met as a child. We do not necessarily look to our parents to get our needs met, but we're still looking for it somewhere. As adults, we either make a decision that we'll never get that need met, or we look for someone outside our parents to get it. For example, nearly every conflict that develops in a marriage situation, or relationship with a significant other, is rooted in unmet needs in our inner child. It's our attempt to get our needs met later in life.

The life we live each day is a result of all the stories we tell ourselves about our lives. When we believe we are victims, we attract situations that confirm that perspective. When we believe we are powerful and inspired, that is how we experience the world. You're always right about your kids because what you really believe about them shows up as a representation in your life. Life is a mirror and gives you information on a daily basis. Your experience will show you what you really believe. You can help your own child create a story about their life that empowers and heals them. And it starts with you taking accountability for yourself.

If you have unintentionally wounded your child at any age, take responsibility for it, go to them and acknowledge what has happened, what you want to change, and what you plan to do. Give them the messages they did not receive at a certain age and change what you are doing. And when you recognize the things you've done right, keep doing them! Recognize the victories in your parent-child relationship and continue them!

It's time. Time to stop wounding your child inadvertently, no matter their age. Time to continue the positive things you're already doing. Time to honor your child's inner nature in the way you treat and talk to them. Time to be the kind of parent that you are meant to be!

Using Your New Found Child Whisperer Skills

Are you feeling like a Child Whisperer yet? I hope so. I hope you have already applied some of the skills you've learned and seen an improvement in your life. I encourage you to be patient with your child, kind to yourself, and remember a few things as you put your new found Child Whisperer skills into practice:

Don't expect to get it all right at once. Parenting is a process, not a destination. Be willing to stay open and keep learning. It's like anything new; you have to practice. And believe me, your children will give you plenty of opportunities every day!

Communicate clearly. Any of the Types will respond to clear communication. Tell your child that you've learned some things and that you want to change things for the better with them. Let them share their own ideas about what you can do together to help them. Share how committed you are to understanding and loving them.

If your relationship has been strained or challenging, consider using a phrase like this: "I haven't understood you completely, not because I didn't want to but because I just didn't know how." Trust yourself that you are taking care of any issues before it is too late (no matter how late it is). Your child will give you feedback along the way, but don't put it on your child to tell you how to be their parent. Just communicate your love and take responsibility for what you have learned.

Make it enjoyable. This is most important of all. Energy Profiling is meant to be a system that supports you, not the other way around. If you ever start feeling limited or confined by the Types, it's time to review the material again and consider which limiting beliefs you need to clear from your life. As your new found Child Whisperer skills become more and more natural, you will start to look forward to the opportunities your children give you to use them.

Just Go For It Now!

Wow, you got through the whole book! Believe me, I never imagined it would be this big of a book, but it's a big topic. Now that you have taken all this in, and have started to put it into practice, take a deep breath and relax! You may feel a bit overwhelmed and uncertain if you can adapt your parenting to the Child Whisperer techniques I teach in this book.

Let me reassure you, the main reason you may feel overwhelmed is what you are learning is not familiar—YET! Yes, it will take more conscious effort on your part to parent your children true to their natures. Yes, it will require more of you if you have several children of different Types. And yes, it will get easier and more instinctive. That is the beauty of becoming a Child Whisperer through Energy Profiling; it is very intuitive and once you understand your child's nature, they will make it easier for you with their constant reminders of what they need from you as their parent.

Something to remember: Your children are their own owner's manual. Every day of their lives, they are telling you what they need! Now that you are becoming a Child Whisperer, you have the skills to know how to read them and intuitively respond in a manner that creates what you really want as a parent: Cooperative children who are developing into confident, successful human beings.

I encourage you to really put to the test what I have just taught you. See if it works. I feel confident in offering you that challenge because I have witnessed hundreds of times over and over these past several years how well this information works when put into practice. I have seen and heard from thousands of parents how much better their family lives are, how much happier their children are, and how much their lives have changed since they put this into practice.

My hope for you is that you will be able to say after using these Child Whisperer tools that your family life is better, that you are closer to your children, that you get along better, and are creating the family life you always wanted. My hope is that you use the tools in this book to create deep and lasting bonds with your children and that they love and honor you as their parent. I want you to have fun, feel connected, get a lot done, and experience the deep love and respect you are meant to have with your children.

This book truly is a manual that you are meant to refer to often. There is much to learn in becoming a Child Whisperer, so return to this book often for reminders, new aha's and inspiration, especially as your children grow through their different stages of development.

Thank you for letting me be an influence for good in your life. My role as a mother has been and continues to be one of my most important commitments and loves. To be able to help parents better understand and love and honor their child is one of the greatest things I could do. Thank you for giving me that chance. May God bless you and your family to be one of the sweetest blessings of your life. I believe God wants that for all of us and is striving everyday to help us achieve that. When we become better parents, we just naturally create a better world. Believe in yourself, forgive yourself, and move forward to make the next moment better. You can do it! (Spoken like a true Type 3!)

Appendix A: Dressing Your Children True to their Type

I am well known for a fashion system called *Dressing Your Truth*. Although this system has been designed for women, the same principles of apparel apply to children and teenagers. You may not have considered that what your child wears makes much of a difference in their behavior. But it does. I have personally seen—both in my own children's lives and the lives of children whose mothers have gone through our online learning program—how much of a difference dressing a child true to their Type can be.

The Surprising Benefit of Dressing Your Truth for Children

Looking good is not actually Dressing Your Truth's primary benefit for your child—although it *is* one of them. The greatest value is something you might not think of at first.

As you have learned in this book, your child expresses a certain quality of movement in their inner nature. When the movement and quality of your child's apparel supports their natural movement, other people naturally align more fully to your child's true nature. Others perceive your children's behavior in harmony with who they really are and your children are naturally disciplined or judged less for just being themselves. Others interpret your child's actions more accurately and treat your child according to their nature. I recommend that you dress your child true to their nature from a young age.

. . . .

SETH'S STORY
A Type 4 Baby

My Type 4 grandson Seth looked silly in bright colors and animated patterns, even as a baby. As soon as my daughter Jenny dressed her son in bold colors with simple lines, he looked much more like himself. While many babies are called cute, people often commented on what a handsome baby Seth was. People acknowledged his more serious, mature nature with a more serious, mature word, even when he was a baby. Not only did Seth's parents honor him, but dressing him true to his nature helped others to honor him as well.

. . . .

So what exactly is Dressing Your Truth? It is a supportive system for choosing apparel that can help your child to feel confident in their appearance as they grow.

Dressing Your Truth contains five elements:

1. Design line
2. Texture
3. Fabrication
4. Pattern
5. Color

These five elements show up in all children's apparel and shoes and hairstyles. As young women grow, they may also add to that makeup, jewelry, and other accessories—all components of adorning the feminine.

We all have a sixth sense of what feels right on our body. Children and teens are naturally drawn to clothes that are supportive of their dominant Type. This is true even of babies. We often don't really realize that the clothing on a baby could make them fussy—not what they're eating or how they're sleeping. What apparel is going next to their skin? What about the texture of the blankets you use? What about diapers?

When you honor your child's nature with what you put on them and next to their skin, your child will be at ease with the world and will grow up being better seen for who they are. I have seen this with all of my grandchildren, who have experienced great levels of ease in their baby stages and as they grow. Dressing Your Truth helps you as a parent to build on and tune into what a child naturally knows would be supportive to them until they are able to make those choices themselves.

Tips for Dressing Each Type of Child

Type 1: Clothes should feel light and free on the body, and the fabric should have a crisp quality to it. Type 1 children should be able to bounce and play without restriction from their clothing. They'll be fussy in clothes that weigh them down. You'll readily find clothing for these children because clothing for children is predominantly Type 1—playful, youthful, animated and fun.

Type 2: Comfort is key, so fabrication is the number one quality to consider. Soft, plush, cozy fabrics will help your child feel held in comfort. Consider everything from clothing to blankets to diapers to towels. Whatever touches their body should have a soft, comfortable feel. Their faces show up more when they wear more muted colors, and softer, subdued patterns.

Type 3: Due to their substantial energy, these children look best in heavier textures, more substantial weaves, and patterns with an earthy quality. They need substance to their clothes, even as babies, and can wear a little heavier weighted items. In fact, if an item is too light, a Type 3 child won't like it—it will feel wispy and look silly. Since many parents don't see textured, heavier clothes as typical baby clothes, you'll find many of them at thrift stores.

Type 4: These children need structured clothes that are fitted to the body. Don't put them in anything with too many extra laces, frills, or embellishments. This issue comes up less often for Type 4 boys. But the girls do encounter many more frills. Their quality of inner stillness needs to be honored. Less is more. Simpler is better. Think solid colors, stripes, and even bold black.

Body Image of Every Type

As children grow into teenagers, they become very aware of their appearance and start to develop an opinion about their body image. Although it is just as important for boys to feel confident and have skills to support a healthy body and image, teenage girls get hit much harder by the media in developing a negative body image.

While Dressing Your Truth principles apply to dressing both males and females, I recommend sharing my Dressing Your Truth program with your teenage daughter in particular. She can learn how to work with fashion and her Type of beauty at a very early age—and bypass the too-common trend of hating her body and how she looks!

If Your Child Doesn't Want to Dress Their Truth

It's not appropriate for a parent to insist that a child dress their truth. When a child becomes active in the role of choosing what to wear, let them! Let them make the choices. Parents who have explored this system have actually found that their children naturally go back to the things that we teach in the Dressing Your Truth program true to their Type. Their children are just naturally drawn to them.

The desire in a child to request something else is just to make sure they have a say in their lives and not be controlled by their parents. That is usually the motive behind not wanting to dress their truth.

Of all the Types, Type 3s and 4s (particularly boys in their teens) have the strongest tendency to blow off this information. Type 3s are just too busy to be bothered. And Type 4s resist if they have not been treated in a way that honors their authority—they don't want to be told how to dress if they don't feel respected. These children tend to get more interested in Dressing Your Truth when they have a say in their choices and they realize that using the program increases their quality of being attractive, which is something every growing child—teenage boy or not—wants to experience.

Dressing Your Truth for Moms

If you are a mother, I encourage you to look into Dressing Your Truth for yourself. You probably spend way too many hours and days frustrated with your body, hair, and appearance. This affects your parenting! When you don't feel good about yourself, inside and out, your confidence is challenged and you are not as capable of meeting your children's needs fully and modeling a healthy self and body esteem to them. I also encourage you to consider Dressing Your Truth as an additional support for you and your child.

See how Dressing Your Truth can help you create
your personal style with my free Beginner's Guide

Visit dressingyourtruth.com

Appendix B: Additional Resources

More Parenting Support

For more support in learning how to become a Child Whisperer, I have created additional resources that can be found at:

thechildwhisperer.com

We continue to add supportive materials to this website on an ongoing basis to help you become a better parent.

These resources include our video library:

"How to Profile Babies, Children and Teens"

These videos will help you better understand how your children's facial features and body language express their dominant Type.

Online Community of Parents

We're in this together! In the Child Whisperer Facebook group, parents ask question, share answers, and post reasons they celebrate their child's Type—which can help you recognize your own child's unique gifts. Search for "The Child Whisperer" on Facebook.

More Support for Living Your Truth

In addition to *Dressing Your Truth*, I have created several online resources, programs, and additional books to support you in living true to your nature.

Explore and enjoy whichever resources seem most important to you right now.

To learn more about the 4 Types, how they express in the nature kingdom, and how they relate to an adult experience:

Visit *myenergyprofile.com*

Read or listen to my book, *It's Just My Nature*

For ongoing support in the areas of personal healing and development along with more parenting support:

Visit *caroltuttle.com*

Read or listen to my book, *Remembering Wholeness*

To learn simple skills to heal emotional baggage, childhood issues, or any other limiting beliefs in your life:

Visit *healwithcarol.com*

I am passionate about helping children and adults live their truth. I hope you find my other resources supportive in your intention to live true to yourself. Thank you for reading.

About the Author

Carol Tuttle is a teacher, speaker, healer, and best-selling author. As an educator, Carol began her career in secondary education and has since taught hundreds of thousands of people worldwide with her inspiring books and life-changing online programs. As a mother, she raised five distinctly different children—and she's been where you are.

She knows that no two children are alike. Some are naturally loud and playful, while others are more reserved. What worked for one of her students or children backfired for another. She knows how important it is to find what works for your child.

Carol discovered that the key to effective teaching and parenting is to customize your approach to each child. Her Child Whispering framework has helped adults worldwide to understand the children they parent and teach on a deep, individual level. As they honor each child's individual needs and gifts, those children thrive and parenting gets so much easier.

This unique approach to parenting helps resolve parent-child conflict quickly, and increases cooperation and harmony. Carol's book turns longstanding parenting assumptions on their heads, and shows how parenting can be an even more intuitive, cooperative, fulfilling experience than you've experienced before.

Carol lives in Utah with Jonathan, her husband of 30+ years. Mother of five and grandmother of ten, Carol takes every opportunity to honor each of her grandchildren's unique natures. She believes we can raise a strong generation of children who know who they are and live true to their natures.